Communities, Crime and Social Capital in Contemporary China

90 0934544 7

364
2HO

University of Plymouth
Charles Seale Hayne Library
Subject to status this item may be renewed
via your Primo account

http://primo.plymouth.ac.uk
Tel: (01752) 588588

Communities, Crime and Social Capital in Contemporary China

Lena Y. Zhong

WILLAN
PUBLISHING

Published by

Willan Publishing
Culmcott House
Mill Street, Uffculme
Cullompton, Devon
EX15 3AT, UK
Tel: +44(0)1884 840337
Fax: +44(0)1884 840251
e-mail: info@willanpublishing.co.uk
website: www.willanpublishing.co.uk

Published simultaneously in the USA and Canada by

Willan Publishing
c/o ISBS, 920 NE 58th Ave, Suite 300
Portland, Oregon 97213-3786, USA
Tel: +001(0)503 287 3093
Fax: +001(0)503 280 8832
e-mail: info@isbs.com
website: www.isbs.com

© Lena Y. Zhong 2009

The rights of Lena Y. Zhong to be identified as the author of this book have been asserted by her in accordance with the Copyright, Designs and Patents Act of 1988.

All rights reserved; no part of this publication may be reproduced, stored in a retrieval system, or transmitted in any form or by any means, electronic, mechanical, photocopying, recording or otherwise without the prior written permission of the Publishers or a licence permitting copying in the UK issued by the Copyright Licensing Agency Ltd, Saffron House, 6–10 Kirby Street, London EC1N 8TS.

First published 2009

ISBN   978-1-84392-405-0 hardback

British Library Cataloguing-in-Publication Data

A catalogue record for this book is available from the British Library.

Project managed by Deer Park Productions, Tavistock, Devon
Typeset by GCS, Leighton Buzzard, Bedfordshire
Printed and bound by T.J. International Ltd, Padstow, Cornwall

Contents

List of figures	*vii*
List of tables	*viii*
Foreword	*ix*
Preface and acknowledgements	*xi*

1	**Introduction**	**1**
	Research background and theoretical framework	3
	Research questions and significance of the study	7
	Overview of the book	9
2	**Taking to the field**	**12**
	Shenzhen: an 'overnight city'	13
	Five communities: model versus non-model	18
	Dilemmas in China studies	22
	Methodological challenges and research methods	27
3	**Community crime prevention and social capital**	**41**
	Patterns of social control in modern Western societies	43
	Context for the emergence of community crime prevention	45
	Conceptualization of crime prevention	51
	Social capital and community crime prevention: the nexus	54
	Community crime prevention and social capital: problems and issues	68
4	**Social capital in China**	**75**
	Confucianism versus legalism	76

	Organization of Chinese society	80
	Guanxi in China	85
5	**Crime and social control in China**	**94**
	Crime in China	95
	Social control in China	111
	Conclusion	125
6	**Building little, safe and civilized communities in Shenzhen: community crime prevention with Chinese characteristics?**	
	Part One: CMSO, and BLSCC development and outcome	**130**
	CMSO: a duality	131
	BLSCC and its development in Shenzhen	142
	Officially claimed outcome of BLSCC in Shenzhen	144
7	**Building little, safe and civilized communities in Shenzhen: community crime prevention with Chinese characteristics?**	
	Part Two: BLSCC Measures	**147**
	BLSCC measures	147
	Conclusion	177
8	**BLSCC in two Shenzhen communities**	**182**
	Community A: order and peace	182
	Community B: disorder and fear	186
	Comparison between the two communities in the survey	189
	Conclusion	209
9	**Conclusion**	**212**
	Theoretical exploration	212
	Empirical testing	215
	The nexus revisited	218
	Looking forward into the future	229
Appendix		233
References		240
Glossary		260
Index		266

List of figures

2.1	Population of Shenzhen 1979–2006	17
2.2	GDP and GDP per capita in Shenzhen 1979–2006	18
3.1	Social capital matters	57
3.2	The basic systemic model of crime	60
3.3	The non-recursive model of crime	63
3.4	Dimensions of social capital and crime level inside a community	68
4.1	The Chinese 'pyramid of morality' or 'pyramid of socialization'	78
5.1	The hierarchy of administrative structure in China	115

List of tables

2.1	Recorded (and reported) criminal cases in Shenzhen 1980–2007	19
2.2	Convictions for public security offences and offenders in Shenzhen 1981–2007	20
2.3	Demographic distribution of the respondents in communities A and B	36
5.1	Reported criminal cases (excluding public security offences) in China 1950–2006 – total, rates per 100,000 population and clearance rates	102
5.2	Categories of reported criminal offences 1981–2006	104
5.3	Proportion of young persons convicted of a crime in the People's Courts 1990–2006	107
5.4	Reported public security offences vs. reported criminal offences 1986–2006	108
5.5	Number of People's Police (units of 10,000) 1988–93	121
6.1	Development of BLSCC in Shenzhen: 1992–1998	143
8.1	Cross-tabulation of area one by community	191
8.2	Perception of intervention in a pickpocketing case	193
8.3	Cross-tabulation of area two by community	197
8.4	Frequency of crime within the two communities	199
8.5	Percentages for 13 types of crimes in the two communities	199
8.6	Cross-tabulation of area three by community	205

Foreword

My first exposure to the study of Chinese criminal justice was a seminar at Yale Law School, where I was a visiting fellow in the autumn of 1976. The reading materials included Cohen's *The Criminal Process in the People's Republic of China*, van der Sprenkel's *Legal Institutions of Manchu China*, and Bao Ruo-Wang's (Jean Pasqualini) *Prisoner of Mao*. At the very beginning of the course, Chairman Mao died, and our professor, Stanley Lubman, advised the class that things were certainly about to change. Indeed they were.

Four years later, as a tourist on my first visit to China, I asked a local guide about the extent of crime. I was advised that 'since the smashing of the Gang of Four', crime was no longer a problem. There may have been more than a grain of truth to this reassurance, for, as we were crossing the border on the train back to Hong Kong, a Western guide warned us, 'You are now leaving the People's Republic of China. Please guard your valuables.'

The changes in China that began during the last quarter of the twentieth century have been staggering. One anecdote will suffice. Among the cities that I visited in 1980 was Hangzhou, the site of the magnificent West Lake. On my next visit to that city 25 years later, I noticed something by the lakeside that I had not seen in 1980: a Ferrari dealership.

The economic transformation of China continues unabated. Not surprisingly, crime has followed opportunity. In this book, the author quotes the quaint Chinese reference to 'flies and mosquitoes coming through the window of reform'. Readers will be intrigued by the author's examples of ideological discourse on crime complete with colourful slogans and reliance on numbers. Chapter 7 will reveal the meaning of the 'Four a's' and the 'Four Haves', among other things.

The continuing economic development of China will produce continuing criminal opportunities. What was once unheard of has now become routine: As one of the author's interviewees put it, 'If you have not been burgled, you don't belong to (Community C).' The extent to which the collectivist ethos will continue to be eroded by the individualism of the market economy and by the abundance of only children since the advent of the one-child policy remains to be seen. Meanwhile, economic stratification intensifies. The floating population of 200 million, less constrained by informal social control and by traditional practices of household registration, constitutes an abundant supply of motivated offenders and suitable targets. Public security is destined to remain high on the public agenda.

Now, a new generation of Chinese criminologists, trained in the West, has begun to analyze Chinese criminal justice. The author of this book, originally from Hunan Province and with a PhD from the University of Hong Kong, will become prominent among them. This book is a great example of contemporary social science. Its treatment of criminological theory in application to contemporary China is both comprehensive and accessible. Its use of multiple research methods, including observation, depth interviews, surveys, and documentary analysis, is exemplary.

Insights on how the state harnesses informal institutions of social control, and the relationship between the public police and the growing private security industry, will enlighten Western readers.

For those who are unfamiliar with Chinese culture and institutions of social control, this book is the place to start. It is a wonderful and fascinating introduction to contemporary Chinese society and to the problems of crime control that accompany it. The reader's attention will be richly rewarded.

Peter Grabosky
Regulatory Institutions Network
Research School of Pacific and Asian Studies
Australian National University

and

Australian Research Council Centre of Excellence in Policing and Security

Preface and acknowledgements

This book was based on my PhD thesis at the University of Hong Kong. The topic of the study was initially development and crime in a transforming China, and the study aimed to examine changes in crime in the modernization process of the country, with a focus on the booming city of Shenzhen. It later evolved into deploying the concept of social capital to examine community crime prevention in Shenzhen, with the initial topic always in the background. The new endeavour has proved especially challenging and rewarding.

The fieldwork was conducted in Shenzhen, which borders Hong Kong on the south-east coast of China. Shenzhen was designated as a Special Economic Zone (SEZ) in the reform era. The former fishing village has witnessed profound economic and social changes during the past three decades. In particular it has become an attractive destination for the huge migrant population from the inland areas of China, and over the years migrants have accounted for a majority of its population. Known as an 'overnight city', Shenzhen leads the whole country in implementing the reform and open-door policy. To some extent, the findings contained in this book have wider implications for China studies and comparative criminology.

Social stability has always been accorded overwhelming priority in contemporary Chinese society, and more so in the reform era when crime has soared rapidly. In the country, the crime rate in 2006 was nearly four times that in 1950. The effort to pursue stability and control crime has become an integral part of the reform and open-door policy. The growth of crime and the development of the economy seem to be moving *pari passu*. Soaring crime rates in the economic reform era have imposed tremendous pressure on the traditional control mechanisms, especially the communitarian ethos in Chinese society. This book aims to shed light on the tensions between growing crime and Chinese commmunitarianism and illustrate to what extent the community approach to crime prevention has adapted to the new social realities.

The book draws on a large amount of material in Chinese. As researchers undertaking cross-cultural studies would understand, it is not easy to negotiate problems in multiple languages. I have tried to be faithful to the original Chinese material and at the same time endeavoured to make the English translations comprehensible. Often I have added in parentheses the *pinyin* form of special terms and phrases, and I have largely followed that system of Romanization of Chinese names, except in common English forms of historical names such as Confucius and Mencius.

In completing the PhD thesis and adapting it into the current book, I owe many more debts – personal and intellectual – than I can possibly acknowledge. I thank Prof. Roderic Broadhurst, my supervisor at the University of Hong Kong, for his guidance, patience, inspiration and encouragement throughout the years. Even while I was in the midst of writing the thesis, he suggested that I should consider publishing the thesis as a book. At a time when I was 'relishing' life without the tensions and anxieties of doing a PhD, he kept prodding me on the book project and even pushed me hard to write a book proposal to Willan Publishing. I am especially grateful for the encouragement and help from Prof. Peter Grabosky at the Australian National University and Prof. Roger Hood at the University of Oxford. They both joined Prof. Broadhurst to encourage me to adapt the PhD thesis into a book and played a pivotal role in the process. Prof. Hood read the first manuscript thoroughly, pointed out patiently all my grammatical errors and sloppy expressions in English, and provided valuable comments on how to improve the text. Prof. Grabosky was the external examiner of the thesis, and his encouraging assessment and constant support gave me extra impetus to take one further step by publishing it.

Since I set foot in Hong Kong to undertake my postgraduate study, I have received valuable help and support from many people at the University of Hong Kong. I wish to thank in particular Dr Philip Beh, Prof. Karen Joe Laidler, Prof. John Bacon-Shone, and Mr David Hodson. I appreciate very much the assistance from Ms Kelly Lee, Mr Davy Lau, Mr Eric Tsang, Ms Clara Wan, and Ms Lavina Tam. I also value very much the sharing of joys and pains of conducting a PhD study with the following postgraduate students: Barbara Ho, Francisca Kwok, Aris Chan, Kent Lee, Crystal Loh, and Marketa Moore.

I am also grateful for the valuable help and moral support from many people in both mainland China and Hong Kong, including Mr Xu Renyi, Ms Zhan Jinyu, Miss Xu Qian, Mr Yang Zhanwei, Ms Sun Junfen, Prof. Chang Siliang, Prof. Xie Yong, Mr Sheng Chengguang, Prof. Chen Daifen, Ms Helen Li, Mr Felix Law, Miss Saulee Cheung, Miss Esther Cheung, Mr Daniel Lam and family, and Mr Simon Peh and family. In particular I appreciate the support and friendship of Miss Liu Xiaohong and Ms Lin Youshi.

I owe thanks to my family: my parents, brothers, sisters-in-law, nieces and nephew. Especially Junhui and Junmei have acted both as elder brothers and mentors. I particularly thank my parents, to whom I dedicate this book. My thanks also go to Andy Xi Xiang whose prodding and support have played an important role in the completion of the book.

Thanks also go to Professor Cheung Yuet-wah and Dr Nicole Cheung Wai-ting at the Chinese University of Hong Kong for their support and encouragement. I thank my colleagues at the Department of Applied Social Studies, City University of Hong Kong.

Finally, I want to thank the wonderful people at Willan Publishing. Mr Brian Willan has extended to me incredible patience and understanding since the very beginning of publishing the book. My thanks also go to the two reviewers, the production editor Ms Emma Gubb, the copy-editor Dr Joseph Garver, and Ms Michelle Antrobus.

Words on the gate of a building in community A:

'Mass prevention and mass management, ensure peace and security; watch out for each other, and close the door upon entry or exit.'

'Watch out for each other and be aware of strangers'. [the telephone number for reporting crime to the local police station and that of the office of housing management]

Slogan on the wall of the seventh building in community D: 'To crack down firmly on thieves.'

To my parents

Chapter 1

Introduction

Among the social problems affecting societies during the past several decades, crime looms large, always staying near the top of the agenda of public concerns. Crime growth and economic development seem to be moving *pari passu*. Escalating crime in a period of prosperity puzzles criminologists (e.g. Young 1999). Yet, crime hits not only the highly industrialized, affluent countries but also the developing economies in eastern Europe, and large urban concentrations in South America and Africa, where many live under the poverty line. So it becomes a paradox that both affluence and poverty seem to breed high levels of victimization (van Dijk 1994). It is observed that 'crime has moved from the rare, the abnormal, the offence of the marginal and the stranger, to a commonplace part of the texture of everyday life' (Young 1999: 30). Or, in the words of Garland (1996: 446), crime has become a 'normal social fact'. Consequently, fear of crime and anxiety about crime penetrate every nook and cranny of social life.

With crime escalating, the theories to characterize the patterns of social control in the past several decades seem to be plagued with inconsistencies and contradictions. For example, Cohen's model (1985) projected a picture of statist decentralization and decarceration, while Melossi (2000) depicted a scene of antipathy towards criminals, who are portrayed as monstrosities, evil forces attacking the very foundation of a social fabric. The contradiction echoes Garland's analysis of social control since the 1960s (Garland 1996, 2000), the essence being that contemporary society sees the coexistence of the strategies of 'preventive partnership' and 'punitive segregation'. According to Garland, the normality of high crime rates and the limitations of the criminal justice agencies have created a new predicament for governments, leading to the volatile and contradictory character of recent crime control policy. He suggests that underlying this dualistic, ambivalent and often contradictory pattern of crime control is a similarly dualistic and ambivalent pattern of criminological thinking: the split between 'criminology of the self' and 'criminology of the Other'. He further stresses that this contradictory dualism displays a conflict at the heart of contemporary policy, rather than a rationally differentiated response to different kinds of crime (Garland 1996).

As Garland and Sparks (2000) argue, the social changes of the last several decades have already stirred the rethinking of the assumptions underlying academic criminology. They observed that the continuing erosion of clear-cut distinctions between the public and the private realms of crime control, coupled with the displacement of the criminal justice state from centre stage in the production of security and crime control, has had a major impact on the ways in which criminology now addresses questions of regulation and control. That is, criminologists have begun to 'think beyond the state' (Garland and Sparks 2000: 4). Indeed, the failure of the welfare state in crime control and the pessimism of 'nothing works' in criminology and policymaking circles have prompted the emergence of various theorizations regarding the state – for example, the death of the social (Rose 1996), the hollowing out of the state (Lash and Urry 1994), the limits of the sovereign state (Garland 1996), and minimal statism (Cohen 1985).

It is exactly in this pervasive climate that the approach of community crime prevention emerged. But in the bulky literature of community crime prevention, the rhetoric seems to imply that, currently, the arena of crime control is dominated by the community approach. So proponents of the community approach should bear in mind Garland's pertinent thesis of dualist coexistence. In fact, that very thesis not only deals a blow to those hardliners who embrace 'three-strikes-and-you-are-out' and mandatory sentencing in the war against crime and disorder, but also pours cold water on the community activists who emphasize such strategies as informal control, naming–blaming–shaming, community policing, and the community alternative to combat crime.

The above discussion on the background against which community crime prevention emerges is totally from a Western perspective. In his influential book *The Politics of Crime and Community*, Gordon Huphes (2007: 1) acknowledged this 'gaping omission' of the East and other geo-historical places and contexts. With a focus on community crime prevention in China, it is hoped that this book will, to some extent, fill this void. Since the initiation of the reform and open-door policy, Chinese society has experienced widespread and penetrating transformations. Bakken (2000) argued that current China is in a period of industrial revolution, similar to what the West experienced more than 200 years ago. Solinger (1999) suggested that the switch from a planned economy to a market economy in China involves an institutional dislocation that has much in common with the decline of the welfare state in the West. Whatever the merits and demerits of the above arguments, it is certain that large-scale social changes are sweeping every stratum of social life in China. Further, in the eyes of Western scholars, the Chinese approach to crime prevention is essentially community-based (e.g. Troyer *et al.* 1989). Thus, it is worthwhile to look at the Chinese approach to crime and crime control in the transforming period of China, in order to shed light on crime and crime control in general.

Research background and theoretical framework

As stated previously, community crime prevention in the West reflects the particular social developments in Western societies since the 1970s. Crime has become a normal social factor for all layers of the social fabric, leading to the public perception that the criminal justice system, particularly the police, is ineffective in fighting crime and safeguarding public security. Moreover, substantial doubt has been cast on the effectiveness of the 'welfare' approach to crime and other social problems. Further, among criminologists and policymakers, it is realized that 'prevention is better than cure', and thus the proactive approach to crime gains recognition. In this atmosphere, community crime prevention stresses the vital role played by the citizenry in crime prevention and the importance of the multiagency partnership and a good police–public relationship. Thus, various strategies under the roof of community crime prevention have been initiated, including neighbourhood/block watch, crime stoppers, citizen patrol, safer cities programme, lighting of the streets, target-hardening, house security survey, community policing and problem-oriented policing, to name just a few. As a result, studies were conducted to evaluate the effectiveness of various programmes and theories were formulated to support the conceptualization of the community approach. However, a deep look into the literature reveals that proponents of the community crime-prevention approach are divided on what measures are intrinsically community-oriented. This confusion is exemplified in the range of classification models of crime prevention, where overlaps and contradictions abound regarding what the concept of community crime prevention implies.

Furthermore, as scholars within the field have observed, at a more theoretical level what 'community' denotes in community crime prevention is vague. As Cohen notes, 'it is not at all clear what community control means and almost anything can appear under the heading of "community" and almost anything can be justified if this prefix is used' (Cohen 1985: 116). The observation of community's symbolic power is echoed by Walklate (1996), who regards 'community' as a 'seductive word'. In regard to the community approach, Nelken (1985) cautions against the confusion of means with ends.

Notwithstanding the enthusiasm of community activists, it is inconclusive whether community crime prevention is effective, especially compared with the traditional approach. It is contentious how effectiveness should be defined: is it judged on the criterion of reduced crime, or the 'consolation prizes' (Ekblom and Pease 1995), such as reduced fear of crime and incivilities or other quality-of-life measures? Another fundamental question is how to distinguish between output evaluation, outcome evaluation and process evaluation. It is suggested that, according to scientific and statistical measuring rods, most evaluation work is inadequate, simplistic and even flawed. Rosenbaum suggests that 'any claims regarding the successfulness of citizen crime prevention activities must not be categorically accepted apart from a studious examination of the integrity of the research designs and data-analysis strategies predicting these assertions' (1986: 20). Ekblom and Pease even claim that some evaluation work 'doesn't even meet the most elementary criteria of evaluative probity' (1995: 86). This is echoed by Sherman *et al.* (1997), who built five levels to measure the integrity of more than $4 bn worth of federally sponsored crime prevention programmes in the United States. Moreover, in terms of programme failure, most of the time it is unclear whether it is theory failure, implementation failure or measurement failure, thus casting doubt on the operational mechanisms of certain initiatives.

There are other fundamental questions asked of the community approach. During the claimed shift from viewing the criminal justice system as the thin blue line in the war against crime to viewing the institutions of civil society as being of prime importance, should or could the community approach *assist, supplement, monitor* or *replace* official provisions of dealing with crime (Nelken 1985)? In other words, should state minimalism be possible (Cohen 1985), or how should the roles of steering and rowing of the state be defined (Crawford 1997)? Or, less ambitiously, does community involvement amount in practice to a covert extension of the criminal justice system (Nelken 1985) or to 'net-widening' (Cohen 1985)? What are we pursuing in terms of the two visions in community crime prevention constructed by Currie (1988): 'symbolic' or 'more complicated' views? Does the rush to embrace the community approach only display nostalgia for life in the 1950s and 1960s and the envisioning of community as a small village, or does it only reveal a moral panic from living in a high-crime society (Cohen 1985, Nelken 1985, Young 1999)? In the quest for target-hardening and defensible space, are we being confined in a gated community, a fortress city and a barrack society? The endless list of questions extends afar.

In the academy, another controversy emerged at the same time as that surrounding the community approach to crime prevention. In her 1961 book *The Death and Life of Great American Cities*, which inspired defensible space theorists in her footsteps, Jane Jacobs explained that the dense social networks in the older, mixed-use neighbourhoods constituted a form of social capital that encouraged public safety. Since the 1970s, the concept of social capital has gained widespread use in disciplines ranging from economics, sociology, and education, to political science. According to Coleman (1990), the concept is in contrast to a broadly penetrated fiction in modern society, a fiction that holds that society consists of a set of independent individuals, each of whom acts to achieve goals that are independently arrived at, and that the functioning of the social system consists of the combination of these actions of independent individuals. In contrast with the nature of atomized individuals, social capital describes the benefits and advantages accruing to individuals when they are involved in networks and broader social structures. Through an analysis of the difference between the well-governed north Italy and the poorly governed south Italy, Putnam (1993a: 37) uncovered the relationship between social capital and economic prosperity by arguing that 'these communities did not become civic simply because they were rich. The historical record strongly suggests precisely the opposite: They have become rich because they were civic.' Lamenting the loss of social capital through the decline of civic participation in American life, Putnam (1995) viewed social capital as a basic element in building a civil society. Lin acknowledged the inescapable vulnerability to definitional contestation, and in order to save it from 'an undeserving death', he defined social capital as *the investment in embedded resources in social networks with expected returns* (2000, 2001a, 2001b).

Even a cursory glance at the two concepts of community crime prevention and social capital reveals certain links or similarities between them. Carson (2004a, 2004b, 2007) put concepts of community and social capital under the roof of communalism and regarded social capital as the 'newer and ostensibly more sophisticated relative' (Carson 2004b: 192) of community. Apart from the seeming affiliation between social capital and community crime prevention, little genuine and substantial efforts have been made to explore social capital's potential application in and usefulness for the community approach to crime prevention.

Turning to Chinese society, social capital plays an important role in all walks of social life, although the concept of social capital *per se* is seldom used. From a Westerner's perspective, China conjures up an image of *'guanxi'*[1] together with the Great Wall, Tiananmen Square, and Changsam, among other things. Traditional Chinese society is credited with generalized collectivism, close interpersonal relationships, institutionalized reciprocity, penetrating informal control, and widespread mutual surveillance within the social fabric (e.g. Dutton 1992, Sigley 1996, Deng and Cordilia 1999). Since the founding of the People's Republic of China (PRC) in 1949, the closely knit informal control web was even intensified with the reinforcement of the household registration system (*hukou*), the establishment of the work unit (*danwei*) with its associated welfare system, the setting up of the grass-roots level organization of the neighbourhood committee (*juweihui*), and the sustained inculcation of communist ideology. Thus, China is credited with a low crime rate in the pre-reform era.

In China's modern history, 1978 signals a significant turning point. In that year, the policy of economic reform and opening up (*gaige kaifang*) was launched in the Third Plenum of the Eleventh Chinese Communist Party (CCP) Congress. Since then, the country has undergone profound and speedy changes. With the ideology of 'socialism with Chinese characteristics', China embraced modernization, industrialization, urbanization and marketization. In the period of transformation, its economy was shifted from a planned economy to a market economy, and the citizens' living standard has been substantially improved. One of the most spectacular successes of the reform era lies in the enforcement of the 'household responsibility system' in the countryside in the early 1980s, which had a double-edged effect: the increase in agricultural productivity and a huge army of surplus labour in the vast rural areas. With the institutionalized discrepancies between rural and urban residents, peasants defied or circumvented the restrictions imposed by the *hukou* system and began to migrate or 'float' to the towns or cities with the aim of gaining a modicum of benefits brought about by the reform policies, or of 'contesting citizenship in urban China' (Solinger 1999). This massive internal migration challenged social institutions and infrastructures in the country, and it virtually shattered the welfare system associated with the *hukou* system, such as rationing of rice and cooking oil, and assignment of jobs. The economic growth and population migration run parallel to a rise of crime in China. Just like immigrants in the Western countries, the Chinese migrants easily became the scapegoat for the increase in crime and other social problems in the cities. Therefore, social control and especially crime control are faced with new challenges in the reform era. One of the initiatives in combating crime is the initiation of a community-based, crime-prevention programme: Building Little, Safe and Civilized Communities (BLSCC).

By drawing on the insights generated in the West surrounding community crime prevention and social capital, I endeavour in this book to capture this unique period in Chinese history to conduct a preliminary examination of BLSCC in the Chinese city of Shenzhen – a city in the vanguard of implementing the policy of 'reform and opening up', with fascinating economic achievements and acute migration and crime problems.

Research questions and significance of the study

The study reported in this book was conducted from late 1998 to mid-2002. It mainly explores four issues:

1 How to define community crime prevention and could the concept of social capital be applied to the examination of community crime prevention?
2 To what extent could the concept of social capital be applied to the examination of Chinese society in general and crime and social control in China in particular?
3 What are the characteristics of BLSCC, a locally initiated, community crime-prevention programme in China?
4 Could empirical data collected in China support the link between social capital and BLSCC?

As crime inflicts harm in both socialist and capitalist societies and drives people to fight back to win the 'war', this enquiry aims to make its contribution to that pursuit. First, this empirical study distinguishes reality from rhetoric regarding crime prevention in China. Here the 'empirical' is stressed because of its rarity or absence in Chinese criminology. Compared with other jurisdictions, the discourse on crime and the policies of crime control in China are more subject to political winds, especially the CCP guidelines. China always takes pride in its low crime rate, and in political ideology the low crime rate is (or at least used to be) treated as a testimony to the superiority of socialism over capitalism. Yet, crime statistics were regarded as state secrets and were unavailable to the public. This sensitivity and over-politicalization associated with crime hinders any sophisticated evidence-based research into crime and crime control in China. Success stories are always supported by anecdotal evidence. This research seeks to refresh policymakers and crime researchers in China in their quest for effective crime prevention measures. It is demonstrated that regarding community crime prevention most of the principles embodied in the Western strategies of community crime-prevention have long been employed or promoted on Chinese soil. So this study to some extent serves to 'dig out' the Chinese strengths in crime prevention so as to put them to better use.

Second, the study explores the Chinese experience of social control and crime prevention. Westerners were either fascinated by the mysterious China (Toryer and Rojek 1989) or returned with great praise and high expectations after they first observed the Chinese justice system (Curran and Cook 1993). However, as Troyer and Rojek admitted, 'knowledge about modern Chinese society is still limited. This is especially true with respect to crime, criminal justice, and the general social control system' (1989: 2). According to He and Marshall (1997: 59), Western knowledge of China has typically been from the perspective of an outsider looking in, resulting in a very sketchy and incomplete picture. Moreover, most Western studies of China are based on secondary data, such as CCP policies, official documents, laws and regulations, and newspaper coverage, although a new shift has been observed to a more microlevel study of more specific groups and localities. Further, a substantial amount of information and observations in the Western literature are outdated. This problem is especially acute considering the fact that China is developing at an unprecedented rate in the wake of economic reform since the 1980s. During his scrutiny of culture, law and policy in England from 1830 to 1914, Wiener (1990) put forward a thesis of 'criminal policy as cultural history'. So this study, conducted by a native Chinese with a cross-cultural perspective, helps to enrich and broaden the understanding of China generally and social and crime control particularly in the West.

Last but not least, this enquiry expands the concept of social capital into the analysis of community crime prevention, especially from a non-Western society. As shown in the literature, the potential of social capital to explain community crime prevention has not been explicitly explored. Thus, this study not only deepens the comprehension of community crime prevention in diverse ideological and cultural contexts, but also enriches the understanding of social capital.

Overview of the book

This book consists of nine chapters. Chapter 2 describes the issues centred on doing the fieldwork. First, it introduces Shenzhen, where the fieldwork for this study was conducted, including *hukou* and migration, population and economic growth, and crime. Second, it provides an overview of the five communities to which access was granted by the authorities. Third, it discusses the dilemmas in the process of conducting China studies, including dilemmas within and dilemmas without. Last, it briefly discusses two obstacles in conducting fieldwork in Shenzhen and introduces the research methods used in this study.

Chapter 3 defines community crime prevention, social capital and the nexus between the two. First, it surveys several prominent explanations of the development of social control in modern Western societies with the aim of providing a broad template for depicting the emergence of community crime prevention. Second, it describes the context for the emergence of community crime prevention, highlighting three interwoven facilitating factors arising during the past several decades: theoretical reorientation, changes in crime, and the perceived inefficiency of the traditional criminal justice system in controlling crime. Third, it outlines the conceptualization of crime prevention in the literature, in order to locate community crime prevention in the general framework of crime prevention. Fourth, it introduces the concept of social capital, and establishes the nexus between social capital and community crime prevention by discussing the criminological theories supporting community crime prevention. Lastly, it highlights the issues and problems surrounding social capital and community crime prevention: the three dyads of formal/informal, public/private, and inclusion/exclusion, and the role of the state.

Chapter 4 examines in detail to what extent social capital can be employed to depict Chinese society and social and crime control in China. It first introduces two theoretical models of the organization of Chinese society, showing that rural society in China, both in traditional times and in the Mao era, was characterized by internal intimacy and external isolation. It then explores the concept of *guanxi*, the indigenous version of social capital, and its application in the Chinese cities in the reform era, demonstrating that *guanxi* plays a remarkable and sometimes even miraculous role in everyday life in Chinese cities, and how *guanxi* converges with the concept of social capital.

Chapter 5 begins with a description of the crime situation in post-1949 China and briefly reviews academic and official discussions of crime and especially its rapid growth in the reform era. Building on the discussion of the Chinese perspective of social capital and the Chinese understanding of crime, the next section examines the basic features of the Chinese control mechanisms. It illustrates how certain Chinese social institutions, notably the household registration system, the neighbourhood committee, the work unit, and the public security bureau, can play an important role in controlling and preventing crime, at least theoretically, both individually and cooperatively, as manifested in the so-called mass line (*qunzhong luxian*). This examination is to show that the Chinese social control system is intrinsically community-based, and how the concept of social capital can be employed to explain its working rationalities. Perhaps the point that in Chinese communities there is inadequate 'bridging social capital' may sound rather unconventional. But it should be pointed out that all the exploration is based on the social, economic and ideological aspects in Chinese society prior to the full-swing development of the economic reform. Thus, it paves the way for a more detailed study of the development of social control concomitant with the economic reform.

Chapters 6 and 7 describe in detail BLSCC, the locally initiated, community crime-prevention programme in Shenzhen. Chapter 6 first introduces the general crime policy, 'comprehensive management of social order' (CMSO), in China, which is characterized by the 'duality' of punishment and prevention. Second, it moves to cover the development of BLSCC in Shenzhen. Third, it briefly discusses the official claimed outcome of BLSCC in Shenzhen. Chapter 7 first describes in great detail the measures taken to implement BLSCC, including organization features, safety measures, civilization measures, and the rating system. Then, it concludes by discussing the officially claimed 'Chinese characteristics' of BLSCC, the difference from and similarities to the social control mechanisms prior to the full-swing economic reform, and the role social capital plays in BLSCC.

Chapter 8 describes the implementation of BLSCC in the microcosm of two contrasting Shenzhen communities, paying special attention to the community survey results. It first reports the qualitative data collected on communities A and B, which are characterized as 'order and peace' and 'disorder and crime', respectively. Then it presents the data from the community survey in detail by contrasting the two communities in terms of three aspects of community life: (1) mutual help, social networks and interaction; (2) crime, fear of crime, and attitudes to the private security guards hired by companies or communities, and the police; (3) awareness and perceived effectiveness of BLSCC. The chapter concludes by discussing both the qualitative and quantitative results in terms of the manifestation of the two aspects of social capital: bonding and bridging social capital in the two communities.

Chapter 9, in conclusion, first summarizes the whole study on the two levels: theoretical exploration and empirical testing. Then it discusses the implication of the findings in relation to the nexus between social capital and community crime prevention in terms of the following aspects: formal/informal social control, public/private control, inclusion/exclusion, and the role of the state. It also examines certain issues unfolding in China to shed light on the future direction of social control and its study in China.

Note

1 *Guanxi* literally means relationships, ties, or links or connections between people, but it can also denote seeking favours through personal connections. For details, see Chapter 4.

Chapter 2

Taking to the field

The study contained in this book was conducted in Shenzhen, a city at the vanguard of the economic reform and opening-up in China. As a Special Economic Zone (SEZ) situated in the Pearl River Delta of the south-eastern coast, Shenzhen underwent rapid economic development in the reform era, and was thus dubbed an 'overnight' city. Designated as a 'laboratory' and a 'window' for economic reform and openness, Shenzhen leads the inland areas in economic transition and social changes, with the slogan, 'Shenzhen today is the interior areas tomorrow'. Its impressive economic achievement, however, ran in parallel with rapid population growth and an escalating crime problem. Thus, compared with those hinterland cities, Shenzhen exhibits both similarities and differences in diverse perspectives of social life. From a methodological viewpoint, the aspect of similarities is important because it is still Chinese, while the aspect of differences signifies the direction of future development of China as a whole. Therefore, through the prism or vantage point of Shenzhen, the past, present and future of China may be crystallized and captured in one picture. However, the specialness of Shenzhen does not translate into less difficulties and challenges in carrying out a criminological study. Moreover, as a native Chinese growing up in China's reform era and as a student of criminology in Hong Kong (a Special Administrative Region since its handover of sovereignty in 1997), I was also confronted with a bitter struggle between the West and the East and between the traditional and the modern. So this chapter is organized into four sections. First, it introduces Shenzhen, where the fieldwork for this study was conducted, including *hukou* and migration, population and economic growth, and crime. Second, it provides an overview of the five communities to which access was granted by the authorities. Third, it discusses the dilemmas in the process of conducting China studies, including dilemmas within and dilemmas without. Last, it briefly discusses two obstacles in conducting fieldwork in Shenzhen and introduces the research methods used in this study.

Shenzhen: an 'overnight city'

Shenzhen borders Hong Kong and was established as a SEZ in 1980. Since then, it has grown from a small fishing village into one of the major metropolises in mainland China. The establishment of Shenzhen as an SEZ, to some extent, served as a pilot study of the economic reform and open-door policy in China. Or, in the words of Deng Xiaoping, 'Cross the river only by the stepping stones.' It is thus dubbed the 'window' of the reform and open-door policy. Shenzhen SEZ includes four districts: Futian, Luohu, Nanshan, and Yantian. Shenzhen SEZ and the two districts of Bao'an and Longgang form Shenzhen City. A barbed wire fence, the so-called 'second border', separates Shenzhen SEZ from the districts of Bao'an and Longgang. In the initial stage, the second border played an important role in preventing migrants from entering Shenzhen SEZ without authorization, as seen in the section on management of the floating population. In recent years, the 'second border' has become less important, with the inland areas catching up in economic development and the central government gradually abolishing the privileged policies favouring Shenzhen SEZ. In this text, Shenzhen refers to Shenzhen City as a whole.

Shenzhen became one of the 'mecca' destinations for migrants, especially rural migrants when they started leaving the countryside for opportunities in the cities, bearing in mind the Chinese proverb that 'water flows down to lower places but people flow up to richer places'. Thus, the economic development of Shenzhen runs parallel to population growth. This section comprises three parts. The first part introduces the *hukou* system and migration in Shenzhen and the country in general, the second part describes the population and economic growth in Shenzhen and the third part depicts the crime situation in Shenzhen.

Hukou and migration in Shenzhen

With the policy of reform and opening up gaining full speed, the *hukou* system became increasingly incompatible with social and economic development. The rural reform centred on the 'household responsibility system' in the countryside, giving rise to millions of surplus agricultural labourers. Some of the surplus farm labourers were absorbed by the township and village enterprises that have blossomed since the end of the commune system in the early 1980s. Many more of them began massive migration to the towns and cities, negotiating the barriers imposed by the *hukou* system associated with the huge social and political disparities between rural and urban residents. This mass transformation created successive waves of the 'floating population' (*liudong renkou*) in China. At the end of 2005, the floating population reached 147.35 million, accounting for 11.28 per cent of the total population (National Statistical Bureau 2006). Migration here mainly refers to rural to urban internal migration. The 'floating population' is defined solely on the basis of the *hukou* status. They are 'floating' because they have not been granted the official *hukou* status in the place where they are currently residing. It is because of the *hukou* status that floating here is not equivalent to the meaning of migration in common usage; that is, simply transferring one's place of residence to a new jurisdiction and remaining there for a specified time (Solinger 1999). This illustrates the significance of *hukou* in the examination of migration. Dutton (1992) noted that even after the implementation of the identity card system in the mid-1980s, the *hukou* system is still needed. Thus, the divide between urban and rural residency, including the associated difference in status, is still maintained on the basis of the *hukou* system.

In the 1980s, the barriers to rural to urban migration were somewhat relaxed. In 1984, the state council issued a directive permitting peasants to settle in towns after obtaining a new kind of non-agricultural *hukou* status: *zili kouliang chenzhen hukou* (literally urban *hukou* for those with self-supplied grain). But it is particularly stipulated that the destination towns are minor, not the seats of county governments. In June 1985, the temporary residence permit (*zan zhu zheng*) was introduced, wherein migrants older than 16 are required to obtain documentation from officials in their native place, and upon arrival in a new destination, they must apply for temporary residence permits from the local public security bureau. But holders of temporary residence permits are not entitled to rationing cards or housing allocation, as are the local residents, and their children have no right to enter schools in their destination urban areas (see

Shi and Meng 1996). Since May 1985, Shenzhen authorities started issuing temporary residence permits, valid for one year, to migrants who had a work contract for over six months (*Shenzhen Political and Legal Yearbook* (SZPLY) 1996: 46).

In the late 1980s, some counties began selling local urban household registration cards (known as blue cards or blue seals) to migrant workers. Shenzhen started a pilot study on blue card *hukou* in 1995, and later blue cards were issued to those who bought housing in the districts of Bao'an and Longgang in Shenzhen. From October 1995 to November 1998, 18,022 households (48,207 people) were granted blue card *hukou*, and 6,534 households (18,679 people) were granted the transfer from blue card *hukou* to permanent *hukou* in the two districts of Bao'an and Longgang (SZPLY 1996–9). It should be pointed out that this blue card *hukou* is premised on property buying, and the two districts involved are outside the Shenzhen SEZ, locally known as the 'second border', which migrants without proper documents cannot cross. Since 1993, the state policies and measures for labour migrants have become more relaxed and have shifted away from exclusion and expulsion to 'active guidance and better management', in the official language.

Earlier observations and comments on migration made inside China tended to focus on the numbers, characteristics, distribution and welfare of the migrants, to treat them as problems to the cities and to reflect panic and fear on the side of the government and city residents. Later studies started painting a less negative picture of the migrants and even examined the government's biased policies towards the migrants. Ma and Xiang (1998: 2) argued that 'peasant migrants, far from being hopeless and simply trying to eke out a precarious living in the cities, are optimistic, energetic and confident, possessing more invisible power than their less than urbane mannerisms would suggest'. From survey data from eastern China, Yao (2001) observed that social exclusion and economic discrimination reinforced each other in the fate of migrants and pointed out that the *hukou* system 'has been the source of the immigrants' [migrants'] lack of political rights and desire for long stays' (2001: 170). He called for 'greater inclusiveness' of migrants. One issue of great interest to this research is the fact that migrants are the focus of official concern over crime and disorderly behavior, and they are typically blamed for most of the social ills and problems. The mass media, official reports, and scholarly research seem to concur in this point with sensational reports. It is beyond the scope of this research to elaborate; hence, I only highlight several salient aspects.

Migration and rising crime occurred simultaneously in China, and thus migrants are easily blamed for the rise in crime and decreased feeling of safety in the wake of the economic reform. But the media and official reports on the proportions of crime committed by the migrants are so inconsistent that we could cast doubt on their accuracy. As Solinger (1999) noted, among the majority of reports on the disproportionately high numbers of migrants involved in crime, with one even as high as 97 per cent, there are reports of a low proportion of 13.1 per cent by a criminologist and newspaper comments such as, 'ninety-nine per cent of the rural migrants are law-abiding'. She even covered a Chinese criminologist's answer to how he could be sure that peasants actually committed the crimes in question: 'Why, because they were arrested.' Solinger (1999) argued that all of the reports on migrants' crime should be viewed in light of three facts: firstly, and most obviously, migrants tend to be the scapegoat of any bad effect experienced by the urbanites in the social transition; secondly, migrants' crime, if it occurs, reflects their status as outcasts, their exclusion from mainstream society; thirdly, most often, migrants are the victims rather than the perpetrators of crime, but they report their victimization less often. The observation of migrants as a scapegoat is in line with that made by Young (1999: 28–29) in relation to immigrants: 'The role of the immigrant is ... more as a scapegoat, an outgroup set up to assuage ontological insecurity rather than a cause of such.' Further, a great majority of migrants are young men; thus, they will account for a higher rate of crime than that of the host population. In China, crime statistics, if available, are seldom broken down, and detailed demographic data, such as migrant status, in relation to criminals, are not available. Thus, it is even harder for academic attempts to verify those sensational reports.

Population and economic growth in Shenzhen

Population in Shenzhen includes two parts: the permanent and the temporary. Migrants in Shenzhen come from other parts of Guangdong Province or other provinces. Some of them successfully applied for Shenzhen *hukou* status and are classified as permanent population in Shenzhen, together with the local residents. The holders of the temporary residence permits and the 'three nos'[1] persons belong to the temporary population in Shenzhen. Figure 2.1 highlights the growth of the total, temporary and permanent population in Shenzhen from 1979 to 2004. In 1979, prior to its establishment as an SEZ, the total population was only 314,100. By 1985, it had grown

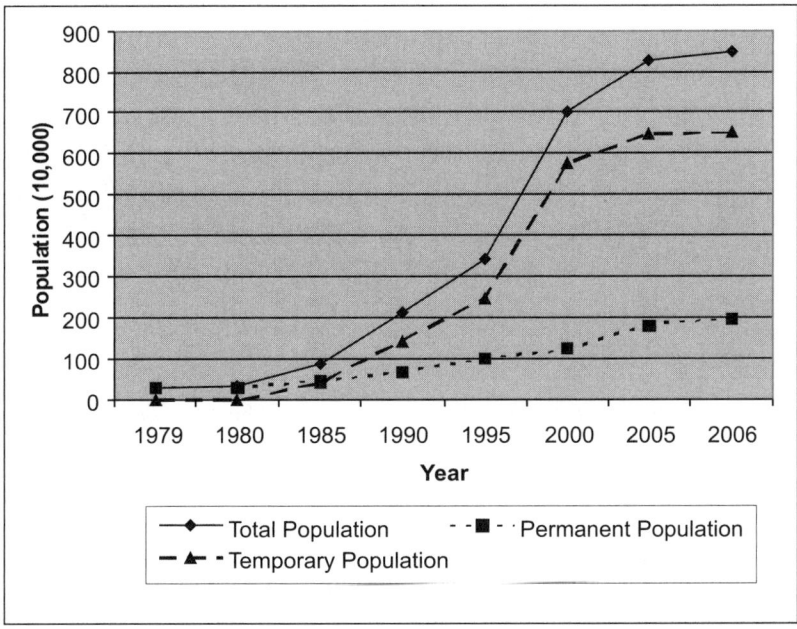

Sources: *Shenzhen Special Economic Zone Yearbook* (1986–96), *Shenzhen Yearbook* (1997–2006) and Shenzhen Statistical Bureau (2007).

Figure 2.1 Population of Shenzhen 1979–2006

to 741,000, 2.8 times that in 1979. In 1995, it reached 3,451,200, 11 times that of 1979. The population in 2006 was 8,464,300, 27 times more than in 1979. Both the permanent and temporary population grew. However, the latter grew more rapidly and accounted for an increasingly larger proportion of the total population. In 1979, the temporary population was only 1,500, accounting for a mere 0.48 per cent of the total population. In 1987, the temporary population first exceeded the permanent population, and subsequently the temporary population kept up its rapid growth, so that in 2006 it accounted for 77 per cent of the total population.

Employing a large influx of migrant labourers and enjoying a wide range of policy privileges as an SEZ, Shenzhen has made truly remarkable economic strides since 1979, as shown in Figure 2.2. In 1979, its GDP was 196 million yuan and its GDP per capita was 606 yuan. By 1985, the GDP had risen to 390 million yuan and its GDP per capita to 4,809 yuan. In 2006, its GDP was 581 billion yuan, the

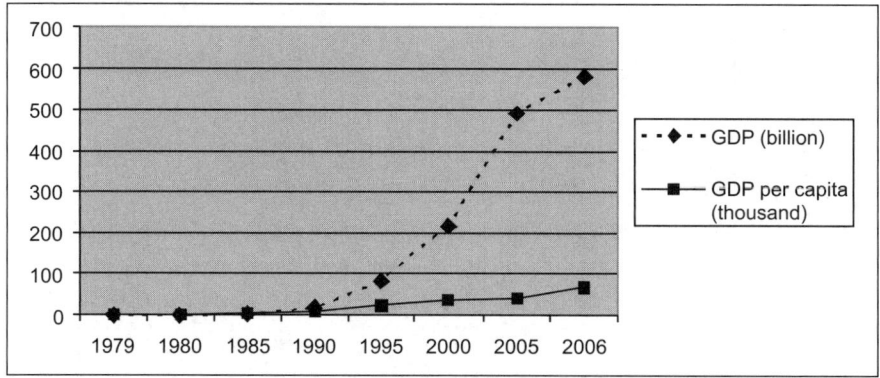

Sources: *Shenzhen Special Economic Zone Yearbook* (1986–96), *Shenzhen Yearbook* (1997–2006) and Shenzhen Statistical Bureau (2007).

Figure 2.2 GDP and GDP per capita in Shenzhen 1979–2006

fourth largest among the main metropolises in mainland China, and its GDP per capita was 69,450 yuan, the highest among the main metropolis in mainland China.

Crime in Shenzhen

Systematic crime statistics are not available, and the following data are gathered from several different sources to depict the crime situation in Shenzhen from 1980 to 2007. Table 2.1 shows the total number of reported crimes in Shenzhen from 1980 to 2007. During this period, there were several sudden increases, the most notable of which were from 1988 to 1999 and from 1999 to 2000. The second jump from 8,733 to 68,863 is very puzzling to me. I double-checked the *Shenzhen Political and Legal Yearbook* and found no clues.[2] The total number of crimes in 2003 (as recorded and publicly reported) was the highest, and in subsequent years it dropped. Table 2.2 shows the total convictions for public security offences and public security offenders from 1981 to 2007. There was a steady increase over the years. The sudden increase from 2005 to 2006 might be attributed to the Public Security Law taking effect in 2006 (see Chapter 5 for the difference between a criminal offence and a public security offence).

Five communities: model versus non-model[3]

Access was granted to five communities, represented as A, B, C, D,

Table 2.1 Recorded (and reported) criminal cases in Shenzhen 1980–2007

Year	Crimes
1980	623
1981	1,165
1982	1,165
1983	1,473
1984	1,374
1985	1,743
1986	1,352
1987	1,352
1988	2,028
1989	7,467
1990	(6,353[1])
1991	(9,965[1])
1992	(8,507[1])
1993	(10,362[1]) 10,500[2]
1994	(12,674[1]) 12,773[2]
1995	13,043[2] (13,073[1])
1996	11,790[2]
1997	8,406[2]
1998	8,060[2]
1999	8,733[2]
2000	68,863[2]
2001	80,282[2]
2002	67,862[2]
2003	106,797[2]
2004	99,678[2]
2005	78,598[2]
2006	70,604[2]
2007	66,740[2]

Sources: [1]figures from Tan and Xue (1997); [2]*Shenzhen Political and Legal Yearbook*, 1996–2008. The remaining figures are from Huang (1996).

and E in order to maintain confidentiality and anonymity. Among the five communities, A was rated a model and the other four were not.[4] Community A is a paradigm for housing reform, estate development, and management in China. It was even designated as 'China's First Civilized Village', and received VIPs, including former president Jiang Zhemin on 5 December 1995. It has over 6,016 households

Table 2.2 Convictions for public security offences and offenders in Shenzhen 1981–2007

Year	Convictions	Convicted offenders
1981	9,533	8,871
1982	4,781	9,505
1983	10,329	13,927
1984	21,744	30,302
1985	11,501	16,075
1986	3,062	5,604
1987	4,233	8,939
1988	5,914	12,203
1989	9,132	23,654
1990	12,207	32,675
1991	19,406	49,169
1992	26,345	59,441
1993	29,482	68,187
1994	33,957	61,469
1995	34,885	63,950
1996	35,869	64,151
1997	34,889	56,296
1998	33,889	56,296
1999	35,551	55,798
2000	32,835	54,129
2001	44,749	69,592
2002	43,139	38,529
2003	50,342	53,889
2004	48,271	68,253
2005	55,147	71,448
2006	209,082	192,191
2007	324,350	254,812

Sources: data for 1981–98 are from the Shenzhen Police, and the rest are from *Shenzhen Political and Legal Yearbook*, 2000–08.

with more than 30,000 residents, among whom nearly 20,000 hold permanent Shenzhen residence status. A large proportion of residents are civil servants or employees in the State-Owned Enterprises (SOE). Community A was administered by the Office of Housing Management (OHM) affiliated to a large housing estate company, rather than by the popular local Neighborhood Committee. The Neighbourhood Committee was overshadowed because the OHM took charge of all the important aspects, such as security. The Neighbourhood

Committees remained responsible for military conscription, family planning, and local elections in the community.

Community B, once a rural village, earned a pass in BLSCC. The reform era saw village annual income increase astronomically after its farming land was taken over by the government to build a very large industrial belt. Its residents were financially compensated and granted urban residential status. Since 1984, a huge number of migrant workers came to the village and various service industries were developed to cater for the large number of factory workers from the neighbouring industry belt. So a village enterprise was created to oversee its own factories, markets, and retail stores. During my fieldwork, there were over 800 permanent residents (250 households) and 9,695 temporary residents in community B. This community is managed by a Neighbourhood Committee.

Community C also earned a pass in BLSCC. It was established in 1984 by the municipal government to provide subsidized accommodation to the workers of SOEs. At the time of the fieldwork, there were 1,360 households including 4,078 residents in 16 buildings, most of whom held temporary residence status. The income level of the residents was average, and a substantial number of residents were laid-off workers. Crime used to be a very severe problem, especially burglary. Among the residents there was a saying, 'If you have not been burgled, you don't belong to community C.' The community was managed by a Neighbourhood Committee that had adapted to the need for a different role in grass-roots governance.

Community D also got a pass in BLSCC. It used to be a village and was urbanized during the reform era. It was well known locally as a 'mistress village' because many Hong Kong men purchased flats in that village to stay with their mistresses. Although I visited the community, my request to do fieldwork was rejected. The streets were dirty and lined with various kinds of shops and sauna parlors. Like community B, its population was dominated by migrant workers. In addition to the alleged prosperity of the local sex industry, this community was also troubled by crime.

Community E also got a BLSCC pass and was developed by the government to cater for the residents in the 'three-no tribes', among whom are many migrant workers. Some migrants, unable or unwilling to pay for housing, put up shacks and other makeshift shelters, while others made money by building such shelters to rent to desperate migrants. Some 'tribes' became hot spots for criminal activities (such as manufacturing bogus food, drinks and other fake products), havens for criminals and fugitives, and warehouses for stolen goods. To address these problems, the Shenzhen government started building cheap temporary housing estates to accommodate migrant workers in every district. Community E is such a housing estate with 65 buildings, including 1,500 flats. My request to interview the local government officials and residents was rejected. Conditions in community E were in stark contrast to those found in community A.

Dilemmas in China studies

To conduct China studies poses enormous challenges. To some extent, they are more acute for a native Chinese growing up in China's reform era and studying at a university in Hong Kong. The challenges are characterized as tension between the traditional and the modern and between the West and the East, for both scholars within China and those beyond the national border. In other words, they are dilemmas within and dilemmas without.

Dilemmas within

For Chinese intellectuals, the balance between the past (*gu*) and the present (*jin*) is always intriguing. For example, Confucius, dissatisfied with the contemporary status quo (*jin*, the present), sought to restore the 'rituals of Zhou' (*gu*, the past), thus 'employing the past to negate the present' (*yigu feijin*). In the Qin dynasty, legalism (*fajia*) became dominant, and Confucianism (*rujia*) was officially banned; this was 'emphasizing the present and denigrating the past' (*houjin bogu*) and led to the notorious 'burning the books and burying the Confucianists' (*fenshu kengru*). With the death of Qin, the Han dynasty revived Confucianism.[5] The Han and later imperial dynasties preserved all the imperial state structures established by the Qin dynasty and inspired by legalist discourse (such as the commandary-county system, the penal and surveillance system, and the bureaucracy), but replaced legalist discourse with the moralism of Confucianism as its orthodoxy. Once the imperial state system was established, pre-Qin Confucianist oppositional discourse became state orthodoxy; this was predicted on and served as a cover for legalism (Yang 1994: 243). The debate on the past versus the present continues to feature in Chinese history, and it culminated in the Cultural Revolution with the 'criticizing Lin Biao and criticizing Confucius' (*pilin pikong*) campaign.[6] In the 1980s, it resurfaced in the intelligentsia, with the past simply dismissed as 'feudal remnants' (*fengjian canyu*)[7] (see Dutton 1992).

The dilemma of the West versus the East (the Chinese) forced itself into the consciousness of the arrogant intellectuals in the 'Middle Kingdom' in the wake of the humiliating defeat of the Opium War, when China was forced to open to the West. The Opium War, in some sense, was a wake-up call for those patriotic modern intellectuals to reposition the 'Middle Kingdom' from a nascent global perspective. In the 1860s, the Westernization Movement (*yangwu yundong*) was initiated with the basic idea of learning from the West especially in areas of technology and weaponry. One of the elite intellectuals who carried the banner for this movement was the great viceroy Zhang Zhidong,[8] who expressly advocated 'Chinese learning should be for its essence, and Western learning for practical use' (*zhongxue wei ben, xixue wei yong*). Understandably, in the late Qing dynasty, such a piecemeal and superficial effort was inefficient to strengthen and reinforce the Great Qing, let alone to counteract the threat of the Western powers. Notwithstanding, intellectuals spared no effort in the pursuit of balancing the West with the Chinese way. In the intervening years of the Republic of China, Western ideas and practices found root in the cities and urban populations. With the founding of the PRC in 1949, the policy was endorsed of 'closing the door to construct [a socialist state]' (*guan qi men lai gao jianshe*). The anticapitalism campaigns continued, together with antifeudalism ones.

With the implementation of the reform and open-door policy in 1978, the door was reopened. But as the metaphor that was often cited by the authorities goes: 'With the windows open, both fresh air and insects, such as flies and mosquitoes, come into the house.' Hence, a series of 'anti-spiritual-pollution' campaigns was launched in 1983. Proceeding and following the 1989 Tiananmen incident, the concern and debate shifted to the advocacy of 'anti-wholesale Westernization' and 'anti-bourgeois liberalization'. Since the early 1990s, 'the Chinese characteristics' (*zhongguo tese*) approach to modernization has been emphasized in every aspect of social and political life, with the launch of the ideology of 'building socialism with Chinese characteristics'. In a sense, the slogan has been abused because often the 'Chinese characteristics' are unknown even to their advocates.[9]

Dilemmas without

Likewise, Western sinologists, including some overseas Chinese scholars, have to deal with the challenges of West versus the East, and the traditional China versus the modern China. As Bakken (2000: 3) observes, Western scholars must be aware of the specific historical and cultural foundations of Chinese society if they are to have any hope of grasping the character of its current development. Apparently, this observation stresses the importance of the Chinese past (*gu*). Apart from the officially claimed 'new China' since 1949, sinologists concur with each other that the present China is not, and should not be, artificially cut off from its past (e.g. Shue 1988; Troyer *et al.* 1989; Dutton 1992; Tanner 1999). But Dutton (1992) cautioned sinologists not to go too far by imprudently consigning everything present in China to the 'grab-bag' of the past. He argued that while Western scholars are right to refuse to employ certain elements of the American past to explain the American present, these very scholars use elements of the Chinese past to explain the Chinese present because they categorize the East as the 'Other' and use 'Other' forms of logic when examining Chinese problems. Thus, Dutton (1992) pointed out a tunnel vision in China studies, that is, indiscriminately reducing everything current in China to its ancient past. Meanwhile he criticized some sinologists for using double standards in the analyses of the West and the East. He argued that Chinese techniques of social policing, for example, are irreducible to their classical forms, partly because they did not emerge from a unilineal historical development, and partly because their original usage could not necessarily determine their current deployment. Nevertheless, he emphasized the irrefutable influence of the Chinese past on its present, regardless of the sweeping economic reform. According to him, the redeployment of certain mechanisms of social control introduced as a result of economic reform served only to '*reinforce* certain tendencies which many liberal social theorists predicted would be *undermined* by the reform process' (1992: 326; emphasis added). Or as Troyer and Rojek (1989: 9) observed, 'The Chinese Communists often drew upon cultural traditions in devising and operating the social control system, and in a few cases, the Communists have attempted major changes; more often, however, they have relied on and used traditional Chinese values in exercising social control.' In this respect, Tanner (1999: 172) is correct in observing that social stability in China, an overwhelming priority for the party/state, was preserved from 1949 through 1979 by 'a mutually reinforcing combination of traditional Chinese morality, Communist Party ideology, and the Communist Party's organization and occupation of social space and time'. However, he claimed that 'in the reform era of the 1980s, these anchors of stability had been swept away by the forces of modernization, while no similar moral principles or institutions had effectively taken their place' (Tanner 1999: 172).

However, drawing on Giddens' discussion of both the dis-embedding and re-embedding effects of modernity, Bakken (2000: 23) argued that the Chinese policy tradition represented the re-embedding tendencies of the process of modernity. That is, 'tradition is the producer of stability within change, order within transformation', or, 'in the official Chinese development model, tradition comes back not as "re-traditionalization" (or "re-Confucianization" for that matter) but rather as a direct instrument of reform and modernization' (Bakken 2000: 22–23). In this regard, Bakken provided an excellent understanding of the Chinese policy tradition, especially considering the official obsession with 'social stability'. Thus, it is undeniable that economic reform and its concomitant social reconstructions have a huge impact on the control system. However, the role of economic reform should not be overstated. Hence, social policing in modern China is a fusion of 'the appearance of traditional continuity' and 'fundamental changes' (Dutton 1992: 234). In other words, it is 'repetition with a difference' (Dutton 1992, 1995; Bakken 2000).

Interestingly enough, regarding the past and the present in China, early Western sinologists, like some native Chinese intellectuals, are also inclined to 'employing the past to negate the present'. As Dutton (1992: 143) observed, for those scholars, their readings of the East are featured by a dramatic shift from 'incredulous amazement' to 'condescending veneration'. The latter refers to a distain for the present in the East coupled with intellectual eulogies of its past. According to Dutton (1992), it is this very 'condescending veneration' that constitutes the hallmark of all that was wrong with Orientalism.[10]

In comparative studies, some Western scholars tend to associate China with 'otherness', the 'exotic Other'. It is sort of cliché that common ground exists between China and the rest of the world, including the ambiguous 'West'. For example, Dikotter (2002) explores the profound effects and lasting repercussions of the superimposition of Western-derived models of repentance and rehabilitation on traditional Chinese categories of crime and punishment during the first half of the twentieth century. According to David J. Rothman, Dikotter's exploration alerts us not only to the extended reach of American and European ideas on prison reform but also to how they fit so neatly with indigenous Chinese theories.[11] Furthermore, communism comes from a European intellectual tradition. The Chinese criminal justice system, especially the Chinese criminal code, is greatly influenced by the Soviet model (Troyer *et al.* 1989).

Xu (1995) argued that Western influences have bearings on Chinese lawmaking, policing, corrections, legal education, and control techniques under the Qing dynasty, the Kuomingtang, and the CCP. She also analysed the imperatives on and motivations of the Chinese to borrow Western control ideas and practices through modernization, denial of ethnocentrism, and participation in the world community. However, Sigley (1996) has warned of the trap for Western scholars in blindly applying Western frameworks and concepts to the examination of China, while disregarding the 'Chinese characteristics'. For example, in examining the apparent contradiction between economic liberalization and authoritarian birth control in the reform era of China, Sigley (1996: 472) pointed out that, on the one hand, the tenets of liberal political philosophy are problematic, and, on the other hand, the critique of liberal political theory, in terms of concepts such as 'action at a distance' and expertise, is misleading. Similarly, Dutton (1992) discussed certain problems in applying the governmentality discourse to the Chinese context. Thus, only with this fundamental difference in mind, could Western scholars possibly ask a series of different questions regarding the government of families, populations, work units and so on in China (Sigley 1996: 477).

Apparently, Klein and Gatz (1989: 169) went too far by claiming that 'The People's Republic of China is different – different from anything that Westerners know.' While we certainly reject the message in the ballad by Rudyard Kipling that 'East is East, and West is West, and never the twain shall meet', it is worthwhile for us to locate the similarities and differences in between, so as to enhance the understanding of human behaviour such as crime and social institutions such as crime control. As Cain (2000: 257) cogently argued, 'Comparison from within either an orientalist or an occidentalist mindset can do more harm than good.'

Taken together, the Chinese social control system is influenced by Westernization, socialism and Chinese characteristics; that is, by both the East and the West, and both the past and the present. Moreover, apart from memories of the past and realities of the present, Chinese social control is also influenced by a forward-looking perspective, 'dreams' of the future (Tanner 1999; Bakken 2000), considering that the official ideology remains to build a socialist society and ultimately a communist society. It should be pointed out that due to its long history and huge territory, Chinese society exhibits incongruous features in time and space.

Methodological challenges and research methods

There are books dedicated to the unique difficulties and challenges of doing field work in China (e.g. Thurston and Pasternack 1983; Heimer and Thogersen 2006). Sometimes articles or monographs have also reported detailed information on conducting fieldwork in China. For example, Zhang *et al.* (2007) highlighted the importance of understanding the Chinese political, cultural, and academic context in order to conduct a large-scale criminal victimization survey in Tianjin, China. The process of conducting the study in this book was characterized by tremendous obstacles. I introduce two of the main obstacles.

The first obstacle concerns misconception of research in the social sciences generally and in criminology particularly. It seems that social sciences research is distorted in the Chinese context due to the public's resistance and even aversion to persistent ideological indoctrination and political propaganda. The downsides of the practice of political education, moral inculcation, and socialist instruction, such as 'boilerplate' texts, 'newspeak' and 'gobbledegook', was generalized by the public to the whole field of social sciences research. Certainly, there are historical reasons for this. During the Cultural Revolution, all the social sciences disciplines were treated as pseudosciences, and it is only in the early 1980s that they were given official 'redress', together with the researchers in those fields. So it should not come as a surprise when people all follow the guideline that 'with a good command of mathematics, physics and chemistry, you are fearless to go anywhere around the globe', especially in the beginning of the reform era. This atmosphere severely obstructs the healthy development of disciplines in the social sciences.

The available official evaluation of social policies and reports of social issues are mostly based on model showcases, anecdotal evidence, or even armchair elaboration. As Chan (1993) and Lu (1998) noted, normally no detailed information was provided to support claims of success, and there were no reports of limitations and operational problems of the socialist system. Klein and Gatz (1989) went as far as to claim that 'China does not have the perspective of social science that we so automatically bring to bear on observing social phenomena', and attributed the situation to the devastating effects of the Cultural Revolution. In Chinese social sciences, research methods and ethics are in the process of coming to terms with the standard approaches, and empirical research has just been recognized and adopted by the younger generations of scholars. Problems of this kind hinder a comprehensive grasp of Chinese reality.

The second problem lies in the unavailability of data and restriction of collecting data. Although the increased openness of Chinese society facilitates decent social sciences research, it still takes time to overcome those embedded problems. On the one hand, the local cadre do not keep complete records of what they do, and there are no clear rules and guidelines of their conduct (He and Marshall 1997; Lu 1998). As in the West, it is not uncommon for local officials to manipulate the available data. On the other hand, the politicization of social sciences investigation imposes taboos on some fields of enquiry, and restricts scrutiny by 'outsiders', especially overseas researchers and even Chinese students studying abroad, including Hong Kong. Crime research in China is sensitive, and crime statistics are usually guarded as state secrets.

For several decades after 1949, the Chinese government did not publish crime statistics, other than occasionally providing a few percentage-point changes for a selected number of specific crimes in an official newspaper for propaganda purposes. It was in 1986 that China first submitted national crime statistics to Interpol (see Yang 1994). Undoubtedly, this secrecy impedes solid criminological research.

To examine the locally initiated, community crime-prevention programme BLSCC in Shenzhen, this study adopts a triangulation of multiple methods. This is based partly on the observation made in the West that the traditional quantitative approach is not sufficient in programme evaluations, and partly on the 'realist scientific approach' proposed by Pawson and Tilly (1994), which 'eschews conventional one-shot quasi-experimentation in favor of repeated manipulations leading to the cataloging of possible mechanisms and consistency of outcome pattern with presumed mechanisms' (Ekblom and Pease 1995: 585). Furthermore, it was not realistic to conduct a quasi-experiment to study the effectiveness of BLSCC.

The fieldwork of this study was conducted from late 1998 to mid-2002. A variety of methods were employed to collect data, including secondary data analysis of official documents, newspaper cuttings and existing literature; individual and group interviews; participant observation; and a community survey. The triangulating of various methods provided me with a more comprehensive view of the research subject and hence enhanced my understanding. I discuss below in detail the methods I used to collect data, giving emphasis to the survey and its data analysis. At appropriate points, I also stress the weaknesses of the data concerned and my strategies for overcoming certain weaknesses.

Secondary data analysis

As unobtrusive measures, secondary data analyses eliminate or minimize reactivity or 'stooge' effects compared with primary data analysis (see Hagan 1997: 224). Although researchers are more fascinated by collecting primary data, they cannot afford to overlook secondary data. In this study, secondary data include existing academic publications, official records and documents, and newspaper reports. Firstly, by overcoming many obstacles, I collected official documents, publications and records about crime and crime control policies, especially the programme of BLSCC in Shenzhen. They included speeches by Shenzhen government officials, or minutes of official meetings, official release of the processes and results of the implementation of BLSCC, and a number of issues of the *Newsletter on BLSCC*, which was published (500 copies every issue) mainly for the high-level officials' reference. I also managed to collect some communities' written presentations to the municipal administration, which covered the local implementation of BLSCC and what had been achieved. These were mainly obtained through repeated requests to my informants working in the Shenzhen municipal administration (the Party Committee and the Government), the Shenzhen Political and Legal Committee, and the Shenzhen Public Security Bureau (PSB), or during my visits to the communities. Since systematic crime data in Shenzhen are not available, I searched the *Shenzhen Yearbook* and the *Shenzhen Political and Legal Yearbook* for piecemeal information about law enforcement, so as to project a picture of crime in Shenzhen since 1980. An in-depth analysis of these data helps to generate a deeper understanding of crime control in China, especially the aspects of BLSCC.

Secondly, I gathered a large number of references in both Chinese and English directly relevant to issues of concern to this study. Some of them were obtained by searching the resource guides, including the *Social Sciences Citations Index*, *Social Sciences Index*, *Criminal Justice Abstracts*, and *UMI Dissertation Abstracts* in the libraries. Some of them were referred to me by my supervisor and my colleagues, or accumulated during my trip back to China. I frequently scanned important periodicals such as *The China Quarterly*, *The China Journal*, *Modern China*, *Criminology*, *The British Journal of Criminology*, *Crime and Delinquency*, *Theoretical Criminology*, and other related journals to keep myself up to date with fresh findings and new developments in the field.

I also gained a more realistic understanding of crime, crime control and the maintenance of order in China. In the absence of systematic crime data, I searched relevant journal articles, yearbooks, and published books to piece together a more or less complete picture of crime in China since 1950 and in Shenzhen since 1980. By reviewing studies by domestic scholars, and cross-cultural commentators and observers, I was able to comprehend the rapid social and economic development in China, the stratification of Chinese society, and especially emerging social problems, such as the widening disparity between the poor and the rich, the special class called the 'floating population', and their impact on crime. From those works, I also gained an understanding of the historical orientation, contemporary adaptation, underlying rationale, reality/rhetorics gap, and West/East comparison concerning the Chinese social control mechanisms.

Scholarly works provide a deeper and fuller understanding of the issues under consideration; however, sometimes they are not up to date. Thus, this study was supplemented by news coverage in both Chinese and English. During my trip back to Mainland China and during my fieldwork in Shenzhen, I always kept an eye on news reports on crime and crime control in China and Shenzhen. During my daily scanning of the Internet Edition of the *South China Morning Post*, an English newspaper published in Hong Kong, I collected articles concerning new crime-control policies, criminal cases, anticrime campaigns, and social control in China, so as to keep abreast of the developments in the Mainland. Generally, materials of this kind are subject to editors' political orientation, individual interpretation, personal stance, or emphasis on news value, so I tried to catch the events, and to be less influenced by the comments and observations contained in the news coverage. I also collected some news coverage in Chinese of community A. Newspaper reporting in the Mainland sometimes amounts to nothing more than boilerplate, newspeak, and propaganda. Thus, I tried to adopt an objective stance to 'reject the dross and assimilate the essence', to use a typical Chinese expression.

Site visits and participant observation

While visiting the five communities, I closely observed what was going on inside each. Apart from community A – the model – the observation inside other communities was very brief and cursory because of the denial of full access, but I still got first-hand experience of the physical environment and social settings of those communities. In community A, I was able to conduct intensive participant observation during the one-and-half-year period of my fieldwork. I stayed with a friend and her family who are residents of the community. From them, I obtained detailed information about both the physical and social life of the community. Besides, I got involved in the daily operation of the Department of Cultural Affairs in community A for a period of one week. I stayed with the staff in the same office, reviewing the newspaper articles they collected, consulting them with problems I could not figure out, and especially observed how things were handled. Sometimes we took meals together and thus we built a sound relationship. But I could not reveal my true identity to them because I was referred to them as an intern journalist at a local newspaper by a Public Security Bureau (PSB) official. They spoke highly of my personality and capacity, and invested great trust in me. They even kindly offered to help me find a permanent job in Shenzhen. This 'fake' identity made me feel very uneasy, but I had to cope with it. Similarly, Lu (1998) during her participant observation in Shanghai, was often known as Dr Lu, a Fudan University graduate, or a lawyer depending on the occasions.

I also participated in the community life as a local resident. Every day, I got up very early to walk around the community, observing what the residents were doing, talking to them, and examining any meaningful event inside the community. I also took down what was written on the noticeboard, and took pictures of some interesting posters and even 'slogans' painted on the entrance gates of some buildings. This observation helped me understand the running of daily life inside the model community and to a large extent corroborated the official reporting. I was greatly impressed by the orderly life in the model community, and thus attempted to do similar observations in at least one non-model community for a comparison. But numerous attempts did not work out.

One major concern about participant observation is whether an observer's presence will change the normal behaviour of the subjects under study, or whether it is really 'unobtrusive'. Given the Chinese cultural emphasis on 'saving face' and the high level of alertness towards outsiders at the local level, it is not easy to observe 'unobstructed' behaviour. However, Lu (1998) argued that it was very unlikely that her Shanghai residence committee members could 'keep up appearances' over a period of three months, but rather likely that she was observing a residence committee behaving at its best. In terms of my involvement with the staff in the Department of Cultural Affairs of community A, my existence probably prompted them to exhibit their best at least to protect the model image. But observations show that the above possibility is very slight. Firstly, the fact that I was only an intern did not put much pressure on them. Secondly, I found that although officials at the higher level were very sensitive, the lower-level personnel were very friendly and helpful, especially when they regarded me as a modest, credible and eager-to-learn new graduate. Thirdly, in this newly constructed community, the local organization was not the conventional 'neighbourhood committee' which is usually dominated by elderly retired cadres (mostly women). Instead, the 'Office of Housing Management' oversees the daily operation of the community, and the staff were mostly young and well educated. Thus, I could communicate with them very easily. My reasoning that my presence did not alter their behaviour is further supported by the fact that in my presence one female employee in the department had an argument with the department head due to her dissatisfaction with the handling of certain issues inside the community.

As for my involvement with the community residents, it is even less likely that my presence affected their behaviour. I just acted like a resident in the community. I talked to the shopkeepers when I was doing photocopying or buying things. Sometimes I initiated a conversation with an old lady who was doing morning exercise in a group by asking her whether I could participate. At other times, I just walked around, observing and listening. Thus, I became confident that the participant observation had provided me with very credible information regarding the implementation of BLSCC, the operation of local social control, and more generally the lifestyle at the grass-roots level.

In-depth interviews

In-depth interviews offered me another means to enrich my understanding of the programme of BLSCC, and various aspects of community life. In communities B and C, I undertook group interviews with the local leaders, including five persons in B and three persons in C. I had individual interviews with the following: two PSB officers of the Shenzhen PSB, one Shenzhen University professor, one employee in the Department of Cultural Affairs of community A, and five local residents. The group interviews were arranged through the official channels, with me posing as a research assistant of the Shenzhen University professor. All the other individuals were referred to me by my friends. Thus, altogether, I interviewed 17 people. The group interviews lasted from two-and-a-half to three hours, and the individual interviews half an hour to an hour.

The questions were unstructured with open-ended responses, and significant points or remarks by the interviewees were followed up immediately, and any unusual body language or facial expressions were taken down. For the group interviews, questions were asked to obtain two aspects of community life: (1) basic information about the community such as demographic composition, the structure of the community administration, and their self-assessment of social order inside the community; and (2) the operation of BLSCC inside the communities, including the agencies involved, the cooperation between the involved agencies, the concrete strategies adopted, the problems encountered, the public response, and the outcomes produced. The interview questions for the employee from the Department of Cultural Affairs in community A followed a similar pattern. For community residents, questions were structured more towards their personal experience of community life, including their attitudes to their neighbourhoods and relations with neighbours, their opinions on migrants, any significant incidents inside their communities, their victimization experience, and their awareness of, participation in and evaluation of BLSCC. For the PSB officers, questions were oriented to enquire how they and their stations got involved with the implementation of BLSCC, their relations with the public, their opinions of migrants and especially migrants' disproportional representation in reported crime statistics, and the problems encountered in law enforcement. For the Shenzhen University professor, questions were more theoretically directed to obtain his opinion of local crime problems, local law enforcement, and the implementation of BLSCC.

I personally did all the interviews in Mandarin. All those who agreed to be interviewed were very cooperative. I tape-recorded the group interview in community C and the individual interview of the employee from the Department of Cultural Affairs in community A, while in all the other interviews I took notes, since most of the interviewees chose not to be tape-recorded when asked. Some interviewees knew my true identity, while others did not. All the interviews were transcribed immediately afterwards, and only the parts included in this study were translated into English. The details of the interviews are mainly contained in Chapters 6, 7, and 8. The interviews also helped me to refine the survey questions so as to suit better the targeted respondents.

Community survey

The survey was administered in communities A and B only. I compared the advantages and disadvantages of the three surveying methods: in-person interviews, mailing surveys or telephone surveys. Considering the local community conditions, I finally decided in-person interviews would be the most suitable. The survey was conducted in the two communities simultaneously on a Saturday and a Sunday. With intensive training, five experienced interviewers from a local university in Shenzhen did the survey. Via a stop-and-ask method,[12] the interviewers approached residents in different parts of the communities, including the entrances to them, shopping malls, pedestrian roads, parks, and retail stores. The interviewers also tallied the number of rejections. Altogether, about 70 per cent of those approached agreed to do the interview, with each interview lasting about 12–18 minutes. Among 120 and 106 questionnaires, collected in the model and non-model communities respectively, 117 and 94 were valid: 211 in all.

Sample
The demographics of the respondents in the two communities are shown in Table 2.3.

Measurement of variables
The variables chosen covered three areas, each addressing a particular aspect of BLSCC (see Appendix). The first area covered social networks, interaction and mutual help within the community. The second area studied the respondents' perception of crime, fear of crime and their attitudes to the security guards and the police. The last area aimed to explore the respondents' evaluation of BLSCC.

Area I: mutual help, social networks and interaction
This was represented by six questions. The first question asks respondents during the last year whether their neighbour had asked them for help; for example, to watch their home or look after their children while they were away. This kind of help is assumed to be very common between neighbours in China. The second question turns to the respondents' own request for the same kind of help from their neighbours.

In the discussion on social capital in China, *tongxiang* was identified as an important relationship for the Chinese people. In the field, I always heard people talking about *tongxiang*. Thus, the

Table 2.3 Demographic distribution of the respondents in communities A and B

Variable	Distribution		
	A	B	Total
Sex			
Male	57 (53.8%)	49 (46.2%)	106
Female	60 (57.1%)	45 (42.9%)	105
Total	117 (55.5%)	94 (45.5%)	211
Age			
Under 25	19 (37.3%)	32 (62.7%)	51
26–35	29 (37.3%)	39 (57.4%)	68
36–45	28 (57.4%)	14 (33.3%)	42
46–55	23 (79.3%)	6 (20.7%)	29
56–65	11 (84.6%)	2 (15.4%)	13
Over 66	7 (87.5%)	1 (12.5%)	8
Total	117	94	211
Period of residence			
Under 1 year	9 (26.5%)	25 (73.5%)	34
1–2 years	34 (60.7%)	22 (39.3%)	56
2–5 years	49 (61.3%)	31 (38.8%)	80
5–10 years	23 (65.7%)	21 (34.3%)	35
Over 10 years	1 (33.3%)	2 (66.7%)	3
Total	116 (55.8%)	92 (44.2%)	208
Hukou			
Permanent	85 (83.3%)	17 (16.7%)	102
Temporary	29 (27.9%)	75 (72.1%)	104
Total	114 (55.3%)	92 (44.7%)	206
Education			
Under junior high	4 (26.7%)	11 (73.3%)	15
Junior high	9 (21.4%)	33 (78.6%)	42
Senior high	40 (51.3%)	38 (48.7%)	78
College	55 (82.1%)	12 (17.9%)	67
Postgraduate	7 (100%)	0	7
Total	115 (55.0%)	94 (45.0%)	209

Table 2.3 continues overleaf

Table 2.3 continued

Variable	Distribution		
	A	B	Total
Job			
Cadres	32 (100%)	0	32
Employees in SOEs	24 (85.7%)	4 (14.3%)	28
Employees in the private sector	20 (27.0%)	54 (73.0%)	74
Employees in foreign enterprises	1 (20.0%)	4 (80.0%)	5
Employees in joint enterprises	7 (46.7%)	8 (53.3%)	15
Teachers	7 (58.3%)	5 (41.7%)	12
Students	10 (71.4%)	4 (28.6%)	14
Unemployed	3 (21.4%)	11 (78.6%)	14
Retired	12 (75.0%)	4 (25.0%)	16
Total	116 (55.2%)	94 (48.2%)	210
Type of housing			
Own	75 (85.2%)	13 (14.8%)	88
Rent	13 (17.3%)	62 (82.7%)	75
Living with relatives	17 (81.0%)	4 (19.0%)	21
Provided by work unit	12 (48.0%)	13 (52.0%)	25
Others	0	2 (100%)	2
Total	117 (55.5%)	94 (44.5%)	211

third question explored the existence and the importance of the respondents' *tongxiang*. The fourth question was intended to measure the respondents' awareness of any activity in the community, since one of the important aspects of BLSCC is to organize cultural and educational activities to enrich residents' life and enhance their legal and moral consciousness.

The fifth question asked the respondents to imagine how their neighbours would react if they were being robbed or attacked. The sixth question asked how they would react if they witnessed a pickpocketing, so as to measure bystanders' behaviour as an indicator of informal social control or self-help. Since the literature suggests that the perpetrator's status influences bystanders' response, the vignette had two versions: a migrant pickpocket and a non-migrant pickpocket. To investigate whether the response would be different if the respondents were outside the community compared with inside the community, a follow-up question was framed, 'If that situation would arise at the same time but outside your own community in the street, what woul you do?'

Mutual help between neighbours, *tongxiang* ties, community activities, the neighbours' reaction to the respondent's robbery or attack, and the respondent's own reaction to an imagined incident of pickpocketing, are all likely measures of social capital in the community.

Area 2: crime, fear of crime and attitudes to the security guards and the police
The first question explored the respondents' perception of major community problems. The list included (a) hygiene, (b) health service, (c) problems with the floating population and house renting, (d) laid-off workers, (e) car parking, (f) the problem of *'zhi'an zhuangkuang'*, (g) public transport services, (h) children's school education, (i) illegal structures, (j) family planning, (k) fire, and (l) others. Here *'zhi'an zhuangkuang'* literally means 'the situation of public security'. Respondents' worries about *'zhi'an zhuangkuang'* actually mean that they regarded crime as a community problem.

The second question measured crime prevalence inside communities. The following 13 types of crime were listed: breaking into houses, bicycle theft, auto theft, violence and fighting, gambling, drunkenness, robbery, sale or use of drugs, prostitution, sexual assault (hooliganism against women), swindling, gang activity, triads, and others.

The third question asked respondents for their perception of migrants' criminality. The fourth question measured respondents' feeling of safety by asking whether they felt safe to walk alone at night in their own communities. The fifth question was about respondents' estimated chance of personal victimization, and the sixth question asked respondents to estimate the likelihood that they would be a victim of a property crime. The seventh question asked them to recall their victimization experience.

The eighth question on this area asked whether there was any security guard in the community and also about their assessment of the importance of security guards for maintaining security in their community. The ninth question measured police presence in the community by asking respondents whether they had seen any policeman from the local police station in their communities. The tenth question asked whether they were satisfied with the police.

Area 3: awareness, and perceived effectiveness of BLSCC
The first question on this area asked respondents whether they had heard anything about BLSCC. If an affirmative answer was given, a question about the usefulness of BLSCC followed.

Questions two to seven asked respondents if they had witnessed any change during the past year in relation to the following six aspects: personal relationships, installation of anticrime measures in the home, physical appearance, *zhi'an zhuangkuang* (situation of public security), feeling of safety, chance of personal victimization, and chance of property victimization.

It should be pointed out that when the questionnaire was administered, the actual sequence of the questions was different from that listed above, partly to facilitate the flow of the questions. For example, the question on the residents' fear of crime was immediately followed by the question on their perception of the change in the fear of crime, but in the analysis the former appears in the second area, and the latter in the third area. But special attention was paid to the sequence of the questions in case of contamination. The questionnaire was modified several times in order to minimize misunderstanding. It was piloted with 10 residents, and based on the pilot results it was further refined. Extra emphasis was paid to the wording of the questions, especially the so-called sensitive questions, such as the satisfaction with the police, so as not to pose any threat to the respondents. All the questions except the one on victimization experience were in the close-ended format.

Three hypotheses
For the survey data, which will be discussed in Chapter 8, the following three hypotheses were generated:

1 In model community A, there will be more social capital, exemplified by more mutual help, more *tongxiang* relationships, and more willingness to intervene in crime, etc., than in the non-model community B.
2 In model community A, crime will be perceived as less serious, there will be less fear of crime, and the residents' attitudes to the police and security guards will be more positive than in the non-model community B.
3 In model community A, respondents will hold more positive attitudes to BLSCC than in the non-model community B.

To conclude, the methodology took shape as the study progressed in the field. To some extent, the triangulation approach and the multiple methods deployed in this study are results of various compromises made in the process, due to the obstacles and cultural barriers encountered in a society where empirical social sciences enquiries are not very common.

Notes

1 'Three-no population' is a locally coined term in Shenzhen to refer to those who have '*no* valid legal documents, *no* legal occupation and *no* legal residence'.
2 I consulted a police friend about this puzzle. He simply dismissed the statistics, and asked me not to use them for academic research. He implied that the statistics had been manipulated. It seems crime statistics in China could be treated as 'recorded and publicly released' at best, and thus we should exercise caution when using the crime data.
3 The description of the five communities has appeared in Zhong and Broadhurst (2007).
4 See Chapter 7 for the rating system of BLSCC, which classifies the communities into model, advanced, pass or failure.
5 Because of the 'burning the books and burying the Confucianists' in the Qin dynasty, many of the extant Confucian classics were written, compiled, or reinterpreted in the Han dynasty, when Confucianism gained a state-endorsed orthodoxy status.
6 This part is mainly based on Yang (1994, Chapter 6).
7 Although the notion of 'feudal' was not defined in the debate, it tended to be associated with, *inter alia*, 'the predominance of collectivism at the expense of individualism, the strength of patriarchalist family and relational networks at the expense of open relations, and the power of despotism' (Dutton 1992: 16).
8 Zhang Zhidong was the great viceroy of the Hu-guang region (including Guangdong, Guangxi, Hunan and Hubei). Other pioneers of this movement are Zeng Guofan, Li Hongzhang, and Zuo Zengtang, all Han mandarins of the Great Qing. To learn from the West, a number of weapon factories and shipyards for warships were built in Tianjin, Wuhan and other major cities.
9 Regarding the discourse of 'West versus East', my observation is that traditional Chinese intellectuals (those who focus on the traditions of China) tend to be mostly associated with the superiority complex (*zida*), and their modern counterparts with the inferiority complex (*zibei*). It is not hard to see that the two extreme complexes are subject to both the perceived and real strength of the Chinese state throughout history.

10 This practice has the equivalent of making a 'museum' of China, such as to reduce it to a manageable subject of intellectual contrast.
11 This comment by David J. Rothman is from the endorsement on the back cover of Dikotter's (2002) book.
12 This stop-and-ask method is similar to the 'mall intercept' method as employed extensively in market research. Rosenbaum and Lavrakas (1995) argued that the 'mall intercept' method could be a useful technique for interviewing users of small shopping areas and for generating typical samples or other types of samples.

Chapter 3

Community crime prevention and social capital

Recent years have seen sweeping changes and interesting paradoxes in societal developments. Giddens (1990, cited in Bottoms and Wiles 1996: 19) has argued that the 'environments of trust' are characterized by a move from the 'overriding importance of localized trust' in pre-modern societies to a context where 'trust relations are embedded in disembedded abstract systems' in modern societies, a move regarded as one of the most important societal changes in recent times. Robert Putnam (1993a, 1993b, 1995, 2000), however, scrutinized the decreasing community participation and civic engagement in US society and regarded it as the epitome of declining social capital in that society. Contemporary communities also appear to be increasingly developing towards, if not becoming dominated by, computer-mediated communication such as electronic mail (e-mail), interactive chat rooms, computer conferences and bulletin boards: emerging virtual communities instead of traditional, face-to-face communities (Blanchard and Horan 2000). On the other hand, in public policy, the past three decades or so has witnessed a drift towards maximizing individual liberty and away from enforcing communal control, as argued by Kelling and Coles (1996). Thus, in this IT age and era of globalization, one cannot help wondering whether it is anachronistic to promote 'community' in crime prevention, or whether it is only a kind of nostalgia, because we seem to be 'perennially tempted to contrast our tawdry today with the golden past' (Putnam 2000: 24).

Apparently, this questioning of anachronism is partly premised on the assumption that 'community' is a localized entity. Community crime prevention stresses the importance of the community – a closely knit relationship, in controlling and preventing crime. This relationship denotes both horizontal and vertical community dynamics, with the latter transcending community boundaries to link a community with external sources. Moreover, in delineating the tendencies towards globalization and localization in late modern societies, Bottoms and Wiles (1996: 15) observed that 'notwithstanding these processes (changes in globalization) in modern societies local milieux not only remain important, but ironically are actually in some respects of increasing significance'. They argued that 'the overall result of the various processes ... is that both globalization and localization (including "niche"-style individualization) occur at the same time' (1996: 16). Indeed, as Sampson et al. (1997) demonstrated, collective efficacy, defined as neighbours' willingness to intervene on behalf of the common good, combined with social cohesion among neighbours, is linked to reduced violence at the neighbourhood level, and the effects remain after individual-level characteristics, neighbourhood characteristics and prior violence at the neighbourhood level are taken into account. Moreover, the 'neighbourhood effects' were manifested as neighbourhood-level variations in a variety of phenomena (e.g. delinquency, violence, depression, high-risk behaviour), especially among adolescents (Sampson et al. 2002). Thus, the overwhelming confluence of globalization seems to be deflated by a concurrent process of localization. Further, in spite of the increasing emergence of virtual communities, it is revealed that when these virtual communities develop around physically based communities and when these virtual communities foster additional communities of interest, social capital and civic engagement will increase (Blanchard and Horan 2000).

As the recent academic discussion has increasingly featured the role of social capital in community building, on the one hand, and as the crime prevention field has shown the growth of the community approach on the other hand, this chapter will examine how the concept of social capital underlies the mechanisms of the community approach to crime prevention. For that purpose, the chapter is organized around the following five aspects. First, it surveys several prominent explanations of the development of social control in modern Western societies with the aim of providing a broad template for depicting the emergence of community crime prevention. Second, it describes the context of the emergence of community crime prevention, highlighting three interwoven facilitating factors arising during the past several decades: theoretical reorientation, changes in crime, and the perceived inefficiency of the traditional criminal justice system in controlling crime. Third, it outlines the conceptualization of crime prevention in the literature, in order to locate community crime prevention in the general framework of crime prevention. Fourth, it introduces the concept of social capital, and establishes the nexus between social capital and community crime prevention through discussing the criminological theories supporting community crime prevention. Lastly, it highlights the issues and problems surrounding social capital and community crime prevention: the three dyads of formal/informal, public/private, and inclusion/exclusion, and the role of the state.

Patterns of social control in modern Western societies

The modern Western history of industrialization, modernization and urbanization has involved continuing change in crime, punishment and, more generally, social control, and a number of paradigms have been advanced to chart the process by classical theorists such as Durkheim, Foucault and Weber. As our society enters a postmodern stage in the process of globalization, contemporary writers, such as Cohen (1985), Crawford (1997), and Garland (1985, 1996, 2000, 2001), have offered their reflections upon the patterns and phases of social control generally and crime control/prevention particularly.

Stanley Cohen (1985) sketched the master patterns and strategies for controlling deviance in Western industrial societies, which he saw as three phases: arbitrary and decentralized control (pre-eighteenth century), rational and state-centred control (from the nineteenth century), and hybrid forms of statist decentralization (from the mid-twentieth century). He argued that the cumulative picture of the first transition – from phase one to phase two – embodied four changes, such as the increasing involvement of the state in the business of deviancy control, and the second transition, from phase two to three, could be expressed as four groups of destructuring movements or ideologies, each supposedly reversing one of the changes identified in the first transition, such as the movement away from the state. The second shift ushered in a major trend in criminal justice rhetoric that stressed the quest for community in the pursuit for social control.

Although Cohen's model is helpful and inspiring, rarely does the development of history exhibit such clear watersheds. Later, Cohen (1989) even cautioned against the identification of distinct master tendencies in the genealogy of social control and recognized the fragmented nature of the phenomenon. Shearing (1992: 422) argued that the triumph of the state was not as complete, nor as secure, as had been believed. Johnston (1992) demonstrated that private policing, in a variety of forms, persisted into the twentieth century, that is, phase two of Cohen's model, which is characterized by the prevalence of the welfare state and professionalism, thus suggesting that public and private domains, instead of exhibiting a clearcut dichotomy of private/public, 'relate to each other in complex, dynamic, contradictory, and sometimes ambiguous ways' (Johnston 1992: 205).

In a similar manner, Crawford (1997) delineated the historical strands of criminal justice discourse with a focus on the British perspective and the ramifications for other Western societies. He argued that prior to the 'new police' of the nineteenth century and Peel's reforms, public safety, policing and crime control had been subject to forms of 'government at a distance'. The period from the late nineteenth century to the post-World War II era saw a process of bureaucratization and professionalization; for example, there was a general move away from local communal justice and towards centralized, state-administered public justice. According to Crawford (1997), since the 1970s, there have emerged the new discourses and practices in crime control that are constructed around three overlapping concepts: 'crime prevention', 'appeals to community' and 'interagency partnerships'. He contended that appeals to 'prevention', 'partnership', and 'community' justify the quest for the legitimacy of the state and the responsibility of individuals, families, groups, and the state in the area of crime control.

The current crime-control policy, as depicted in the above two models, stresses the emergence of the community approach from the late twentieth century. However, far from being a widespread and dominant practice, the community approach accounts for only one part, if not a small part, of the whole picture of society's response to crime and disorder, which is illustrated by Garland's depiction of the current landscape of social control in contemporary society: the coexistence of two strategies: 'adaptive' and 'non-adaptive' (1996, 2000, 2001). This description of current social control is built on his theory of cultural adaptation, which argues that policy shifts are conditioned by prior changes occurring at the level of social structures and cultural sensibilities (Garland 2000, 2001). In the wake of the crisis of the welfare state, there emerged a 'new predicament' of crime control, which was characterized by 'high crime rates as a normal social fact', 'the limits of the criminal justice state', and 'the myth of the sovereign state and its monopoly of crime control' (Garland

1996, 2000, 2001). In response to the new predicament, crime-control policies become volatile and contradictory, with different kinds of policy at different times and at different points in the crime-control field. But he particularly stressed that this 'contradictory dualism' essentially displays a conflict at the heart of the contemporary policy, rather than a rationally differentiated response to different kinds of crime.

The merit of Garland's thesis lies in the argument that the current domain of crime control is not dominated by one single perspective.[1] Rather, it is vacillating in a 'contradictory dualism', subject to political winds and populist demands. Adaptive responses, which Garland previously referred to as 'preventive partnership' (1996, 2000), to a large extent, converge with the community approach. Thus, all the three models, to varying degrees, point out the emergence of the community approach to crime control since the 1970s. Or, in the words of Huphes (2007), it is the 'preventive turn' in criminology. The following section is to identify, in more detail, certain factors in that very context of the recalibration of crime control.

Context for the emergence of community crime prevention

The above models all stress the social, economic, political and cultural impact, especially the rise of advanced capitalist mode of production and markets, on the transformation of crime control in modern Western societies. In that big picture, certain 'proximal' factors, mostly related to criminology and criminal justice, stand out and facilitate the rise of the community approach to social control. Here three factors are identified: (a) theoretical reorientation, (b) crime change in modern societies, and (c) the perceived inefficiency of the traditional criminal justice system in reducing crime and safeguarding safety.

Theoretical reorientation

The last several decades have witnessed shifts in the theoretical front to explain crime and victimization, and these theories in turn condition the strategies to prevent crime. Basically, the theoretical terrain is dominated by the following dyads: individuals/community, offender/offence, and offender/victim. The preference of academic researchers shifts between the units of each dyad, and even the meaning attached to a certain unit of a particular dyad also undergoes changes with time.

Dyad of individuals/community

According to Reiss (1986), there are two modern criminological research traditions that focus respectively on individual victims and offenders, and on the variability in community crime rates. In the first tradition, some theories centre on 'what causes only some persons to behave as delinquents rather than about what causes delinquency', and other theories explain 'why some people become victims instead of what causes victimization by crime' (Reiss 1986: 3). Thus, the individual-oriented theories fail to account for variation in crime in time and territory. The second tradition takes as its major point of departure the weakness of the first tradition, the variation in crime over time and territory, especially variation among communities at one time (cross-sectional) and among communities over time (longitudinal), which is the focus of the Chicago School of Criminology and the work of Bursik and Grasmick (1993). According to Reiss (1986), differences in the concentration of crime in space can also be explained by 'ecological and information search and processing decision theories', which later fully developed into 'rational choice' and 'routine activities' theories. They take into account the findings that both offenders and victims are concentrated in areas with high crime rates. One means of linking the two traditions together is to explain differences in victimization rates of individuals (see review by Reiss 1986: 7).

Bursik and Grasmick (1993) suggest that theories explaining crime and delinquency have been characterized by a historical cycle of between group dynamics and individual differences. The recent shift of focus to community, a unit of the first dyad of individual/community, is in parallel with the rise of the community approach to crime prevention.

Likewise, in the theoretical framework, the representation of 'offender', one unit of the individual/community dyad, has also changed over time. Melossi (2000) argued that the representations of crime and the criminal oscillate between two different social attitudes in modern history: (1) the sympathetic attitude that sees criminals as innovators fighting against an unjust and suffocating social order; and 2) an attitude of antipathy that regards criminals as monstrosities, evil forces attacking the very foundations of a social fabric and a moral order that should be defended at all cost. Correspondingly, the punishment and control measures are liberal and conservative, respectively. Melossi (2000) regarded the period after 1973 until today as one in which an attitude of antipathy has prevailed. However, for Garland (1996, 2001), the period since the 1970s has seen coexistence of the adaptive and non-adaptive responses, as referred to earlier.

Garland argued that the adaptive and non-adaptive responses to crime are corresponding to 'the criminology of the self' and 'the criminology of the Other', respectively.

Dyad of offender/offence
The second dyad of offender/offence also impinges on the theoretical orientation. Pease (1994) divided theoretical traditions into offender-focused and offence-focused. The former approach sees offenders as motivated by genetic influences, the experience of unfairness, strain, social disorganization, the inadequacy of social control, or personality characteristics such as extroversion or impulsivity. Thus, to prevent crime is to tackle those individual or social factors that fuel or sustain crime. However, given the difficulties in changing offenders, or potential offenders, Pease (1994) argued that theories shifted to focus on offence, including lifestyle theory (Hindelang *et al.* 1978), the routine activities theory (Cohen and Felson 1979), and the rational choice theory (Cornish and Clarke 1986). The focus on offence has generated significant crime-prevention initiatives, especially the opportunity-reduction model (situational crime prevention). Addressing overemphasis on either the offender or the offence, Ekblom and Tilley (2000) proposed the concept of 'resourceful offender' to integrate the two approaches. Community crime prevention, Ekblom and Tilley (2000) suggested, applies a mix of offender-oriented and situational approaches, focusing not on the level of individual offenders or crime situations, but on whole communities.

Dyad of offender/victim
The third dyad of offender/victim manifests itself in the rise of victim status in the criminal justice discourse. Until recently, the victim's interest was subsumed within the public interest, according to which, in the long run, the rehabilitation of offenders will work to the interest of both the offender and the public at large, including the victims. The recent shift of attention to victims takes into account the interests and feelings of victims – actual victims, victims' families, potential victims, and the projected figure of 'the victim'. According to Garland (1996, 2000, 2001), this rise of the victim is a response to the crime complex of 'high crime rates as a normal social fact'. Thus, at the theoretical level, the victim is featured at the centre, not periphery, in the new 'criminologies of everyday life' – rational choice theory, routine activity theory, crime as opportunity, and situational crime prevention (Garland 1996, 2000, 2001). In particular, the routine activity theory holds that a crime occurs when

three elements converge in time and space: a motivated offender, a suitable victim, and the absence of a capable guardian (Cohen and Felson 1979).[2] Further, Young argued that the nature of crime should include 'the *form* of crime, the *social context* of crime, the *shape* of crime, its trajectory through *time*, and its enactment in *space*' (1992: 26; emphasis in original). The form consists of two dyads: a victim and an offender, and actions and reactions. A square of crime is constructed: a victim, an offender, formal control and informal control. Thus, the responsibilities for preventing crime are redistributed between the state, and the public, i.e. the potential victims. This line of thinking is reflected in target-hardening measures and self-defence strategies, a manifestation of the community approach to crime prevention.[3]

The above section has charted the main theoretical developments in criminology during the past several decades. It should be pointed out that, considering the complexity of the field, this review is more appropriately treated as some snapshots instead of a panorama. The theoretical reorientation set the tone for the emergence of the community-based approach to crime prevention. This shift of emphasis in crime prevention from police to community is directly related to the limits of the state in public affairs in general, and the criminal justice system in crime prevention in particular.

The changing nature of crime problems

Apart from the theoretical reorientation, the emergence of the community approach to crime prevention is also intimately related to changes in crime problems during the last several decades in Western societies. Thus, the change in the quantity and quality of crime shapes the orientation of crime control and prevention practices.

Young (1999) argued that the rise in the crime rate began in most advanced industrial countries before the early 1970s and then continued to rise, often at a greatly augmented rate. Fukuyama (1999) also depicted the rising crime rate, based on official data, in Western societies despite widespread social amelioration. In addition, as Rosenbaum (1988) and Cain (2000) have observed, national crime surveys over time demonstrate that crime is not a random set of events, distributed evenly across all segments of American society.[4] With aggregate crime growing in most societies, crime at the community level presents some interesting features. One prominent feature is that, in high-crime communities, residents are most commonly victimized by other residents. Thus, offenders are not external to the communities and crime is from inside, not outside (see e.g. Hope 1995, Walklate 1996). As witnessed by the Priority Estates Project experiment in the UK, the residential concentration of the young poor fostered a 'subterranean community' both victimized and victimizing (Foster and Hope 1993).

Apart from the rise of 'common' and 'serious' crime (the focus of the policing activities), drug sale, drug use and related crimes, disorder and incivilities inside communities became rampant. The apparent worsening of disorder and incivilities, such as drug dealing, prostitution, panhandling, homelessness, and public drunkenness, stimulated Wilson and Kelling (1982, 1989) in the 1980s to advance the thesis of 'broken windows', which builds the links between disorder, fear, serious crime and urban decay. Not only did the last several decades see an escalation in crime rates, but they also witnessed its repercussions on the public's perceptions of crime, and media portrayals of crime (Heath 1984; Williams and Dickinson 1993). For urban dwellers, crime is no longer a marginal concern, an exceptional incident in their life, but has become an ever-present possibility, causing considerable public anxiety (Young 1999). This point converges with Garland's thesis of 'high crime rates as a normal social factor' and a high level of fear of crime. However, studies show that there is always a gap between the level of fear and the actual extent of crime, and the level of fear appears to be independent of actual risk of crime (Baker *et al*. 1983; Young 1988; Lupton 1999; Farrall *et al*. 2000) and is unevenly distributed (Killias and Clerici 2000; Pantazis 2000; Tulloch 2000). From a left, realist perspective, Young (1999: 35) pointed out that 'rises in crime became signs, not so much of any changes in the "real" crime rate, but of increased governmental and public responses to crime, represented sometimes as smokescreens for the vested interests of those in the criminal justice system, sometimes as metaphors for wider social anxieties unrelated to crime.' Nevertheless, some, if not most, crime-prevention initiatives, could substantially reduce reported levels of fear and insecurity, although they have failed (apparently) to reduce actual crime rates. Thus, fear of crime is taken seriously (Brown and Polk 1996), and reduced fear of crime starts to feature in the measures of programme effectiveness.[5]

With crime escalating and public anxiety aroused, the penal population grew rapidly. For example, the rate (per 100,000 resident population) of sentenced prisoners under jurisdiction of State and Federal correctional authorities in the United States increased from 139 in 1980, to 292 in 1990, to 478 in 2000, and to 491 in 2005.[6] In particular, as Rose (2000) pointed out, despite the proliferation of non-custodial punishments, there has been no reduction in the prison population in Britain and the United States. There is an uneven distribution of incarceration rates in American neighbourhoods (Sherman *et al.* 1997) and a disproportionately high level of blacks under the control of the penal apparatus in the United States (Mauer 1997, Wacquant 2001). Arrests and prisoners associated with drugs are increasing rapidly, and the increasing prison population related to drugs is disproportionately represented by African-Americans (see e.g. Tonry 1995). Moreover, the costs of crime are alarming in industrialized countries (see e.g. Waller and Welsh 1999).

Hope (1995: 66) argued that the various community prevention paradigms of the past have arisen as responses to contemporary perceptions of the problem of crime in urban areas, and any assessment of the development of community crime prevention needs to comprehend the changing nature of the crime problem in the urban environment. With increasing crime, higher levels of public fear of crime, a large penal population, and huge costs of crime, doubt has been cast on the efficiency and effectiveness of the traditional approaches to crime, a subject to be examined in the following section.

Perceived inefficiency of the criminal justice system

Ever since the rationalization and professionalization of the functions of the welfare-state, the locus of responsibility of government and social control has been shifted from the citizens to the police (Engstad and Evans 1980). However, with the changes of crime problems in the late twentieth century, this assumed responsibility and expectations of the police have been shaken. The questioning of the welfare state and the criticism of the rational/deterrent model of policing spurred the examination of the effectiveness of policing (Banton 1980; Hough and Clarke 1980), albeit with substantial methodological challenges.[7] Some studies also showed the failure of past policing strategies (e.g. Rosenbaum 1986, 1988; Rosenbaum *et al.* 1998; Sherman 1990; Kelling and Coles 1996). This points to the importance of the police working with the public. In fact, even early in the 1960s, Jacobs (1961: 41, cited in Hope 1995: 42) made the following cogent observations, 'The first thing to understand is that the public peace – the sidewalk and street peace – of cities is not kept primarily by the police, necessary as the police are. It is kept primarily by an intricate, almost unconscious, network of voluntary controls and standards among the people themselves, and enforced by the people themselves.... No number of police can enforce civilization where the normal, casual enforcement of it has broken down.' Studies have shown that the police are mainly dependent on the public for information about crime, and in the work of the police a very large proportion of police time is devoted to matters either unrelated to crime or only marginally related to crime-fighting objectives (Hough and Clarke 1980). Kelling and Coles (1996) stated that the failure of the criminal justice system lies in two aspects: (1) it does not recognize the links between disorder, fear, serious crime and urban decay;[8] (2) it ignores the role of citizens in crime prevention. Thus, crime prevention entails the public–police cooperation and multiagency approach to crime, and the police taking responsibility for the 'broken windows'. The failure or limits of the criminal justice system are well documented in the literature, as in the emergence of restorative justice in response to the failure of the traditional correctional paradigm (Braithwaite 1999; Levrant *et al.* 1999). The situation calls for a refocus on the community as the solution to crime and on the preventive perspective (Miller and Hess 1998), and the mutual dependence between formal justice and social institutions in crime prevention (Hope and Shaw 1988).

Conceptualization of crime prevention

Generally, the types of crime of greatest concern for government and especially locally initiated crime-prevention programmes are street crime and property crime. But there is no consensus whether white-collar crime (such as company fraud, tax evasion and insider trading) and nuisance offences (such as rowdyism among groups of youths and aggressive begging) should be targeted (Graham and Bennett 1995, Bennett 1996). As Crawford (1998) argued, crime-prevention programmes tended to 'orient attention towards public displays of unruly behavior and away from offending which takes place in "private spheres", behind people's back or which involve a less visible and more indirect relationship between offender and victim'. Recently, with the emergence of the 'broken windows' theory and its various strategies, crime prevention typically pulled into its orbit behaviours associated with incivility and disorder, and not just purely legally defined criminal actions (Skogan 1990, Kelling and Coles 1996). It is widely recognized that crime prevention is not merely to prevent crime or disorder per se. The other objectives of crime prevention include reduction of damage (van Dijk 1990); reduction of perceived fear of crime (Lab 1988); strengthening of community cohesion, such as informal social control (Rosenbaum 1988); and the 'consolation prizes' of reduction in fear and incivility (Ekblom and Pease 1995). An even broader definition of crime prevention includes reduction of risk factors for crime, such as gang membership, and increases in protective factors, such as completing high school (Sherman *et al.* 1997).

Many theoretical models have been offered to classify crime-prevention interventions and behaviours. Notwithstanding the collectively confusing nature of the categorizations of crime prevention (Ekblom 1996), this section will review the main models in order to show how community crime prevention is incorporated into the general framework of crime prevention.

Public health model

Based on the principal population target, crime prevention distinguishes between primary, secondary and tertiary prevention. However, this approach is subject to a series of diverse interpretations. According to Brantingham and Faust (1976; see reviews by Pease 1994; Graham and Bennett 1995; Crawford 1998; Rosenbaum *et al.* 1998), primary prevention targets the general population and intends to prevent crime from ever occurring; secondary prevention aims to prevent crime among at-risk population based on the prediction of their predispositional factors; and tertiary prevention aims to prevent known offenders from committing further offences. Addressing the inadequacy of the one-dimensional classification paradigm of the model, van Dijk and de Waard (1991, cited in Crawford 1998) proposed a two-dimensional approach, which divides each of the three categories into situational, offender-oriented and victim-oriented measures. Crawford (1998: 16) recommended another two-dimensional approach to crime prevention by taking into account the collectivities as prevention target. In this model, 'community/neighbourhood-oriented' replaces 'situational' from van Dijk and de Waard's (1991) model; thus, 'community/neighbourhood' orientation is explicitly included within the public health approach to crime prevention. Crawford proceeded to argue that the introduction of 'community-oriented intervention' allows for physical or social strategies by the audiences of collectivities, such as social groups, organizations, associations and communities. In his model, 'community' is a place which is both the victim of crime and the site of criminogenic conditions. This is supported by the research findings that areas and communities with high concentrations of offenders also suffer from high levels of victimization.

Social/situational approach

The distinction between social and situational approaches offers another perspective in crime prevention by addressing the nature of the intervention. Social crime prevention is concerned with measures aimed at tackling the root causes of crime and the dispositions of individuals to offend (Crawford 1998; Rosenbaum *et al.* 1998), as demonstrated by Currie's (1996) strategies at both the macrolevel and microlevel and Young's (1992) twofold agenda for social prevention. Whereas social crime prevention addresses the root causes or *ultimate/push* factors of crime, situational crime prevention involves the management, design or manipulation of the immediate physical environment so as to tackle the *proximate/pull* factors of crime with the aim of reducing the opportunities for specific crimes (see e.g. Clarke 1995, 1997; Newman *et al.* 1997; Crawford 1998; Rosenbaum *et al.* 1998; Siegel 1998). Thus, the underlying rationale of social crime prevention is that crime is the product of complex social, economic and cultural processes, while, for situational crime prevention, crime is opportunistic and can be controlled through the manipulation of the physical environment.

Tonry and Farrington's four-level model

In Tonry and Farrington's typology (1995), crime prevention is classified into four categories: law enforcement, developmental, community, and situational prevention. Crime prevention by law enforcement emphasizes the general prevention in enacting and implementing the criminal law. It achieves the goal indirectly through effects on socialization and directly through deterrence, incapacitation, and rehabilitation. Situational crime prevention, as referred to earlier, is based on the premise that a large proportion of crime is contextual and opportunistic. Therefore, crime can be blocked by adopting target-hardening measures such as locking the door, shuttering the windows, purchasing dogs, and installing alarm systems. But of concern are the consequences of the 'fortress society' (Blakely and Snyder 1997). In terms of its effectiveness, 'displacement' and 'diffusion of benefits' are two issues of concern (Clarke and Weisburd 1994; Crawford 1998).

Community crime prevention refers to actions intended to change the social conditions that are believed to sustain crime in residential communities. It is premised on the insight that individuals' criminality is related to the community where they live and, therefore, changing the community may change the behaviour of its residents. This ecological approach has been revived in recent years and is further developed by scholars following its tradition (e.g. Bursik and Grasmick 1993; Sampson 2002; Sampson *et al.* 1997). Prevention by the community approach has focused on altering the physical and social organization of communities, as in community organizing, tenant involvement, resource mobilization, and community defence (Hope 1995). Apparently, there are overlaps between community crime prevention and situational crime prevention. The last category in Tonry and Farrington's typology is developmental prevention. Through locating the risk factors and protective factors in childhood, the links between developmental processes and later delinquency are clarified. Thus, interventions in children's development process, by decreasing risk factors and increasing protective factors, can have either delinquency-reducing effects or beneficial effects on other indicators (e.g., school performance, hyperactivity, and impulsivity) that are associated with reduced offending probabilities. The addition of community crime prevention to this model is explicitly proposed, notwithstanding the overlaps between the different levels, such as those between developmental and community prevention, and those between community and situational prevention.

The development of community crime prevention has had three phases, albeit not mutually exclusive: informal social control, opportunity reduction and the partnership approach (see Zhong and Broadhurst 2007). Programmes of informal social control have stressed the importance of citizen input in crime prevention, such as neighbourhood watch and citizens' patrol. The phase of opportunity reduction is premised on the conviction that crime is opportunistic, and thus reducing opportunities can prevent crime, as manifested, for example, in target-hardening measures, such as 'defensible space' and 'crime prevention through environmental design'. The partnership approach stresses the importance of synergy between various governmental agencies, community organizations, and the public in preventing crime.

Social capital and community crime prevention: the nexus

The concept of social capital

Although the concept of social capital has gained increasing popularity, it seems to mean different things to different people. So a multidimensional approach has been used to interpret social capital. According to Dasgupta and Serageldin (2000), social capital is identified with such features of social organizations as trust, is thought of as an aggregate of behavioural norms, is viewed as social networks, and is even a combination of all the preceding. Onyx and Bullen (2000) identified three themes in the literature of social capital: more or less dense interlocking networks of relationships between individuals and groups, reciprocity, and trust. Similarly, Lin (2000, 2001a, 2001b) argued that in the literature social capital is basically represented as social networks, as civic engagement, and as trust. Apparently, scholars such as Putnam (1993b, 1995) and Coleman (1990) embrace more than one conceptual perspective of social capital. Coleman (2000) conceptualizes social capital as networks and trust. Putnam seems to conceptualize social capital as all three – civic engagement, networks and trust – when he defines it as 'features of social organization, such as trust, norms, and networks, that can improve the efficiency of society by facilitating coordinated actions' (Putnam 1993b: 167).[9] This study adopts Lin's (2000, 2001a, 2001b) conceptualization of social capital as *'the investment in embedded resources in social networks with expected returns'*.

The analyses of social capital by Bourdieu (1985) and Coleman (1990) have been grounded on relationships between actors or between an individual actor and a group. For example, Coleman (1990) argued that 'social capital inheres in the structure of relations between persons and among persons'. Thus, social capital is basically an individual property, with benefits or advantages accruing to actors because of their involvement in networks and broader social structures. But for political scientists such as Putnam (1993a, 1993b, 1995, 2000) and Fukuyama (1999), the concept has been extended to display the features of collectivities, such as a community, a city and even the whole country. In so doing, according to Portes (1998), it could lead to logical circularity. Lin argued that relations among individuals are uniformly recognized as the building blocks of social capital, and social capital *'is rooted precisely at the juncture between individuals and their relations; and it is contained in the meso-level structure or in social networks'* (2000: 3; emphasis in original). That is, individuals and their relations form the basis of the social capital, and this has microconsequences for the individuals as well as macroconsequences for the collectivity.

When employing social capital to display the features of the larger human groups and organizations, Putnam (1993b) identified two types of social capital: localized social capital and bridging capital. The former, also known as bonding social capital (Putnam 2000), accumulates in the course of informal social interactions that families and people from the same locality engage in through their daily lives. The latter, originally termed by Putnam 'generalized social capital', connects communities and organization to others. Localized social capital and bridging social capital are sometimes referred to as 'horizontal' and 'vertical' capital, respectively. According to Putnam (2000), bonding social capital is exclusive because it is, by choice or necessity, inward-looking and tends to reinforce exclusive identities and homogeneous groups, while bridging social capital is inclusive because it is outward-looking and encompasses people across diverse social cleavages. However, he claimed that, depending on the circumstances, both bridging and bonding social capital could have powerfully positive social effects. Thus, he further argued that bonding and bridging are not 'either-or' categories into which social networks could be neatly divided, but 'more or less' dimensions along which we can compare different forms of social capital.

This distinction between bonding and bridging is, to a large extent, parallel to the discussions of 'strong ties' versus 'weak ties' or 'closure' versus 'structural holes'. As shown in Bourdieu's class perspective and Coleman's calculation of social capital (1990: 313–15), network density and closure of social networks are the basis of social capital. Lin (2000) argued that the linkage between network density or closure and the utility of social capital denies the significance of bridges, structural holes, or weaker ties, and thus is too narrow. The idea of 'strength of weak ties', developed by Granovetter (1974), refers to the power of indirect influences outside the immediate circle of family and close friends to serve as an informal employment referral system (see Portes 1998). Likewise, 'structural holes' exist between contacts who are non-redundant, in the sense of being neither directly nor indirectly strongly linked to one another, nor similarly located in the pattern of relationships in sociometric space (Burt 1992, 2001). In this case, social capital is based on the relative paucity of network ties rather than their density. Burt (2001) reviewed empirical evidence to support the 'hole' argument over closure. However, he argued that the role of closure could not be simply dismissed. He constructed the model shown in Figure 3.1 to illustrate how network closure and structural holes could be integrated.

In Figure 3.1 the X-axis refers to the network closure and the Y-axis to the structural holes. Performance is an undefined mixture of innovation, positive evaluation, early promotion, compensation and profit. According to Burt (2001), performance is highest in quadrant A, where in-group closure is high (one clear leader, or a dense

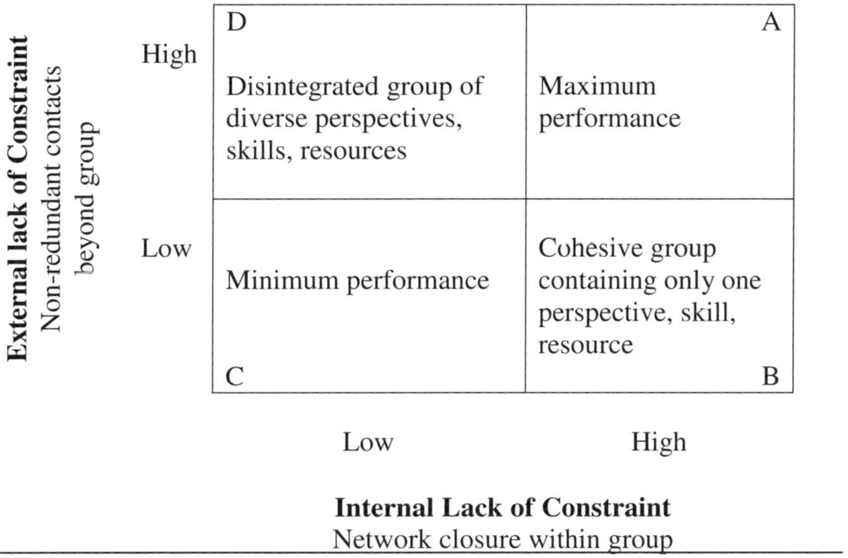

	D	A
High	Disintegrated group of diverse perspectives, skills, resources	Maximum performance
Low	Minimum performance	Cohesive group containing only one perspective, skill, resource
	C	B
	Low	High

External lack of Constraint — Non-redundant contacts beyond group

Internal Lack of Constraint
Network closure within group

Source: Burt (2001: 48).

Figure 3.1 Social capital matters.

network connecting people in the group), and there are many non-redundant contacts beyond the group (member networks into the surrounding organization are rich in disconnected perspectives, skills and resources). However, performance is lowest in quadrant C, where in-group closure is low (members spend their time bickering with one another about what to do and how to proceed), and there are few non-redundant contacts beyond the group (members are limited to similar perspectives, skills, and resources). Burt (2001) further observed that the mechanisms for structural holes and network closures are distinct. Closure describes how dense or hierarchical networks lower the risk associated with transaction and trust, and this can be associated with performance. On the other hand, the hole argument describes how structural holes are opportunities to add value with brokerage across the holes, and this, again, is associated with performance. Thus, structural holes and network closure, subject to certain conditions, can both generate social capital. So studies should first conceptualize for what outcomes and under what conditions a denser or sparser network might generate a better return, and then deduce a hypothesis for empirical examination (Lin 2001a).

Taken together, the discussions on bonding/bridging social capital, and network closure and structural holes illustrate the importance of both the internal and external dynamics of a social structure. In other words, a certain social structure should be both inward-looking and outward-looking. In current times with more technological breakthroughs and shifts in economic demand, it is especially compelling for a social structure to bridge with outside entities. This point is well expressed in Woolcock's (1998) conceptual framework of social capital. Put simply, Woolcock (1998, cited in Colletta and Cullen 2000) incorporated in a comprehensive framework four dimensions of social capital: strong ties between family members and neighbours, weak ties with outside communities and between communities, formal institutions (including laws and norms), and state–community interactions. This integrated model will be more thoroughly investigated in the application of social capital to community crime prevention in the next section.

The nexus between social capital and community crime prevention

In the literature, social capital seems to play a role in crime prevention and deviance control. For example, to demonstrate the effects of social capital, Coleman (1990) gave the example of a mother moving from Detroit to Jerusalem, where the normative structure ensures that unattended children will be looked after by adults in the vicinity; Portes (1998) argued that informal social control could be one of the consequences of social capital; and Putnam (2000) suggested that social capital could contribute to lower crime. A series of empirical studies have been conducted to test the relationship between social capital and crime (e.g. Kennedy *et al.* 1998; Saegert *et al.* 2002; Lederman *et al.* 2002; Rosenfeld *et al.* 2001; Messner *et al.* 2004), recovery from drug addiction (Cheung and Cheung 2000), and prisoners' re-entry to society or recidivism (Sampson and Laub 1992, 1993; Laub *et al.* 1998; Liu 1999; Rose and Clear 2002). Although social capital is variously defined, generally a positive relationship between social capital and crime has been established, except in Messner *et al.* (2004), in which the relationship is different for different dimensions of social capital. Moreover, there is a tendency to assess the reciprocal relationship of social capital with crime and other social outcomes. However, little effort has been explicitly made to demonstrate that social capital is closely related to the community approach to crime prevention. The following section shows how social capital represents itself in the following theories of community crime prevention: social disorganization theory, opportunity-reduction theory and broken windows theory. More specifically, this exploration is to investigate whether and how the concept of social capital theoretically underlies the community approach to crime prevention. Social capital offers an explanatory approach which brings together, in a coherent fashion, those main elements which are embodied in the community approach to crime prevention. Hence, it offers both a framework within which previous research can be synthesized, and a valuable stimulus for future research on crime prevention.

Social disorganization theory
Social disorganization theory holds that disorganized communities are characterized by high rates of economic deprivation, residential instability, and population heterogeneity (Shaw and McKay 1969). Regarding why social disorganization accounts for higher crime, Bursik (1988: 521, cited in Bursik and Grasmick 1993: 33) offered a control-theoretic approach: (1) institutions pertaining to internal control are difficult to establish when many residents are 'uninterested in communities they hope to leave at the first opportunity'; (2) the development of primary relationships that result in informal structures of neighbourhood control is less likely when local networks are in a continual state of flux; and (3) heterogeneity impedes communication and thus obstructs the quest to solve common problems and attain common goals.

Lanier and Henry (1998) argued that ever since the 1960s, social ecology theory has taken four distinct, although related, new directions. First, design ecology relates to the issue of space and design. It aims to 'design out' crime through means such as 'defensible space' and 'crime prevention through environment design (CPTED)'. Second, critical ecology tries to take into account economic and political forces that create the social disorganization that in turn produces crime. Third, systemic ecology suggests that what is required in crime control is a systemic approach that focuses on the regulatory capacities of relational networks in neighbourhoods and between them. Lastly, integrative ecology attempts to integrate ecological theory with biological, social learning, routine activities, rational choice, and cultural theories. Design ecology will be discussed in more detail later in the opportunity model. Critical ecology's emphasis on social and economic forces fits into bridging social capital and into the conceptualization of community that crosses community physical boundaries to tap external forces and sources. Integrative ecology will not be considered explicitly. So the following section moves to systemic ecology, developed mainly by Bursik and Grasmick (1993).

Bursik and Grasmick (1993) reformulated the social disorganization model into a basic systemic model by linking it with Hunter's (1985) three levels of social control: private, parochial, and public. This reformulation of social disorganization shows how ecological factors influence various levels of social control, and is best captured in Figure 3.2.

The basic systemic model illustrates how social disorganization inside a neighbourhood can affect its networks and resources, its levels of social control, and finally its crime rates. Residential instability and racial/ethnic heterogeneity lead to disrupted or limited primary relational networks, the existence of which weakens private social control. The parochial social control, built on the secondary relationship networks, reflects the capacity of local communities to supervise the behaviour of their residents. There are three forms of parochial social control (Bursick and Gramick 1993: 35): (1) informal surveillance: the casual but active observation of neighborhood streets that is engaged in by individuals during daily activities; (2) movement-governing rules: the avoidance of areas in or near the neighbourhood or in the city as a whole that are viewed as unsafe; (3) direct intervention: questioning strangers and residents of the

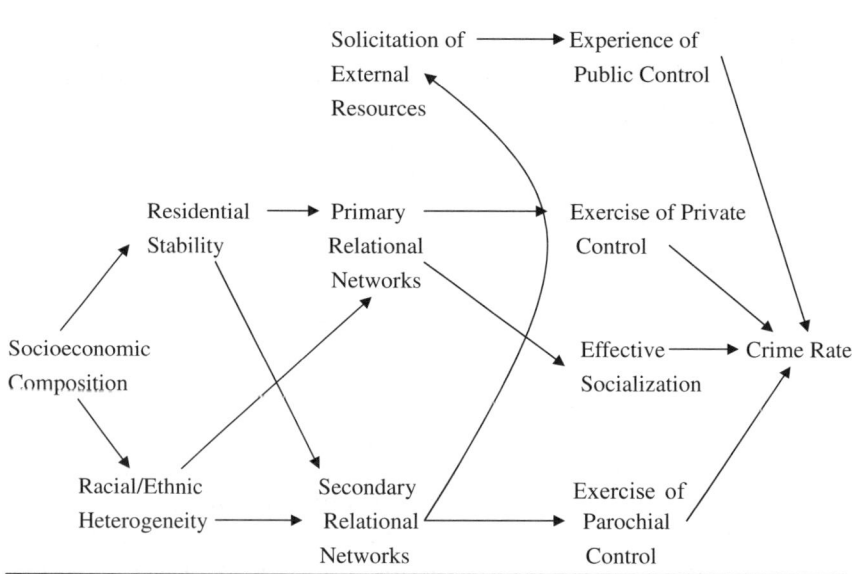

Source: Bursik and Grasmick (1993: 39).

Figure 3.2 The basic systemic model of crime.

neighbourhood about suspicious activities, which may also include chastening adults and admonishing children for behaviour defined as unacceptable.

Without doubt, these forms of control and supervision among residents are important at the local level. But in those communities with higher instability and heterogeneity, parochial control is substantially weakened. The exercise of primary and parochial control affects the effectiveness of socialization in preventing deviance. Together, they have an impact on crime rates inside the community. Bursik and Grasmick (1993) argued that perhaps the greatest shortcoming of the basic social disorganization model is the failure to consider the relational networks that pertain to the public sphere of control. To transcend the community boundaries, they introduced 'solicitation of external resources' and its corresponding 'exercise of public control'. Understandably, the solicitation of external resources entails relationships crossing the community boundaries, which I call 'bridging relational networks'. Through this bridging, individual communities are connected to external forces and sources and public control, instead of being isolated islands. This runs in parallel to Hope's (1995) discussion of community crime prevention, which emphasizes both the horizontal and vertical relationships of individual communities. It also fits Crawford's (1998b) description of 'political economy of community'.

Empirical studies also support this open-minded perspective of community crime prevention, which balances both the external and internal dynamics of community life. Bellair (1997) tested the effects of neighbours' social interaction on the rates of three serious crimes (burglary, motor vehicle theft, and robbery) across 60 urban neighbourhoods. Findings showed that neighbours' interaction, defined as getting together once a year or more with neighbours, had the most consistent and generally strongest effect on the three types of crime. Moreover, this form of interaction explained a significant proportion of the effect of ecological characteristics on community crime. The study by Sampson et al. (1997) on 'collective efficacy' also cogently demonstrated the effects of social cohesion and informal social control on violent crime at the community level.

Studies have also shown the inadequacy of confining 'community' to mean only internal mechanisms. Using rates of total and individual violent crimes for census tracts in Columbus, Ohio, for 1990, Peterson et al. (2000) investigated whether local institutions matter in controlling neighbourhood violence. They examined both those conventional institutions that help control crime, and those that facilitate violence. Their findings showed that communities may reduce violent crime somewhat by developing a larger base of certain types of conventional crime-control institutions (such as recreation centres) and preventing the encroachment of the latter type (such as bars). However, such institutions do not explain why economic deprivation and residential instability are strongly related to violent crime. According to Peterson et al. (2000), the findings suggest that efforts to substantially reduce violence in local communities must counter the macrostructural forces that increase economic deprivation and lead to inner-city decline.

As Rose and Clear (1998) observed, social disorganization theory is implicitly based on the notions of social and human capital, although the terms are not explicitly adopted. In the basic systemic model, the primary, secondary and bridging relational networks, on the one hand, and the resources embedded in those networks, on the other hand, are the two basic elements of social capital: networks and embedded resources, as discussed earlier. The Chicago Area Project in the 1930s launched by Shaw and McKay was a crime-prevention initiative through the strengthening of social capital of the community. Under the project, 22 neighbourhood centres were established in six areas of Chicago. It attempted to organize existing community structures to develop social order in otherwise disorganized slums. The project was run mainly by committees of local residents. The centres had two primary functions: (1) to coordinate community resources such as churches, schools, labour unions, industries, clubs, and other groups in addressing and resolving community problems; and (2) to sponsor a variety of activity programmes including recreation, summer camping and scouting activities, handicraft workshops, discussion groups, and community projects (see Vold and Bernard 1986: 180). Apparently, those measures and activities could serve to strengthen community relational networks, and to create more social capital. The project also campaigned for community improvements in such areas as education, sanitation, traffic safety, physical conservation, and law enforcement (see Siegel 1998: 188). Thus, external resources were likely to be tapped for the benefit of community development. It is easy to see from the literature that ensuing community crime-prevention initiatives have been similar to the Chicago Area Project.

While it is heuristic, the basic systemic model delineates a one-way process inside individual communities, from networks and resources to social control and to the crime rate. In the words of Rose and Clear (1998), it is recursive, disregarding a reciprocal relationship between those three levels of analysis. They argued that the community crime level and the consequent public control measures could give feedback on the structures, networks and control levels inside the community. Their argument is captured in the non-recursive model (Figure 3.3), a revision of the basic systemic model.

In this model, Rose and Clear (1998) used levels of incarceration to illustrate the reciprocal relationship. They incorporated a feedback loop and subsumed primary and secondary relational networks and the solicitation of external resources under the heading 'human and social capital'. That is, the stock of social capital of a community affects its crime rate, and in turn the crime rate affects the supply of social capital of the community. Perhaps this reciprocal relationship between social capital and crime rate can resolve one confusion of the social disorganization model. This confusion lies in the fact that Shaw and McKay sometimes did not clearly differentiate the presumed outcome of social disorganization (i.e. increased rates of delinquency) from disorganization itself (Bursik and Grasmick 1993: 34). In some instance, a delinquency rate is treated both as an example of social disorganization and as something caused by social disorganization. This confusion can be clarified, to some degree, by understanding

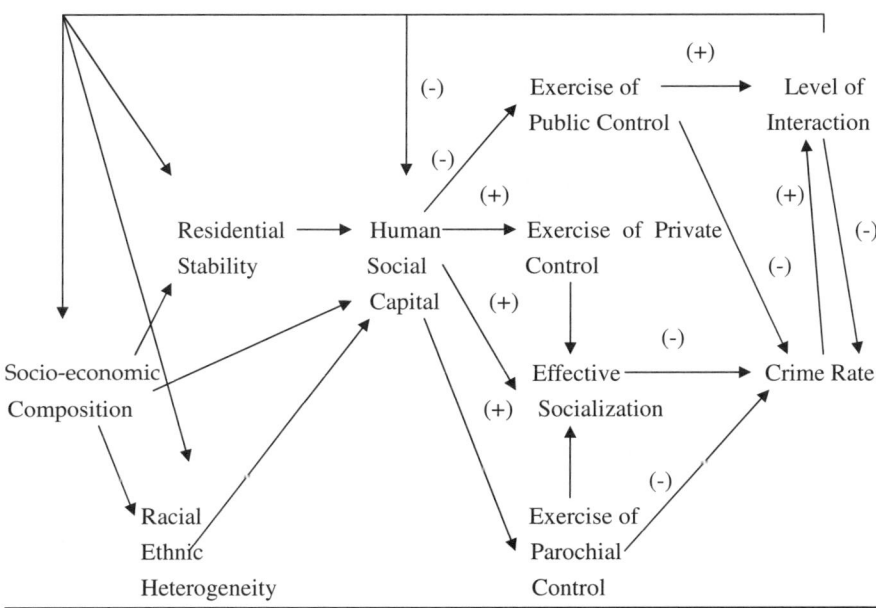

Source: Rose and Clear (1998: 468).

Figure 3.3 The non-recursive model of crime.

the reciprocal effects of crime rates on social disorganization. That is, disorganization leads to a higher crime rate, which in turn causes more disorganization. Thus, disorganization is the cause and crime is the effect. Indeed, Markowitz *et al.* (2001) demonstrated a feedback loop in the relationship between cohesion, crime and disorder, fear and cohesion. Research on social capital and crime, as referred to earlier, indeed demonstrated a reciprocal relationship between social capital and crime.

Opportunity reduction
The opportunity-reduction model is premised on several theoretical initiatives, including lifestyle theory, routine activities theory, and rational choice theory, as referred to earlier. The model stresses the significance of 'opportunities' (location, time, and circumstances) in a specific criminal behaviour; therefore, removing or reducing those opportunities will lead to a reduction in that specific crime.

According to lifestyle theory, people are victimized because they have a lifestyle that increases their exposure to criminal offenders (Hindelang *et al.* 1978; Clarke 1995, 1997; Siegel 1998). The theory is stimulated by National Crime Victimization Survey (NCVS) and Uniform Crime Reports (UCR) data showing that victimization risks grow with such behaviours as staying single, associating with young men, going out in public places late at night, and living in an urban area. It shifts the focus from offenders to victims. According to Sigel (1998), three hypotheses underlie this theory. First, the equivalent group hypothesis holds that victims and criminals share similar characteristics. Research shows that crime victims also self-reported significant amounts of criminal behaviour. Second, the proximity hypothesis states that people become victims because of their physical proximity to criminals. In this view, where the victims live plays an important role in their victimization risks. Thus, neighbourhood crime levels are more important in determining the chances of victimization than individual characteristics. Third, the deviant place hypothesis, which is derived from the proximity hypothesis, regards some areas as intrinsically deviant. Apparently, the second and third hypotheses are closely related to social disorganization theory in that places or ecological factors affect criminal activities, although the former focuses on victims and the latter on offenders. In this respect, the crime-prevention measures conforming to social disorganization theory could be applied to reduce the opportunities for criminal exposure. Clearly, in the crime-prone areas, lifestyle theory suggests that criminal offenders are from inside. So, apart from those 'target-hardening measures', if victims and potential victims are organized to strengthen informal control, such as watching out for each other, their victimization opportunities will be lowered. On the other hand, the crime-prone areas are also usually desperate for external resources and may be hostile to law enforcement. So if residents actively seek external resources and assistance or cooperate closely with law enforcement agencies, it should make a difference. In this regard, social capital can play its role.

Routine activities theory holds that criminal activities are determined by the interaction of three factors: motivated offenders, suitable targets, and capable guardians (Cohen and Felson 1979). Felson (1986) refers to them as 'the web of informal crime control', and added one more factor 'intimate handler', namely someone who knows the offender well enough to be able to exercise informal control over him. Siegel (1998) argued that the convergence of routine activities theory with lifestyle theory lies in how routine living arrangements can affect victims' risk. He further cited Miethe and Meier (1994) in listing the four factors that explain the congruence: (a) proximity to criminals; (b) time of exposure to criminals; (c) target attractiveness; and (d) guardianship. Therefore, following the discussions on its role in lifestyle theory, social capital also supports crime-control and prevention activities inspired by routine activities theory. In particular, the two factors of routine activities theory, 'guardianship' and 'intimate handler', clearly indicate the importance of social capital in frustrating motivated offenders. Potential guardians include mechanical devices, such as security fences or burglar alarms, as well as persons, such as law enforcement officers, hired security guards and citizens. Efficiency and willingness to 'guard' send a signal to discourage potential offenders. Fellow citizens' intervention and vigilance demonstrate a form of social capital inside the community. Guardians can also form partnerships, such as between the public and the police, to enhance efficiency and effectiveness, a manifestation of bridging social capital. On the other hand, the factor of intimate handlers entails a caring relationship, and the availability of intimate handlers shows the amount of social capital possessed by the offender. In a local community, the more intimate the handlers, the closer the relationship, the more social capital there is, and the more likely that potential offenders will be deterred.

Rational choice theory, developed from the classical school of criminology, views criminal behaviour as a result of rational choice based on the balance of potential gains and losses. According to Siegel

(1998), rational choice theory dovetails with routine activities theory. The former provides a microview of why individual offenders decide to commit specific crimes, while the latter provides a macroview of crime, predicting how social and economic changes bear on overall crime and victimization rates. Apparently, for offenders, the interaction of the four factors in routine activities theory is a process of rational choice: to balance their own needs, the victim's characteristics, the efficiency and possibility of guarding activities, and any discouraging factor from their intimates. Lanier and Henry (1998: 77) argued that contemporary rational choice theory differs from its classical counterpart in the degree of rationality attributed to offenders. They claimed that the literature on rational choice and routine activities theories shows that criminal decisions are neither fully rational nor thoroughly thought out, and the decision-making process is subject to a variety of individual and environmental factors.

In terms of prevention, rational choice theory, like lifestyle theories and routine activities theory, focuses on the situational factors. But the emphasis on physical environment and hardware has produced a series of criticisms, such as passiveness and pessimism, victim-blaming, siege mentality, fortress society, and crime displacement. Needless to say, defensible places, hardened targets, and personal and household prevention behaviour could act to thwart potential crimes. But those measures are not infinite due to 'arms race' effects, that is, potential offenders' incentive to catch up with modern technology. More importantly, as critics argue, they lead to huge financial and social costs. Financial cost could restrict the access to those measures by economically disadvantaged individuals and groups, thus causing crime displacement and intensifying victims' suffering. In terms of social cost, society, with individuals and families hiding behind their metal doors and bars, is more atomized. As indicated above, high levels of fear of crime lead to citizens' physical and social withdrawal from public places, attenuating informal social control. In other words, the stock of social capital in a local community is diminished.

As reviewed previously, studies have demonstrated that social/demographic variables are more important in predicting crime rates than are the characteristics of physical environment. Accordingly, community crime prevention puts more emphasis on the social aspect, so as to reduce social cost, increase informal social control, and ultimately reduce crime. In this respect, it is through informal social control that crime prevention is achieved in community crime prevention. There is accumulating evidence that fear of informal sanctions may have a greater crime-reducing impact than the fear of formal legal punishments, and informal sanctions may be most effective especially in highly unified areas where people know one another and crime cannot be hidden from public view (see Siegel 1998). This displays the utility of social capital. Moreover, the analyses of the three theories shows the importance of public–police cooperation in discouraging criminal behaviour, illustrating the role of bridging social capital. In a nutshell, social capital could play its role in community crime prevention by reducing opportunities.

Broken windows theory
'Broken windows' theory theoretically supports the partnership approach in community crime prevention. Its thrust lies in the argument that visible signs of minor disorder in a local community, such as broken windows, will gradually evolve into large-scale social disorder and even crime. The metaphor is as follows: a broken window is interpreted as an unattended building, and thus more windows are broken. This ultimately leads to the abandonment of the streets, leaving them to deviants and criminals (see Kelling and Coles 1996). As the non-recursive model by Rose and Clear (1998) reveals, small-scale social disorder decays into crime, which then produces more, large-scale social disorder, a reciprocal relationship.

Community policing and problem-based policing are policing styles derived from the broken windows theory. But community policing can develop into two extremes. One is top-down, getting-tough, 'zero-tolerance', aggressive policing, and the other is bottom-up, problem-solving policing. As Rose and Clear (1998) argued, the former involves street sweeps and widespread arrests, and it thus may undercut private and parochial social control processes. The partnership approach to community crime prevention is bottom-up, and centres on problem-solving. The local problems are identified and solved with cooperation and coordination between the local residents, law enforcement agencies, and other government agencies. This is aligned with bridging social capital.

In sum, the concept of social capital underlies the three models of community crime prevention. That is, for the purpose of preventing crime, social capital is directly related to social disorganization theory, the opportunity-reduction model should pay more attention to the stock of social capital in a particular community, and community policing should focus more on the bottom-up, problem-solving policing. Thus, social capital can be employed as a useful theoretical framework to integrate those various measures of community crime prevention. More specifically, the localized social capital and bridging social capital of a community affect its crime levels. Thus, the stock of social capital of individual communities could show four combinations, as shown in Figure 3.4. A represents the maximum amount of social capital: both bridging and localized social capital are strong, and we have the lowest crime level. In contrast, D represents the minimum amount of social capital: both bridging and localized social capital are weak, and we have the highest crime level. For B and C, one form of social capital is strong and the other is weak, and thus the total amount of social capital stays in the middle. Regarding the crime level, it theoretically varies between the highest and the lowest. Thus, it sums up social capital's significance in community crime prevention. However, its validity can be tested only in the examinations of practical crime-prevention activities.

Community crime prevention and social capital: problems and issues

In the proceeding sections, community crime prevention and social capital have been reviewed and the links between the two established. People might legitimately ask why such a digression should have been made. In this process, I have endeavoured to grasp the main themes threading through the discussion of community crime prevention and social capital, in the hope of shedding some light on certain intriguing issues and problems. Below, four such issues and problems are identified: the three dyads of formal/informal, public/private, and inclusion/exclusion, and the role of the state.

Bridging Social Capital

	Strong	Weak
Strong	**A** Lowest crime level	**B** Mixed crime level
Weak	**C** Mixed crime level	**D** Highest crime level

Localized Social Capital

Figure 3.4 Dimensions of social capital and crime level inside a community.

Formal/informal social control

The issue of the relationship between formal and informal social control has been featured in protracted, albeit inconclusive, debates. Black (1980) hypothesized an inverse relationship between the two. As Rose and Clear's (1998) non-recursive model showed, over-reliance on public social control, such as large-scale incarceration, would lead to diminished informal social control (which, according to them, includes primary and parochial control), higher crime rates, and more social disorganization. The review of community crime prevention and social capital demonstrated that emphasis should be on informal social control inside the community and on the community's connection with external entities, that is, the partnership approach and bridging social capital. Hence, the informal social control mechanism plays an important role in local crime prevention and at the same time cooperates with the formal mechanisms in order to maximize the benefits. The question remains: is it difficult, if not impossible, to achieve that in practice? Higher-crime communities are always characterized by social economic deprivation, physical and social isolation, racial/ethnic heterogeneity and a strained relationship between the local community and the public agencies. So, imaginably, it is difficult to harmonize local relationship across various lines and rebuild bridging networks with the public agencies. For example, regarding the multiagency approach to crime prevention, Sampson *et al.* illustrated its complexities and power differentials running between different state agencies, and concluded that 'multi-agency strategies can undoubtedly have an impact on the lives of people within a locality, but these are not always the outcomes that are intended' (1988: 478). Therefore, regarding the formal/informal dyad, it is necessary to distinguish the rhetoric from the reality.

Public/private social control

By the same token, the relationship between public and private control poses another unresolved issue for academics, practitioners, and policymakers, although to a certain extent it converges with the previous dyad. In building communities with social capital, Potapchuk *et al.* (1997: 130–131) made the following observations: 'In reality, a mix of private and public sector approaches to governance is common in most communities. Social capital is created at the intersection of market and government, public and private, creating community out of individual interest and collective good.' The question remains: how to operationalize this mix 'in reality'? In the state welfarist era, the state, that is, the public agencies, shouldered a wide range of responsibilities for the citizens. Apart from the fiscal pressures to reduce the role of the state, an argument has emerged recently in political and ideological circles to diminish that role and to increase the responsibilities of individuals. As Rose (2000: 191) commented, 'The dream of the social state gives way to the metaphor of the facilitating state, the state as partner and animator rather than provider and manager.... in exercising prudence, individuals cannot look solely to the public police and the formal mechanisms of the legal system.'

However, as Nelken (1985) and Cohen (1985) suggested, the thesis of the minimal state actually further strengthens state control. This controversy is fully captured in Garland's (1996: 454) observation, 'It should be emphasized that the responsibilization strategy does not entail the simple off-loading of state functions.... The reponsibilization strategy leaves the centralized state machine more powerful than before, with an extended capacity for action and influence. At the same time, however, this strategy serves to erode the notion of the state as the public's representative and primary protector.' Therefore, in light of the above contradictory arguments, and considering the differential interests between the private and public sectors, it is not clear, either theoretically or in practical terms, what this mix can or should be.

A good epitome of this dyad and its difficult settlement in criminal justice is public and private policing. As Shearing (1992) observed, a state-centred view of police functions has given way to a laissez-faire view that embraces 'private-public partnerships' and sees private policing as an industry providing both a service and a public benefit. However, in operationalizing the 'partnerships', there is always public and police resistance to public–police cooperation, and there seems to be a 'turf war' concerning the demarcation of junior partners, senior partners and equal partners. In particular, Shearing (1992: 419) suggested that 'if the community and the state are united as a single integrated system then the need for individuals to protect themselves from the state and from state intrusion falls away. The private becomes the public, and the public the private.'

Inclusion/exclusion

Last but not least, the dyad between exclusion and inclusion reveals even more significant problems. As Putnam (2000) argued, bonding social capital is inward-looking and exclusive, while bridging social capital is outward-looking and inclusive. According to Young (1999), 'late modernity' is characterized by a movement from an inclusive society of stability and homogeneity to an exclusive society of change and division. He listed three levels of exclusion in this late modern world: economic exclusion from labour markets, social exclusion between people in civil society and the ever-expanding exclusionary activities of the criminal justice system and private security. Likewise, Rose (2000) observed that the contemporary control strategies could be broadly divided into two groups: those that seek to regulate conduct by enmeshing individuals within circuits of inclusion and those that seek to act upon pathology through managing a different set of circuits, circuits of exclusion. Thus, the critical issue lies not in moral judgement about inclusion's goodness and exclusion's badness, but on how to face the reality. Whatever the reasons are, there has always been an 'underclass' (Crowther 2000), although politically and rhetorically it is a taboo term.

Regarding the benefits of social capital, Putnam (1995: 67) observed that 'dense networks of interaction probably broaden the participants' sense of self, developing the "I" into the "we", or (in the language of rational-choice theorists) enhancing the participants' "taste" for collective benefits.' Certainly, the shift from 'I' to 'we', that is, to ascend from a focus on individual benefits to one on collective goods, is laudable. However, as Currie (1988) argued, in community crime prevention the 'we' is in contrast to the 'they' and thus a focus on the former will exclude the latter. To counteract this 'exclusion', the concept of 'bridging social capital' is introduced. However, in reality, higher-crime communities with limited localized social capital always tend to lack the capacity to build bridging social capital. However, even if external resources are granted to them – for example, a foundation invests in a crime-prevention programme – those resources cannot be put to greatest use because of the disorganized internal structure of those communities. Perhaps that is why in the literature crime-prevention programmes are the least reported and least successful in higher-crime communities. On the other hand, middle-class communities, with residents economically and socially better off, are more capable of soliciting bridging social capital. Thus, although residents in some middle-class communities are less socially interactive with each other, the crime rates are lower. That is why for B and C in Figure 3.4, I cautiously stated, 'regarding the crime level, *theoretically* it varies between the highest and the lowest.'[10] Therefore, again, there emerged the gap between reality and rhetoric.

The role of the state

Taken together, the three dyads centre on the role of the state in postmodern societies. Regarding the role of the state, a wide range of metaphors emerge: the 'hollowing out of the state', the 'death of the social', the 'minimal role of the state', 'governance at a distance', etc. Skocpol (1985) proposed to 'bring the state back in', a shift from society-centred theories to a renewed interest in states. Skocpol (1985: 7) took Max Weber's definition of states as 'compulsory associations claiming control over territories and the people within them'. She echoed Stepan (1978) that 'the state must be considered as more than the "government"', and 'it is the continuous administrative, legal, bureaucratic and coercive systems that attempt not only to structure relationships *between* civil society and public authority in a polity but also to structure many crucial relationships within civil society as well' (Skocpol 1985: 7; emphasis in original).

She further argued that under the influence of the society-centred theories, the pluralists and structure-functionalists were reluctant to speak of states, and the critically minded neo-Marxists were unwilling even to grant true autonomy to states. She traced this tendency to the birth of the modern social sciences along with the industrial and democratic revolutions of Western Europe in the eighteenth and nineteenth centuries. At that juncture, it is understandable, Skocpol (1995: 6) argued, to perceive 'the locus of societal dynamics – and of the social good – not in outmoded, superseded monarchical and aristocratic states, but in civil society, variously understood as "the market", "the industrial division of labour", or "class relations"'. To reverse that trend, Skocpol's (1985) thesis of 'bringing the state back in' took the state as an independent actor, with autonomy and capacity, and thus put the research of the 'state' per se on the intellectual agenda.

In the earlier discussions about the patterns of social control in modern Western societies, the frameworks advanced by Stanley Cohen, Adam Crawford and David Garland all point out the emergence of the community approach to crime since the 1970s. But in their frameworks, the state did not recede from the scene of social control. In fact, as Garland contends, the current scene is dominated by a 'contradictory dualism': the coexistence of the preventive and populist approaches. In the preventive aspects of community crime prevention, the communities are supposed to form a partnership with the external state agencies in order to maximize efficiency and effectiveness in preventing crime. This, in the terms of social capital, shows the role of bridging social capital. In fact, the state constitutes one important dimension of the comprehensive framework of social capital, as developed by Woolcock (1998). The problem is that current understanding in academia seems to be still dominated by the 'state–society' dichotomy. This 'either-or' mentality hampers the exploration of the extent to which the state plays a role in social and crime control, as for example, in China, as will be shown below.

Up until now, the above exploration has been almost solely based on the Western context. I quote Robert Putnam to conclude this chapter and move to the focus on China in this book.

> Many students of the new democracies that have emerged over the past decade and a half have emphasized the importance of a strong and active civil society to the consolidation of democracy. Especially with regard to the post communist countries, scholars and democratic activists alike have lamented the absence or obliteration of traditions of independent civic engagement and a widespread tendency toward passive reliance on the state. To those concerned with the weakness of civil societies in the developing or post-communist world, the advanced Western democracies and above all the United States have typically been taken as models to be emulated. There is striking evidence, however, that the vibrancy of American civil society has notably declined over the past several decades. (Putnam 1995: 65)

Although China publicly claims to be a communist society and its dominant ideology centres on Marxism, Leninism, Mao Zedong's thoughts, Deng Xiaoping's theories, Jiang Zeming's 'three representations', and Hu Jintao's 'building a harmonious society', due to its clear market orientation since the implementation of the reform and open-door policy, China could still be grouped among Putnam's 'post-communist countries'. Thus, following the discussions in the Western academia and holding them as a prism, it should be interesting and worthwhile to have a close look at what is happening in China. The rest of the book aims to make the journey, with the problems and issues identified above as the guiding compass.

Notes

1 Ayres and Braithwaite (1992) constructed a pyramid to integrate restorative, deterrent and incapacitative justice. Starting from the bases of the pyramid, it is restorative justice, deterrence and incapacitation gradually, each of which corresponds, respectively, to an assumption of

a virtuous actor, rational actor, and incompetent or irrational actor (see Braithewaite 1999: 61). There are some similarities between Garland's framework and this model.
2 The three elements were further developed by Felson (1986) as 'the web of informal crime control' and one more element was added: the 'intimate handler' of the offender, namely someone who may exercise informal control over a person motivated to offend.
3 Certainly, the emphasis on victims sometimes went to extremes. One extreme is the thesis of crime precipitation (see e.g. Siegel 1998); that is, the victims are to be blamed for, or at least implicated in, their victimization; the other extreme manifests itself in the political logic wherein being 'for' victims automatically means being tough on offenders, and therefore a zero-sum policy game is assumed wherein the offender's gain is the victim's loss (see Garland 2000: 351).
4 For example, research in Boston and Minneapolis showed that fewer than 10 per cent of the addresses from which the police received calls accounted for more than 60 per cent of those calls; and a study of domestic homicides in Kansas City revealed that in 8 out of 10 cases the police had been called to the incident address at least once before; in half the cases, they had been called five times or more (Wilson and Kelling 1989, cited in Miller and Hess 1998: 25). Likewise, Sherman (1992) showed that less than 3 per cent of street addresses and 3 per cent of the population in a city produced over half the crime and arrests. For the UK, see Hope and Hough (1988) for the pocketing of crime, based on the 1984 British Crime Survey.
5 Regarding fear of crime, some community programmes actually lead to increases in the fear level in some circumstances. Moreover Curtis (1988: 198) noted the differentiated reduced fear: some for white, middle-class home-owners and nothing for less affluent black renters. Thus, Curtis viewed it as an abused bureaucratic convenience, as it is often easier to show changes in fear levels than in crime itself.
6 It is from Sourcebook of Criminal Justice Statistics Online, available at: http://www.albany.edu/sourcebook/pdf/t6292005.pdf.
7 Considering the police effects on crime, there are issues of validity, as discussed by Maxfield and Babbie (2005). See also Sherman (1992).
8 Robert Sampson and associates, however, challenged the link between disorder and crime, and argued that crime stems from the same sources as disorder – structural characteristics of certain neighbourhoods, notably concentrated poverty (see e.g. Sampson and Raudenbush 2001).
9 Putnam (1995: 67) used a similar definition of social capital: 'features of social organization such as networks, norms, and social trust that facilitate coordination and cooperation for mutual benefit'.
10 My understanding is that in light of their importance based on empirical studies, the two forms of social capital could be assigned weights statistically. Needless to say, it is not easy to do that. But this line of thinking is useful to clarify the points made above.

Chapter 4

Social capital in China

With its focus on the frameworks and practices of community crime prevention and social capital in the West, the previous chapter laid the foundation for the following chapters on the Chinese perspective. As discussed previously, social capital embodies two interlinked aspects: the relational networks and the resources flowing between. When employed to describe the features of large entities, such as a community, a distinction is made between 'bonding' and 'bridging' social capital. Under this definition, social capital is further identified as the underlying mechanism of the community approach to crime prevention in the West, with bonding social capital and bridging social capital depicting the internal and external dynamics of community life, respectively. Thus, regarding social capital, probably anyone with a basic sinological sense will not doubt its lineage in the Chinese cultural heritage. Chinese society, by and large, is closely associated with *guanxi*, which could be regarded as the Sino-version of social capital. Based on the definition of social capital introduced earlier, this chapter mainly locates those elements in Chinese culture and society that are either intrinsically social capital or are closely related to social capital.

More specifically, discussions in this chapter will unfold along three dimensions. First, we briefly sketch Confucianism, the doctrine that shapes the Chinese ethos and psyche, by juxtaposing it with legalism, so as to provide a landscape in which to locate the entrenchment and embeddedness of social capital in Chinese culture and society. Second, we outline two models of describing the organization of Chinese society, in an attempt to illustrate how the concept of social capital can be incorporated into the depiction and understanding of Chinese society. Last, we explore the concept of *guanxi*, an indigenous version of social capital. This includes how *guanxi* is interpreted from both a popular and an official point of view, and how individuals in their routine daily lives and institutional forms actually practise and observe, or embody and negotiate *guanxi*.

Confucianism versus legalism

In the Qin dynasty (221–206 BC), the first unified central state in Chinese history, legalism gained the dominant status. However, it was in the following Han dynasty (202 BC – 220 AD) that Confucius's thoughts achieved the status of an orthodoxy – Confucianism. From then on, it maintained this status in dynastic China, although it was transformed and reshaped according to the vicissitudes of the dynasties. There are suggestions by Western scholars that the legalist tradition was 'scientific' in politics, and was very close in spirit to modern Western nineteenth- and twentieth-century social sciences in its utilitarian realism, its amoralism, and its behaviouralism (see Yang 1994: 174–175). Thus, based on the antagonism between Confucianism and legalism, on the one hand, and the intimacy between legalism and modern Western thought on the other hand, I juxtapose the two doctrines to help readers with a Western background grasp Confucianism.[1]

The two doctrines had emerged with the movement of 'a hundred schools contending with each other' (*Baijia Zhengming*) in the periods of the Spring and Autumn (*Chunqiu*), and Warring States (*Zhanguo*). Confucianism advocated the revival of the past Zhou rituals to stem the turmoil and social disorder at that time. Legalism, with Shang Yang and Han Feizi as pioneers, stressed reform and a legal code as the remedy for the social chaos of those times. It is said that legalism played a key role in Qin's victory over the other warring states and the establishment of the first unified central state in China.

According to Yang (1994), the essence and antagonistic nature of the two schools could be summarized as four pairs of relationships. First, we have that between government by kinship and government by state. Confucianism stressed kinship relations that are based on a hierarchical order. Even the state was modelled on the family, and represented an extension of kinship principles. On the contrary, legalism sought to emphasize the overriding importance of the monarch and the state, and challenged the relational ethics of kinship and friendship as threats to the well-being of the state. Thus, while in Confucianist discourse, the 'state' was only a part of the hierarchical kinship order, in legalist discourse the strengthening of the state became the *raison d'être* of all social life (Yang 1994: 222).

Second, we have the relationship between the power of *li* and power of the law. In Confucianism, *li* was of paramount importance and a return to the *li* and music of the Zhou era was advocated. '*Li*' is variously translated as manners, ritual, etiquette, propriety and rites. According to Dutton (1992), *li* incorporates the notion of virtue, but is irreducible to virtue; more accurately, *li* is 'the obligation, manner and knowledge of virtue as these existed and were articulated within the traditional Chinese family structure' (1992: 22). In other words, *li* is both the awareness ('knowledge') and acting-out ('articulated') of virtue at the locus of the family, from where it also reaches out. The Confucian reasoning is like this: cultivation of the self through observing *li* ensures good management of the family, which in turn allows effective government of the state and finally achieves peace under heaven (*xiushen, qijia, zhiguo, pingtianxia*). This is well articulated in the famous passage from the Confucian classic 'Great Learning' (*Daxue*).

> The ancients who wanted to illustrate illustrious virtue throughout the kingdom first ordered well their own states. Wishing to order well their states, they first regulated their families. Wishing to regulate their families, they first cultivated their persons. Wishing to cultivate their persons, they first rectified their hearts. Wishing to rectify their hearts, they first sought to be sincere in their thoughts.... From the Son of Heaven down to the mass of people, all must consider the cultivation of the person the root of everything besides. (cited in Bakken 2000: 42)

Of foremost importance among all the *li*, is 'filial piety' (*xiao*), because 'the duty of children to their parents is the foundation whence all other virtues spring, and also the starting point from which we ought to begin our education' (*The Book of Filial Piety*, cited in Dutton 1992: 21).

Instead of the power of *li*, the legalists called for the state to make, publicize and indoctrinate laws. Moreover, under legalism, Confucian hierarchical order should give way to objectivity, by which both the high and the low class should bear the same responsibility for lawbreaking. Thus, a new bureaucratic system was established to supervise and execute the laws. This runs in stark contrast to power by *li*, which has no legal form.

In the arena of social control, the Confucian 'power of *li*' is well articulated in the following text from the *Analects*:

> If the people be led by laws, and uniformity sought to be given them by punishments, they will try to avoid the punishment, but have no sense of shame. If they be led by virtue, and uniformity sought to be given them by the rules of propriety, they will have the sense of shame, and moreover will become good. (cited in Dutton 1992: 22)

In fact, for Confucius, shame, virtue, and, as a result, the internalization of social norms and values, constitute the ideal and highest stage of the socialization process. Bakken (2000) observed that in the Chinese discourse, the themes of discipline and control could be found in both 'morality' and 'education'; moreover, the disciplinary and the educational infiltrated each other. Figure 4.1 summarizes the Confucian tenets on social control.

Third, we have the relationship between the segmentary state and the bureaucratic state. The segmentary state implies a centralizing force in the form of a royal clan gathering a number of local segmentary lineages, clans, and even tribes into a larger comprehensive entity in which the segments maintain their independence (see Yang 1994: 234). This is exactly what early Confucianists aspired to. The segments of the Zhou and its preceding three dynasties were

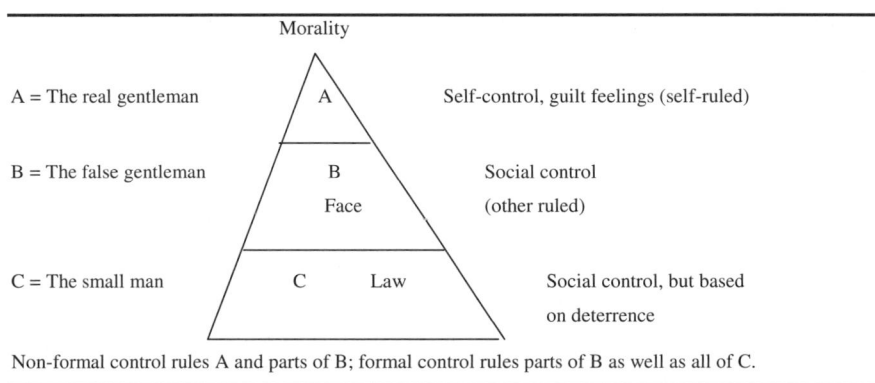

Source: Bakken (2000: 91), originally by Chen, Z. (1989).

Figure 4.1 The Chinese 'pyramid of morality' or 'pyramid of socialization'.

held to the centre by kinship, ritual performance and gift-exchange relations. However, since the Qin dynasty, the state had relied on a well-developed administrative machinery of taxation, bureaucracy, and laws to ensure centralized control. One of the means to maintain basic control was population registration. This registration system combined registration by occupation (military, household, royal clan, official, market, criminal, bondservant or slave, and perhaps scribe) with the complicated system of ranking based on military merit and heredity. Just because of this mixture, Yang (1994) observed that the old kinship hierarchy based primarily on heredity was to be replaced only by a state classification system no less hierarchical.

Last, there is the contrast between Confucianism and legalism in attitudes to the past and the present. Confucianism 'employed the past to negate the present', while legalism 'emphasized the present and denigrated the past' (Yang 1994).

It should be pointed out that ever since Confucianism had been appropriated by the state in the Han dynasty, its character had changed throughout all the later dynasties better to serve the interests of the state. The Han and later imperial dynasties preserved all the centralized state structure inspired by legalism and placed it under the cover of state Confucianism. So, in some sense, the later version of Confucianism may seem less antagonistic towards legalism in terms of the four aspects reviewed above. For example, although Confucianism conforms to 'employing the past to negate the present', except for occasional reformist attempts, state or imperial Confucianism used the past to strengthen the present imperial power. Thus, *li* became the instrument of state. Moreover, as Yang (1994: 243) observed, 'the state "overcoded" its logic of centralized organization onto the segmentary kinship units of local communities so that they formed concentric circles revolving around the same central trunk for the state, all resonating with each other.'

Certainly, the juxtaposition of Confucianism with legalism to facilitate the understanding of the former does not mean that the Chinese tradition is merely a confluence of Confucianism and legalism, with the former being dominant. There are other elements, such as Mohism, Daoism, and Buddhism, which together contribute to Chinese culture as a whole. For example, Bakken (2000: 8) discovered that it is one of the fundamental assumptions in the Chinese theory of learning that people are innately capable of learning from models. In addition, rule by morality is more widespread in traditional China than rule by law. Thus, the combination of the educational (learning from the models) and the disciplinary (rule by morality) constitutes

Bakken's (2000) conceptualization of China as 'an exemplary society'. But he argued that the current practices of the 'exemplary society' result from the interaction of many schools of philosophy in China.

Organization of Chinese society

There are several models, with insightful analogies, to describe the organization of Chinese society. Here I focus on the 'ripple' model developed by Fei Xiaotong[2] in the 1940s, and the 'cellularity' model initiated by William Skinner in the 1960–1970s and the 'honeycomb' model developed by Shue (1988) from the 'cellularity' model.

Fei's 'ripple' model

Fei distinguishes between *cha-xu-ge-ju* and *tuan-ti-ge-ju* to capture the different patterns of social structure in China and in the West, respectively. His metaphor goes like this: Western society is represented by straws collected to form a haystack, while Chinese society is represented by the ripples flowing out from the splash of a rock thrown into water. A whole haystack is formed by making separate straws into small bundles, the small bundles into larger bundles and then into stacks and finally into the whole haystack. For Fei (1992), therefore, Western society is formed from individuals to organizations. This is his metaphor of *tuan-ti-ge-ju*: the organizational model of association. Hence, in society, each organization has its distinct boundaries, which distinguish members from non-members. On the contrary, according to Fei, Chinese society is characterized by *cha-xu-ge-ju*: the differential model of association. Thus, in the words of Fei, in society, 'everyone stands at the center of the circles produced by his or her own social influence. Everyone's circles are interrelated. One touches different circles at different times and places' (Fei 1992: 62–63). He further gave concrete examples to clarify his points. In the West, families are organizations with clearly demarcated boundaries. However, in China, for families or kinships there is a centre and ever-expanding circles, but no distinct boundaries. Moreover, he argued that those social circles are highly elastic, expanding and contracting according to a change in the power of the centre, and that is why the Chinese are particularly sensitive to changes in human relationships. He further pointed out that although there is always a self (either an individual, a family or a kinship) at the centre of each web of elastic networks, this notion of the self amounts to egocentrism, not individualism. The rationale lies in the following:

> With individualism, individuals make up organizations in the same way that parts make up the whole. The balance between parts and whole produces a concept of equality: since the position of each individual in an organization is the same, one person cannot encroach on the others. It also produces a concept of constitutionality: an organization cannot deny the rights of an individual; it controls individuals merely on the basis of the partial rights they have willingly handed over. Without these concepts, such organizations as these could not exist. However, in Chinese traditional thought, there is no comparable set of ideas, because, for us, there is only egocentrism. Everything worthwhile rests on an ideology in which the self is central.
> (Fei 1992: 67)

Thus, with egocentrism, Fei depicts Chinese society as centred on the individual and built from networks created from relational ties linking the self with discrete categories of other individuals (Hamilton and Zheng 1992). Moreover, with egocentrism, Chinese society is not group oriented. According to Hamilton and Zheng (1992), this is a view contrary to most modern interpretations of that society. But the mode of differential association highlights the paramount importance of overlapping networks in Chinese society. Hamilton and Zheng (1992: 20–21) summarized the four key features of those networks. First, networks are discontinuous. That is, since networks centre on the individual, different people have different networks. Second, each link in a Chinese person's network is defined in terms of a dyadic social tie (*gang*). These interpersonal ties are termed in Chinese '*guanxi*'. Each tie is simultaneously normatively defined and strictly personal.[3] Third, networks have no explicit boundaries. Networks pre-exist through kinship, marriage, and reproduction. Moreover, networks can be built. In principle, any two people can arrange a linkage through an intermediary or through a relational category in which they can situate themselves. Thus, in society, there are no sharp boundary lines, but only ambiguous zones of more or less dense and more or less institutionalized network configurations. Lastly, the moral content of behaviour in a network society is situation specific. What is considered moral behaviour depends on the situation and on the social categories of the actors, rather than on abstract standards universally applicable to autonomous individuals.

Fei's model of Chinese society is essentially based on Chinese rural areas because, for him, Chinese society is fundamentally rural, and the rural society and the grass-roots class are truly the foundation of that society (Fei 1992: 1). This point is echoed by Shue (1988). In surveying the applicability of various models to the Chinese experience with socialism, Shue argued it was his 'hunch' that many of the seemingly special complexities and unusual syndromes in China could be ascribed to 'the vastness of the peasant social base, with the sheer weight of the peasantry in the overall constitution of the polity' (1988: 2).[4] Another reason is that Chinese city residents are former migrants from the rural areas, both in traditional times[5] and in the PRC era. For example, Lau (2001) argued that 'the PRC's industrialization was carried out by a peasant-based party creating a new working class of rural migrants engaged in non-market production and exchange.' Still another imperative reason for me to touch upon the rural nature of the Chinese society is that the location for this study, Shenzhen, was built overnight from a fishing village, and migrants account for a substantial part of its total population. Moreover, one of the two communities where the survey was administered was transformed from a village.

Shue's 'honeycomb' model

In his important work on traditional Chinese marketing systems, Skinner first came out with the concept of a cellular pattern of organization of the rural periphery in the China of late imperial times (generally the Ming and Qing periods).[6] Basically, according to this model, the rural areas are dotted with individual small towns, which are surrounded by adjacent rural villages, constituting the cellular pattern. But Shue argued that Skinner's model emphasized 'not the discreteness of the rural cells he sketched, but rather the means of their linkage into quite far-flung networks, which, through commerce and social intercourse, brought about more than a modicum of integration between urban and rural socioeconomy before the revolution' (1988: 4).

Rural China in the PRC era has undergone three waves of development, namely, communization from 1957 to 1978, the implementation of the household responsibility system from 1978 to 1984, and the rise of rural enterprise and commercial activities from 1985 to the present (Chen 1998). Drawing upon the insights from Skinner, Shue (1988) depicted the rural periphery under Mao (prior to 1978) as 'honeycomb' and that under Deng (since 1978) as 'webs of commerce'. He suggested that in the years following the revolution a highly localized, highly segmented, cell-like pattern came to typify the organization of social and economic life in the Chinese countryside. He further identified and discussed the means by which local officials and cadres manipulated the relationship between their localities and the central government in response to the honeycomb structure, on the one hand, and to the particular policies and political rhetoric emanating from the centre on the other hand. He argued that, due to the ubiquitous state penetration and planning efforts under Mao, such as the principle of 'self-reliance' and the slogan of 'taking grain as the key link', the basic units in the countryside (e.g. teams, brigades, villages, communes and even counties) were rather discrete, isolated, and cell-like, and tended to 'thicken ties' within themselves while 'dissolving ties to the outside' (Shue 1988: 132).

Thus, under Mao, 'peasant production and marketing outside the state planned sector was reduced to a trickle, and all the various sorts of horizontal linkages between peasant communities that rested on the trellis of the rural free marketing network were further weakened' (Shue 1988: 135). However, according to Shue (1988), it is undeniable that this 'localist' and 'departmentalist' pattern of isolation, as a result of the leftist policies, held important advantages for China in meeting the larger challenges of development; for example, the emphasis on grain quotas guaranteed the urban population enough to eat, the state's trade monopolies prevented serious inflation, and the restrictions on personal mobility saved China from the miseries of uncontrolled urbanization so visible elsewhere in Asia. The last benefit arising from lack of personal mobility is of special interest to this study on crime and crime prevention, and will be further discussed in detail later.

The most spectacular reform policy in the countryside was the implementation of the household responsibility system, which was characterized by the assignment of land to individual peasants, division of village collective properties, and lease of the village enterprise by individual peasants. Rural reform further saw the dismantlement of the people's commune in 1984. W. Chen (1998) argued that these rural reform policies have greatly weakened the organizational and institutional linkage between the state and peasantry, and, as a result, the Party has lost its material and organizational basis for political leadership in the countryside. According to Shue (1988), under Deng since the late 1970s, both the old cellular structure of rural life and the subcultures of localism have been attacked. The weapon for the double attack is the rapid expansion of the role of market relations in the economy and society, and the actual work of the local government. Thus, collectivization has given way to peasant household farming, and because of that the salience of the village community as a central unit of social life has been greatly reduced. This commodification of the rural economy has created new networks of social relations that successfully extend the horizons of peasants and cadres well beyond the old cellular community units of the past. More specifically, internally, rural villages are becoming less socially homogeneous, and therefore there is less solidarity; and, externally, they are swiftly being enmeshed in the spreading webs of commerce (Shue 1988: 149). With the expansion of the market economy in rural areas, there emerged a new, growing, and potentially very powerful economic elite side by side with the old (also transforming) local government elite.

Up until now, two models sketching the organizational pattern of Chinese society, with a focus on the rural areas, have been discussed. Fei's model was proposed in the 1940s but still makes sense in current Chinese society (see Hamilton and Zheng 1992). The model by Skinner and Shue provides an overview of Chinese society stretching between two turning points: the communist 'liberation' in 1949 and the reform era since the late 1970s. They differ in degree, but not in essence. Fei's model covers social relationships at both the individual and collective level: individuals and collectivities, such as a family, or a kin, are self-centred with social circles expanding outward. Essentially, for Fei, individual collectivities are isolated and disconnected. Fei identified one of the special characteristics of rural society as immobility and isolation. For example, in the village, which Fei regards as the basic unit of Chinese rural society, rural life is 'parochial', and characterized by 'solitude and isolation' (1992: 41). But he stressed again that when he referred to solitude and isolation, his target was a group, such as a village, not individuals (Fei 1992: 40–41). He further elaborated on why village life was isolated and parochial. But inside villages, life is based on familiarity due to little mobility, and consequently a combination of 'consanguinity and regionalism'[7] prevails. The isolation of villages in Fei's model runs parallel to the patterns of 'cellularity' and 'honeycomb' described by Skinner and Shue, respectively.[8] In fact, Skinner and Shue also referred to the tight relationship inside the 'cells'. For example, Shue (1988) discussed in detail how villages, communes, and counties under Mao became 'self-contained' units 'with little lateral intercourse with one another' (1988: 134), and how local cadres manipulated the relationship with the higher levels of the hierarchy to defend and protect the local interest.

Upon closer scrutiny, the village life, both within and without, sketched by Fei, Skinner and Shue fits ever so neatly with the framework of social capital discussed in the previous chapter. That is, internally, the bonding social capital is strong while, externally, the bridging social capital is weak. This is largely due to the immobility of rural residents in traditional China and the period under Mao. With the strong bonding social capital due to immobility of rural residents and isolation of rural communities, local social control was strong and, understandably, the crime level was low. However, the reform in the rural areas saw the breakdown of immobility and isolation. The surplus rural labourers started moving out to the cities for job opportunities and a better life. Hence, local social relationships, both internal and external, underwent tremendous changes. Internally, rural villages became less socially homogeneous, and therefore there was less social solidarity; and externally, they were swiftly becoming immersed in the 'webs of commerce' (Shue 1988). So what are the impacts on social control and crime levels in the countryside and especially in the cities? The following section seeks to elaborate upon *guanxi*, the Chinese version of social capital and further explores how social capital could be applied in the examination of urban Chinese life. This is necessary partly because Shue's observation, appearing in the late 1980s, is an early and rough sketch of the transformation of social relationships in the wake of the market expansion, and partly because, until now, discussion of the organization of Chinese society has mainly focused on the countryside.

Guanxi in China

Guanxi is literally translated as relationships, ties, links or connections between people, between objects, or between people and objects. The aspect of '*guanxi*' of interest here refers to relationship (or ties, links or connections) between people. Based on that, *guanxi* further denotes two layers of meaning. First, it refers to relationships in their 'physical', and 'natural' sense, such as, husband–wife, kinship, and friendship. Thus, the concept settles on the existence of the complexity of human interactions. Second, also more commonly, *guanxi* denotes relationship in its 'social' sense. For example, sentimentally, love or care between people, or, instrumentally, mutual interest, benefit or favour between individuals of a particular network. In everyday usage, the second dimension of meaning seems to be given currency.

Three conceptualizations of Guanxi

In fact, there are multiple conceptualizations of *guanxi*, and Bian (2001) divided them into three models. First, *guanxi* refers to the web of extended familial obligations. According to this view, the family is the core of the social structure and the original source of social relations in Chinese society, and *guanxi* is the web of extended familial ties and familial obligations. In sum, given this definition, *guanxi* exhibits the following four characteristics: the relational bases of *guanxi* are family and pseudofamilies;[9] the sources of *guanxi* capital[10] lie in the ego's reputation for fulfilling the moral obligations to family and pseudofamilies; *guanxi* capital is understood in terms of face, and the ego earns face from 'alter' because of high sentiment and closeness between ego and 'alter';[11] and finally the strategy of accumulating *guanxi* capital is to extend the ties of familial sentiments and obligations to all social relations (Bian 2001: 277–278). Second, *guanxi* refers to exchange networks of particular instrumental ties. This view does not automatically reject the idea from the first model that *guanxi* is a web of extended familial obligations. It argues that the defining character of *guanxi* is the instrumentality of particular ties (family ties included) that facilitate *favour exchanges*. Thus defined, *guanxi*'s relational bases are no longer limited to family and pseudofamilies, but also include a broad range of social and work-related connections.

The above two models emphasize either the sentimental basis or the instrumental uses of *guanxi*. The third model, proposed by Lin (1998), refers to *guanxi* as social-exchange networks of asymmetric transactions. To convey this conceptualization, Lin first distinguishes economic exchanges of symmetric transactions from social exchanges of asymmetric transactions.[12] Then he classifies *guanxi* as a type of social exchange, being asymmetric and thus permitting instrumental uses and favour-seeking purposes. Apart from emphasizing the instrumental uses of *guanxi*, Lin also stresses the sentimental basis of *guanxi* by arguing that 'it is the relationship that is valued and must be maintained, not the value of the favor transacted per se', and hence 'instrumental action becomes the means and *guanxi* (building) becomes the end' (Lin 1998: 22, cited in Bian 2001: 279). Thus, the third model is a combination of the previous two models. Like the second model, the relational bases of *guanxi* become very broad, including all kinds of kin and non-kin relations.

Treating the sentimental and instrumental uses as ends and means, respectively, the third model is ideal, if not utopian. Its actual rendition in everyday life, either in its sentimental or instrumental sense, has been subject to empirical studies and is to some extent governed by the perceptions of those involved. Further, the instrumental uses of *guanxi* are usually associated with its negative meanings, such as, nepotism, favouritism, cronyism, particularism, bribery, and corruption, especially in China currently. Thus, an overemphasis upon its instrumental uses greatly diminishes the vigour and applicability of *guanxi*, and ultimately damages the acceptability of the concept of social capital in the Chinese context. Yet, an underestimation of its instrumental uses runs counter to the practice and reality, as in China at present.

Guanxi *and* guanxi-xue *in urban China*

Yang (1994) provides an elaborated account of *guanxi* in the instrumental sense in contemporary China. She notes that *guanxi* had become so sophisticated and widely practised in different walks of life that it has been elevated to *guanxi-xue* (the art or knowledge of *guanxi*).[13] According to her, *guanxi-xue* is a term hardly ever heard outside the new socialist society in Mainland China. She observes that the satiric connotation of *'guanxi-xue'* lies in its elevation of the art of cultivating personal relationships into a fully-fledged scholarly branch of knowledge equally valid and just as necessary as any other academic specialization. *'Guanxi-xue'*, or the art of *guanxi*, involves the exchange of gifts, favours, and banquets; the cultivation of personal relationships and networks of mutual dependence; and the manufacturing of obligation and indebtedness (Yang 1994). Moreover, according to Yang (1994: 8), 'In *guanxi-xue* can be found the elements of "the obligation to give, to receive, and to repay", a mixture of disinterested and instrumental generosity, of voluntary and coerced reciprocity.' Apparently, in the above observation, the instrumental uses of *guanxi* are taken to its extreme.

Given the sophistication of *guanxi*, Yang (1994) conducted an ethnographical investigation of the micropolitics of *guanxi* in the socialist setting of China. She covers *guanxi* dialects and vocabulary; the scope and use contexts of *guanxi*; the 'art' in *guanxi-xue*: ethics, tactics and etiquette; and the recent past of *guanxi-xue*: traditional forms and historical (re-)emergence (see Yang 1994: Chapters 1–4). Here I extract several of her arguments that are of relevance to this study.

Popular and official discourses of guanxi-xue

Yang (1994) noted that there are two discourses of *guanxi-xue* in the reform era of Mainland China: popular and official discourses. Its popular discourses are 'the forms of language and types of attitudes in everyday life which one finds expressed in localized and delimited spaces within the family; among friends, relatives and neighbours; and between friendly but anonymous strangers on trains and buses' (1994: 51). In its popular discourse, *guanxi-xue* includes three dialects: the pejorative, the mixed, and the morally neutral and pragmatic. First, it can have the pejorative connotations of an antisocial practice, an aberrant instrumental behaviour based on self-interest, which should be morally rejected (1994: 51); for example 'go through the back door' (*zou hou men*) and 'special privileges' (*te quan*). A second approach to explaining the art of *guanxi* takes the instrumental aspect of *guanxi* relations into account, but also stresses that *guanxi* operates according to a morality of its own and serves a necessary social function (1994: 54). Third, the morally neutral understanding of *guanxi-xue* is a position that either suspends judgement or finds it irrelevant to a realistic view of human limitations.

Unlike popular discourse, what typifies official discourse is its monophonic character. Yang argued that official discourse does not mean that its speakers and writers are only officials; rather, it means the style of language that projects the authority and the political correctness that play a hegemonic role in unifying public discourse. This is reflected in its definition of the art of *guanxi* solely as a negative social phenomenon and in its moral and political condemnation of *guanxu-xue* for its corrupting influence on proper socialist ethics (1994: 58). It attributes *guanxi-xue* to three forces from three historical periods. First, it is 'traditional remnants of the past' because of 'the persistence of a backward ethical system whose particularistic ethics of interpersonal relations hamper the development of universalistic loyalty to the country and the "socialist system"' (Yang 1994: 59). Second, it is the 'Cultural Revolution of the recent past'. And finally, it is 'the open-up of the most recent' with the 'introduction of polluting influences such as "bourgeois individualism"' (*zichan jieji geren zhuyi*) from abroad, where human relations have been reduced by the case nexus into impersonal instrumentality' (Yang 1994: 59). According to Yang, what is embodied in the popular discourse on *guanxi* are the contradiction of condemnation on the one hand and admiration and even approbation of the art of *guanxi* on the other hand.

Use contexts of guanxi

The popular 'admiration' and even 'approbation' of *guanxi-xue* result from the fact that *guanxi* could play a remarkable, sometimes even miraculous role in everyday life. For example, there was a popular saying in the reform era which reflects a rather pragmatic view of the academic disciplines: 'With a good command of mathematics, physics, and chemistry, you may fearlessly go anywhere around the globe.' But the importance of academic performance reflected in this saying is dwarfed by the significance of *guanxi*, as articulated well in another cliché, 'A good command of mathematics, physics, and chemistry is not worth as much as having a good father' [i.e. having *guanxi*]. The range of occasions where *guanxi* can be put to use covers all facets of everyday life. Yang (1994: 91–99) provided 'a mere sampling' of the variety of its use contexts: obtaining goods in short supply, of better quality, or at lower prices; obtaining employment, job transfers, and promotions; enabling geographical mobility; maintaining good health; obtaining housing; promoting political security and advancement; facilitating transportation; obtaining better education; and enjoying recreational activities.

Guanxi exchanges can be carried out only between two parties who have established, in one way or another, a basis of familiarity. The range of *guanxi* bases in urban society can be subsumed under the following categories: family and kinship, neighbours and native-place ties, non-kin relations of equivalent status (classmates, co-workers and friends), and non-kin superior–subordinate relations (teacher–student, master–apprentice, and others) (Yang 1994: 111–119).

Apart from the social exchange between individuals, *guanxi* also has its corporate and administrative uses, that is, in a *'danwei'* (work unit). In Chinese work units, whether corporate organizations or administrative agencies, *guanxi* serves to maintain general goodwill not only with other units at the same level, but also with offices at superior administrative levels, and even with units ranked administratively lower because both horizontal and vertical relations can affect a unit's well-being. However, Yang (1994) stressed that *guanxi* between units is carried out on a personal instead of a formal, unit-to-unit basis, mainly through personal ties between their staff members or representatives.

Guanxi, indeed, is not a phenomenon concomitant only with socialist China. As reflected above, it is embodied in Confucian ethics and philosophy. It is also suggested that *guanxi* has two other sources: the knight-errantry tradition and Buddhist notions of retribution (see

Yang 1994: 149). Apart from its cultural rooting, Yang (1994: 153–172) charts the trajectory of *guanxi* in socialist China: (1) the post-revolutionary decline and rise of *guanxi* in the Cultural Revolution; (2) from 'use-value' to 'exchange-value' in social exchanges, that is, the so-called money relationship, with the entrance of market forces; but the art of *guanxi* does not retreat. Dubbing the playing of *guanxi* as 'gift economy' in the contemporary political and cultural economy of China, Yang (1994) argued that the gift economy coexists with two other distinct modes of exchange or domains of power techniques: (1) the state distributive economy; (2) the gift economy; (3) a resurgent commodity economy.

Yang's fieldwork was done in the 1980s and she wrote in the late 1980s, but her prediction makes sense in current China. In fact, *guanxi* in China is widely practised,[14] and I personally experienced the force and etiquette of *guanxi* in my fieldwork. In some sense, *guanxi* and *guanxi-xue* could even be regarded as a cultural assumption by Chinese everywhere. For foreigners, *guanxi* has become a cultural icon of Chinese society. When foreign companies invest in China, the orientation programme for staff begins with *guanxi*.

In contrast to social capital, which is widely seen to provide benefits and to improve performance in economic life, *guanxi* is always associated with underperformance, disruption, irregularity (e.g. non-compliance with accounting ethics in Chang 1998), or collusion and corruption in the thesis of crony capitalism, as advanced by Krugman in the wake of the Asian financial crisis (1998, cited in Chan and Cheung 1998).[15] Apparently, the convergence between social capital and *guanxi* is often overlooked or, given the stigma often associated with the latter, deliberately suppressed. Thus, in the works on its positive effects on either individuals or corporations, most often, especially in Asia countries, social capital might be presented, explicitly or implicitly, as social networks, particularism or broadly Confucianism (or neo-Confucianism), but seldom as *guanxi*.[16] As noted before, in the case of social capital, we should never overemphasize its positive effects. By the same token in the case of *guanxi*, we should not overemphasize its negative effects. Rather, a balanced approach should be adopted. For example, Chan and Cheung (1998) pointed out that it is not a sign of intellectual maturity to appraise Asian culture in general and Confucianism in particular, in view of the 'East Asian Miracle', and blame them because of the recent financial crisis. In their analysis of Confucianism, particularism and the Asian financial crisis, Chan and Cheung (1998) questioned the thesis of crony capitalism, and approached particularism, a synonym of *guanxi*, both as a problem and as a solution to potential problems in economic life.

Apparently, so far, *guanxi* has shown a strong resemblance to social capital. In parallel to the concept of social capital introduced in the previous chapter, *guanxi* exhibits both positive and negative effects. Thus, the stigma or association of it only with something bad should be dismissed, and a balanced approach should be adopted. If we take *guanxi* in this sense as an examination of social capital in China more at a microlevel, and the organization of Chinese society in the previous section as more at a macrolevel, then it is not hard for us to see that social capital fits squarely into the examination of Chinese society.

Notes

1 Here I have used Confucianism rather loosely, with no strict definition. Moreover, although Confucianism had a revival in the reform era, I am not intending to advocate using the return of a 'Confucian ethic' to explain today's China. In this regard, Bakken (2000) provided a good example. In the process of describing the 'exemplary society' of China, he rejected a wholesale resort to Confucianism. Instead, he examined the return of specific patterns of social control to which Confucianism has contributed together with traces of legalism, Mohism, and other contemporaneous sources of governmentality.
2 Fei is a native Chinese sociologist who was trained in the West, and is 'the grand old man of Chinese sociology', in Bakken's (2000: 32) words. See Hamilton and Zheng (1992: 4) for 'the making of a Chinese sociologist'. His model on the organization of the Chinese society originally appeared in the book *Xiangtu Zhongguo*, a set of his essays written in Chinese shortly after World War II. The book was later translated by Hamilton and Zheng and published as *From the Soil: The Foundations of Chinese Society* (Fei 1948/1992). Essentially, the theory contrasts China and the West in order to understand the distinctiveness of Chinese society. With the Marxist social analysis becoming intellectual orthodoxy throughout China since the Communist Party came to power in 1949, 'Fei's sociology of Chinese society runs directly counter to a Chinese Marxist interpretation of Chinese society. It offers a very different view of the society and recommends a very different course of action for facing China's economic and social problems.... In fact, Fei's *Xiangtu Zhongguo* represents one of the few and certainly one of the most insightful efforts to build a sociology of a non-Western society' (Hamilton and Zheng 1992: 4).
3 According to Hamilton and Zheng (1992: 22), each tie is normative in the sense that it consists of an explicit category of social relationship

that requires specific, prescribed 'ritual' (li) behaviour. The tie is strictly personal in the sense that the specific prescribed actions needed to maintain the link are based on norms of reciprocity and are defined as personal obligations on the part of each individual, particularly the subordinate in the dyadic relationship: obligations of the child to the parent, the wife to the husband, the official to the ruler, and the younger to the older.

4 Even more than two decades into the economic reform era, China's rural population still constitutes over 60 per cent of the total population. Moreover, China has impressively managed to feed about 24 per cent of the world's population with about 7 per cent of the world's arable land.

5 Wright (1977) noted that theories of the city had little place in the systematic writings of the traditional elite. He made the following observation: 'It was a cliché of imperial Confucianism that rural life fostered virtue while cities were centers of vice and corruption. This standard view was belied by the behavior of the elite in later dynasties, when they came to use cities as bases of their wealth and power; but perhaps this cliché accounts in part for the relatively insignificant place of city theory in the literary tradition' (Wright 1977: 34).

6 Concerning Skinner's Chinese market theory, Shue (1988) pointed out that the *locus classicus* is G.W. Skinner (1964, 1965a, 1965b). See also G.W. Skinner (1971).

7 Consanguinity (*xueyuan* or, literally, 'blood ties') means that people's rights and obligations are determined by kinship, the relationship constituted by reproduction and marriage. Regionalism (*diyuan* or, literally, 'geographic ties') refers to relationship tied to a specific place. Fei argued that in stable societies with little migration regionalism is no more than an extension of consanguinity and cannot be separated from it (Fei 1992: 120–121).

8 But both Fei's model and the model of cellularity by Skinner and Shue contradict the observations made by Dutton (1992). In comparing the Foucaultian reading of the carceral and the Chinese *hukou*, Dutton (1992: 236–237) argued that while the former was 'constructed around a notion of isolation, separation, and quarantine', the latter 'was not designed to isolate one village from the next nor one family from another' and 'segregation has played no role in either the contemporary or classical Chinese systems'. He further elaborated that both contemporary and classical systems rely on particular forms of 'collectivity', and 'these disciplinary regimes never utilized the family or the compound household to isolate and quarantine. Rather, they were a form of technology which demarcated units in a regime centering upon mutual policing.' In my view Dutton's argument seems to be more congruent with the common understanding of Chinese society. Perhaps it is because, for him, Chinese society is group oriented, contrary to Fei's thesis, as discussed above.

9 According to Bian (2001), 'pseudofamilies', as conceptualized by Lin (1989, 1998), refer to those communities extended from the family and kinship ties, and pseudofamily ties refer to intimate friendships.
10 Bian (2001) argued that the term '*guanxi* capital' is implied in various theories under the first model that 'the capacity to mobilize social resources from *guanxi* networks lies in ego's reputation for fulfilling moral and ethical obligations to one's family and pseudofamilies' (2001: 277).
11 In the context there is no explanation of 'alter'. I tend to understand it as an equivalent of 'alter ego', i.e. an intimate friend or a constant companion.
12 Bian (2001) explained the underlying rationale of both economic exchanges and social exchanges, and why they are symmetric and asymmetric, respectively. 'The rationale of economic exchange is to focus on short-term transactions of valued resources and the relative gain to loss in the resources transacted between the parties involved, while the rationale of social change shifts the focus to long-term commitment to maintaining relationships in which resources are embedded. In social exchanges, transactions of resources are asymmetric in that resources flow from favor giver to favor receiver, and this is also true when the resource flow in social networks is access to other ties (in this case, favor giver performs as a network bridge). But the favor giver does gain – by being recognized as resourceful. The spread of recognition in social networks enhances the reputation of the favor giver, thus helping him/her maintain and strengthen his/her network centrality' (Bian 2001: 279).
13 'Xue' as a verb literally means 'to study'. As a nominative suffix, it can be appended to mean a discipline or specialization, 'the study of', '-ology', '-ics', or '-try', as in the words of 'biology', 'physics' and 'chemistry'.
14 As a native Chinese myself, I was even frequently struck by *guanxi*'s omnipresence. The packages of some necessities and utensils, e.g. a scarf, an electronic cooker or some special local food, were always labelled, 'this product is the best choice for gift-giving' (*kui zeng jia pin*).
15 The 2007 Transparency International Corruption Perceptions Index for China is 3.5, ranked 72 among the 180 countries surveyed by Transparency International (see http://www.transparency.org/policy_research/surveys_indices/cpi/2007).
16 Recent years have seen the emergence of a number of works explicitly addressing both the positive and negative effects of *guanxi*, as, for example, in the labour markets (Bian 1994, 1997; Bian and Ang 1997), and management (Xin and Pearce 1996).

Chapter 5

Crime and social control in China

In depicting crime and social order in contemporary Western society, Garland (2001) utilized the 'history of the present' framework. He argued that his motivation in proposing the history was not a historical concern to understand the past but a critical concern to come to terms with the present. In other words, his genealogical account of 'the culture of control' is not to think historically about the past but rather to use that history to rethink the present (Garland 2001: 2). Likewise, Dutton (1992) was influenced by this method in his portrayal of policing and punishment in China. Similarly, in her genealogy of *guanxi*, Yang (1994) traced it to an ancient transition from a kinship order to a centralized state order, when conflict first occurred between the two discourses of Confucianism and legalism. She rationalized this strategy by drawing upon the guidelines provided by 'history of the present', in that 'a genealogy looks for thematic and structural similitudes that bring to light certain aspects of the present, instead of predictable linear developments of cause and effect' (1994: 220).

The goal of the whole study in this book is to capture the present form of social/crime control in China. Drawing upon the 'history of the present', better to capture that very present, it is pertinent to trace the history of dominant discourses and conceptual frameworks regarding crime and social/crime control in China.[1] This chapter begins with a description of the crime situation in post-1949 China and briefly reviews academic and official discussions around crime and especially its rapid growth in the reform era. Building on the discussion on the Chinese perspective of social capital and the

Chinese understanding of crime, the next section examines the basic features of Chinese control mechanisms. It illustrates how certain Chinese social institutions, notably the household registration system, the neighbourhood committee, the work unit, and the public security bureau, can play an important role in controlling and preventing crime, at least theoretically, both individually and cooperatively, as manifested in the so-called mass line (*qunzhong luxian*). This examination will show that the Chinese social control system is intrinsically community-based, and how the concept of social capital can be employed to explain its working rationalities. The chapter concludes with a brief discussion of some inherent strengths and weaknesses of the Chinese social control system, critically drawing upon certain Western concepts and frameworks.

Prior to this adventurous attempt, it should be pointed out that the undertakings outlined above are rather ambitious. For this chapter is only a rough, if not simplistic or naive, stroke upon the vast and complicated drawing of China through the perspective of crime and crime control. But it is hoped that this brief sketch sheds light on understanding, particularly in the West, of China, one part of the 'mysterious East', while simultaneously revealing the universal concern about crime and social control.

Crime in China

Since the launch of the economic reform and open-door policy in 1978, the market forces have permeated and transformed every nook and cranny of social life in China. With the advent of the so-called 'second revolution', profound economic and social changes have swept China. In the process of urbanization, modernization, and industrialization, China shifted from a low-crime country to one with growing crime rates, worsening social order, and decreasing feelings of security. Based on official statistics, public perception, mass media and academic research, these trends are now the subject of growing concern and state intervention. Thus, the classic question on the relationship between development and crime looms large in China. This section first reviews the literature, mainly Western, on the relationship between development and crime. Then it introduces the crime situation in China, applying official statistics and official ideology. Finally, it reviews how the nexus of development and crime has already been approached inside China, and contemplates how the nexus should be approached.

Development and crime

The issue of development and crime has drawn scholarly attention as far back as in the initial stages of modernization in Western Europe. Certain scholarly work as well as folk wisdom seems to take rising crime as the price that modernization must pay. Among the early pioneers in the pursuit of the effect of modernization on patterns of criminality are Tarde, Durkheim, Marx, Engels, and those who further advanced Durkheim's thesis, such as the Chicago School, Robert Merton, and Travis Hirschi (see Shelley 1981; Vold and Bernard 1986). Durkheim, mainly drawing upon French society, argued that industrialization and urbanization result in the breakdown of traditional values and norms, leading to a state of anomie, which in turn causes crime of all types.[2] Following Durkheim's thesis, there emerged a large volume of research either to refute or confirm his findings (e.g. reviews by Liu 2005, 2006). Generally, consensus has been reached that crime should not be taken as a generic concept, and increasingly it is necessary to differentiate between property crime and violent crime. Further, another consensus is that modernization should be differentiated between its initial stage and mature stage. Among the empirical studies taking into account the two points, Shelley's (1981) research stands out. Her work covers both capitalist societies (and further distinguishes between developed and developing capitalist countries) and socialist societies. She drew the following conclusions:

> The process of urbanization accompanying industrialization has had a rapid and direct impact on crime in urban and rural areas in the nineteenth and twentieth centuries in both capitalist and socialist countries. During the initial transition to modernization, commission rates for property offenses and crimes against the person increase in urban areas, while rural areas experience a drop in criminality as a result of the population exodus to the burgeoning cities. While the level of criminality changes in rural areas, the crime patterns of agricultural areas are still characterized by higher rates of violent crime.... (C)ities during the initial phase of urbanization experience increased rates of violence simultaneously with new levels of property crime. Only as urbanization progresses, as migration into urban centers subsides, and as the newly arrived urban inhabitants adjust to city life, does the total crime rate decline. Crimes of violence cede their once preeminent place to offences against property. (Shelley 1981: 138–139)

While observing that under both capitalism and socialism 'the transition from a society dominated by crimes of violence to one characterized by property offenses is the hallmark of modernization' (Shelley 1981: 35–36), Shelley also noted certain important exceptions to the generalization of the linkage between higher crime rates and economic development. As for Japan and Switzerland, 'the uniqueness of their developmental process, the preservation of a close family structure, and the participation of the citizenry in the fight against crime have served as powerful deterrents to increased frequency of crime commission' (1981: 76). As for the claim of socialist societies that socialism has made them exempt from many of the crime problems associated with capitalism, she argued, 'the fundamental differences between crime patterns in capitalist and socialist societies are explained by the strong controls exercised over the populations of socialist countries, an effect attributable more to the political system than to the form of economic development chosen by these societies' (1981: 143). That means that crime rates are subject to political forces, and social and cultural factors, as well as economic growth.

In contrast to the modernization paradigm is the civilization paradigm (see Garland 1990; Heiland *et al.* 1991; Johnson and Monkkonen 1996; Eisner 2001). Elias's civilization theory fosters the link between the long-term structural change and the alteration of personality structures with two central arguments most useful to the analysis of crime and social control (Heiland *et al.* 1991). Firstly, the ninth to eighteenth centuries witnessed an ever increasing refinement of customs and manners, an obvious pacification of the conditions of daily life and an intensification of instinctive and affected inhibitions. Secondly, during the civilization process, institutions, i.e. the emergent state monopoly of power, the capitalist production system, became increasingly dominant and influential in the formation of social structures. With the development of civilization, sanctions controlling individual actions shifted from outward to inward, that is, from external pressures to internal self-control. Elias' 'civilizing process' has the following substantive implications for crime and crime control: (1) control of violent behaviour emanating from courts; (2) urban centres would have more 'civilized' behaviour; (3) areas where the state system had not yet penetrated would be more impulsively violent; and (4) over time, violence would decline (see Johnson and Monkkonen 1996: 5). This hypothesis has been supported by the research findings that crime, in particular personal violence, in the Western world has declined since the early Middle Ages until very recently (see e.g. Johnson and Monkkonen 1996, Eisner 2001).

In both paradigms regarding crime and development, there are methodological difficulties and limitations. The most difficult problem remains to ensure the credibility and even availability of both crime data and indicators of social-economic development across time and space. For example, Shichor (1985) pointed out the classic problems associated with crime data: (1) different crime definitions across countries; (2) data are subject to influences, such as the actions of criminal justice agencies, the rules of evidence required in trials, and readiness to report crimes; (3) citizen crime reports may differ from reality; and (4) crime statistics are prone to political manipulation. Likewise, Eisner (2001) discussed the following problems of interpreting pre-modern homicide data: (1) the legal concept of intentional killing was not fully developed in earlier periods; (2) population estimates for pre-modern society are notoriously imprecise; (3) the extant data are probably incomplete; and (4) the advance of medical technology would have distorted the difference over time in the number of homicides.

In addition to the problems of data reliability, there are also methodological inadequacies in processing the data. For example, Bennett (1991) pointed out that research tends to assess the effects of change by using cross-sectional designs and variables that measure level of, rather than actual change in, economic development. This is echoed by Liu (2005) on the use of cross-national design. When discussing the inevitable imperfections of the measuring rod of criminal statistics, Radzinowicz and Hood (1990: 110) pointed out the 'remarkable variations in the incidence of crime recorded, and in its mode of prosecution' in terms of comparing cross-country crime data.

Apart from the modernization and civilization paradigms, there are other theories exploring the relationship between development and crime. For example, the 'opportunity thesis' of LaFree and Kick (1986; see reviews by Bennett 1991), basically aims to explain findings from cross-national studies that modernization and development affect property crime (mostly measured by theft) positively and violent crime (mostly measured by homicide) negatively. Property crime increases because modernization and development increase the amount of goods available for theft, and urbanization increases the pool of potential offenders. On the other hand, violent crime decreases because of the attenuated interpersonal ties between former intimates and acquaintances. In a word, the difference is because opportunities for property crime increase and those for violent crime decrease. Another theoretical approach, proposed by Heiland *et al.* (1991: 4), is to integrate the concept of the centralization of power structures and processes with the conceptions of civilization and modernization. Although originally from the modernization perspective, they acknowledged the importance of the civilization process in explaining the nexus, and proceeded to suggest that the triad of modernization, power and civilization should lead to a comprehensive, macrostructural explanatory framework to explain different criminological developments in a wide diversity of societies. Taken together, all the theories have their own merits, and are applicable to certain societies at certain times. China is currently in the full speed of modernization, and what is applicable in the Chinese context concerning modernization and crime remains to be seen. The following section introduces crime statistics in post-1949 China.

Crime statistics in China

In the literature generally, there is concern with the quality and accuracy of the Chinese crime statistics (see e.g. Troyer *et al.* 1989, C. Yang 1994; He and Marshall 1997; Tanner 1999; Bakken 2000, 2004; Liu 2005, 2006), a concern more acute when compared with that in the West. Crime statistics were classified as state secrets at the national level until 1986 when China first submitted national crime statistics to Interpol. The *China Law Yearbook* started reporting national crime statistics in its first issue in 1987, which stretched back to include data from 1981–6. Notwithstanding this concern, I use the official crime statistics to illustrate crime change in China since the 1950s by incorporating other sources.

China's rising crime rate can be seen as an unbidden guest, so to speak, who has slipped in through the open door of reform. Or as the official Chinese metaphor goes, crime is 'flies and mosquitoes coming through the window of reform'. The official statistics on criminal cases are presented in Table 5.1. According to Cao (1997), five waves of crime emerged from 1950 to 1996. The first wave was in the early 1950s, with a peak in 1950. The second wave appeared in the so-called period of 'three difficult years' with a peak in 1961. The third wave occurred during the Cultural Revolution, with a peak of 535,000 cases in 1973. The fourth wave came in 1978 and peaked in 1981, which saw the first 'strike hard' campaign in 1983. The fifth wave started in the early 1990s, and reached its peak in 1995 and the first quarter of 1996 prior to the launch of the second 'strike hard' campaign.[3] Table 5.1 also contains information on the clearance rates throughout those years. In view of the law enforcement criteria in

Table 5.1 Reported criminal cases (excluding public security offences) in China 1950–2006 – total, rates per 100,000 population and clearance rates

Year	Total	Rate	Clearance rate (%)	Year	Total	Rate	Clearance rate (%)
1950	513,461	93	70.4	1981	890,281	89	73.1
1951	332,741	59	77.5	1982	748,476	74	77.4
1952	243,003	42	66.8	1983	610,478	60	70.6
1953	292,303	50	44.5	1984	514,369	50	76.9
1954	392,226	65	66.3	1985	542,005	52	78.8
1955	325,829	53	59.1	1986	547,115	52	79.2
1956	180,075	29	66.2	1987	570,439	54	81.3
1957	298,031	46	70.9	1988	827,706	75	75.2
1958	211,068	32	93.7	1989	1,971,901	182	56.4
1959	210,025	31	97.5	1990	2,216,987	201	57.1
1960	222,734	44	90.5	1991	2,370,000	210	61.7
1961	421,934	64	78.4	1992	1,580,000	135	68.2
1962	324,639	48	74.2	1993	1,616,879	141	75.0
1963	251,226	36	79.4	1994	1,660,734	142	78.2
1964	251,352	31	77.8	1995	1,690,407	143	79.9
1965	216,125	30	65.9	1996	1,600,716	134	79.9
1966–71	–	–	–	1997	1,613,629	134	72.6
1972	402,573	46	54.2	1998	1,986,068	159	63.7
1973	535,820	60	63.6	1999	2,249,319	179	61.1
1974	516,419	57	65.3	2000	3,637,307	287	45.2
1975	475,432	52	68.9	2001	4,457,579	349	42.9
1976	488,813	52	64.9	2002	4,336,712	338	44.4
1977	548,415	58	73.0	2003	4,393,893	340	41.9

1978	535,698	56	72.0
1979	636,222	66	69.1
1980	757,104	77	71.1
2004	4,718,122	363	42.5
2005	4,648,401	356	45.1
2006	4,653,265	354	47.5

The sharp decrease in 1992 was due to the revised monetary threshold for stolen goods. Prior to 1992, the threshold was 80 yuan in the cities and 40 yuan in the countryside. But since 1992, it has been raised to 300–500 yuan in general, and in the areas with a more rapid economic development, it could even increase to 600 RMB. Guo (1998) argued that in 1992 the total of criminal cases should not be lower than that in 1991. In fact, the reported cases to the public security bureaus nationwide reached 5,000,000.

Sources: The annual data 1950–79 are from He and Marshall (1997), and those for 1981–2006 are from *China Law Yearbook* (1987–2007). Clearance rates 1951–95 are from Guo (1998), and clearance rates 1996–2006 are from *China Law Yearbook* (1987–2007).

the West, the Chinese clearance rates are incredibly high. The lowest was 44.5 per cent in 1953. The rate was 50–59 per cent during the four years of 1955, 1972, 1989, and 1990. During the remaining years, the rate ranged from 61.1 per cent to 97.5 per cent. It is noticeable that the highest clearance rates appeared in 1958 (93.7 per cent), 1959 (97.5 per cent) and 1960 (90.5 per cent). As the Great Leap Forward was initiated in 1958, when there was a tide of inflated figures of all kinds, the incredibly high clearance rates during the three years should not come as a surprise.

Table 5.2 lists the number of recorded crimes in every category of criminal offence and its proportion in the yearly total from 1981 to 2006. Apparently, with the economic reform deepening, the categories of crime changed to accommodate the new and more sophisticated crimes, especially so-called economic crime (see Tanner (1999) for its ambiguous definition and corresponding difficulties in prosecution, and Liu (2005) for its relation to economic development). It should be noted that here only the proportions, not their rates, are presented. But Table 5.2 offers an overview of the composition of the categories of crime. Their changing rates were depicted in the two figures in Liu *et al.* (2001: 12–13). Moreover, as Liu *et al.* (2001) cautioned, an in-depth examination of changes in crime rates should take account of the changes of definition of crime, reporting and collecting behaviour, and historical events.

Crime by young people always arouses great concern in China, and in this respect it is not particularly different from Western societies. Both public perception and statistics show the growth of crime by young people, and its alarming percentage of the total number of criminal cases. But in China, 'young people' always refers to those under the age of 25 (*qin shao nian*, the youth), and this is different from the criterion in the West of under the age of 18. The proportion of the number of young (under the age of 25) to total number of persons convicted of a crime stayed rather stable from 1950 to 1979, increased dramatically from 1980, and reached the peak of 75.7 per cent in 1988 (Bakken 2000: 385). The high youth crime in the early 1980s triggered the launch of the holistic approach of 'comprehensive management of social order' (Tanner 1999: 67–68), which is to be introduced in the next chapter. As seen in Table 5.3, the proportion of convictions in which the person was under the age of 25 declined in the 1990s, and the lowest was at 31.1 per cent in 2002.

In China, there is a distinction between criminal cases and public security cases (or administrative offences). According to the 1997

Criminal Law (Article 13, Chapter 2), 'all acts that endanger state sovereignty ... and that, according to law, should be punished, are crime; but if the circumstances are clearly minor and the harm is not great, they are not to be deemed crime'. The Law of the People's Republic of China on Administrative Penalties for Public Security (hereafter public security law), which took effect on 1 March 2006, stipulated that 'All acts that breach social order, disrupt public security, infringe upon citizens' personal rights or public and private property and that, according to the Criminal Law of the People's Republic of China, constitute crime, should be held criminally responsible; if they do not warrant a criminal penalty, and should be given public security punishment, they should be punished by the public security organs according to the penalty meted out in this law' (Article 2, Chapter 1). Four kinds of 'administrative penalties for public security' are meted out in the public security law: (1) warning; (2) a fine; (3) administrative detention ranging from 1 to 15 days; and (4) revoking of licences issued by the public security organs. But certain offences are subject to 're-education through labour' (*laojiao*),[4] which is normally two years but could be extended to three years. Thus, a public security offence differs from a criminal offence in three aspects: (1) it is defined in the public security law, not by criminal law; (2) it is handled by the police; (3) unlike other non-criminal offences handled by the police (e.g. speeding and parking violations), it is similar to criminal offences in terms of its nature and constitutive elements. For example, since the revised threshold of theft in the criminal law in 1992 (over 300–500 yuan in most areas and over 600 yuan in economically developed areas), a theft with a value of lower than the threshold is a public security offence and is therefore punished according to the public security law.

Most of the 'six evils' fall under public security offences.[5] For example, among the 770,000 people involved in 213,000 'six-evils' cases in 1990, only 6,129 people (0.8 per cent) were given criminal convictions, 5,650 (0.73 per cent) were given a period of re-education through labour under the administrative law, and the remaining 586,000 (76 per cent) were punished under the public security regulation (the predecessor of the public security law) (see Dutton and Lee 1993). Table 5.4 lists the total and rate of public security offences and criminal offences from 1986 to 2006. It also shows that the ratio of the former rates to the latter rates ranges from 0.9 to 2.2 during the period.[6]

Table 5.2 Categories of reported criminal offences 1981–2006

Year	Homicide		Injury (aggravated assault)		Robbery		Rape		Human trafficking		Larceny	
	Cases	%	Cases	%	Cases	%	Cases	%	Cases	%	Cases	%
1981	9,576	1.1	21,499	2.4	22,266	2.5	30,838	3.5	–		744,374	83.5
1982	9,324	1.3	20,298	2.7	16,518	2.2	35,361	4.7	–		609,481	81.3
1983	–		–		–		–		–		–	
1984	9,021	1.8	14,526	2.8	7,273	1.4	44,630	8.7	–		395,319	76.8
1985	10,440	1.9	15,586	2.9	8,801	1.6	37,712	7.0	–		431,323	79.6
1986	11,510	2.1	18,364	3.4	12,124	2.2	39,121	7.2	–		425,845	77.8
1987	13,154	2.3	21,727	3.8	18,775	3.3	37,225	6.5	–		435,235	76.3
1988	15,959	1.9	26,639	3.2	36,318	4.4	34,120	4.1	–		658,683	79.6
1989	19,590	1.0	35,931	1.8	72,881	3.7	40,999	2.1	–		1,673,222	84.9
1990	21,214	1.0	45,200	2.0	82,361	3.7	47,782	2.2	–		1,860,793	83.9
1991	23,199	1.0	57,498	2.4	105,132	4.4	50,331	2.1	26,507	1.1	1,922,506	81.3
1992	24,132	1.5	59,901	3.8	125,092	7.9	49,829	3.2	17,168	1.1	1,142,556	72.2
1993	25,380	1.6	64,595	4.0	152,102	9.4	47,033	2.9	15,629	1.0	1,122,105	69.4
1994	26,553	1.6	67,864	4.1	159,253	9.6	44,118	2.7	11,367	0.7	1,133,682	68.3
1995	27,356	1.6	72,259	4.3	164,478	9.7	41,823	2.5	10,670	0.6	1,132,789	67.0
1996	25,411	1.6	68,992	4.3	151,147	9.4	42,820	2.7	8,290	0.5	1,043,982	65.2
1997	26,070	1.6	69,071	4.3	141,514	8.8	40,699	2.5	6,425	0.4	1,058,110	65.6
1998	27,670	1.4	80,862	4.1	175,116	8.8	40,967	2.1	6,513	0.3	1,296,988	65.3
1999	27,426	1.2	92,772	4.1	198,607	8.8	39,435	1.8	7,257	0.3	1,447,390	64.4
2000	28,429	0.8	120,778	3.3	309,818	8.5	35,819	1.0	23,163	0.6	2,373,696	65.3
2001	27,501	0.6	138,100	3.1	352,216	7.9	40,600	0.9	7,008	0.2	2,924,512	65.6
2002	26,276	0.6	141,825	3.3	354,926	8.2	38,209	0.9	5,684	0.1	2,861,727	66.0

Crime and social control in China

Year	Grand Larceny Cases	%	Theft of non-motor vehicle Cases	%	Fraud Cases	%	Smuggling Cases	%	Counter-feiting Cases	%	Others Cases	%
2003	24,393	0.6	145,485	3.3	340,077	7.7	40,088	0.9	3,721	0.1	2,940,598	66.9
2004	24,711	0.5	148,623	3.2	341,908	7.3	36,175	0.8	3,343	0.1	3,212,822	68.1
2005	20,770	0.5	155,056	3.3	332,196	7.2	33,710	0.7	2,884	0.1	3,158,763	68.0
2006	17,936	0.4	160,964	3.5	309,872	6.7	32,352	0.7	2,569	0.1	3,143,863	67.6

Table 5.2 Categories of reported criminal offences 1981–2006 (continued)

Year	Grand Larceny Cases	%	Theft of non-motor vehicle Cases	%	Fraud Cases	%	Smuggling Cases	%	Counter-feiting Cases	%	Others Cases	%
1981	16,873	1.90	–	–	18,665	2.10	–	–	1,649	0.19	–	–
1982	15,462	2.07	–	–	17,707	2.37	–	–	1,763	0.24	–	–
1983	–	–	–	–	–	–	–	–	–	–	–	–
1984	16,340	3.18	–	–	13,479	2.62	–	–	707	0.14	–	–
1985	34,643	6.39	–	–	13,157	2.43	–	–	491	0.09	–	–
1986	42,192	7.71	–	–	14,663	2.68	–	–	497	0.09	–	–
1987	58,661	10.28	–	–	14,693	2.60	–	–	436	0.1	–	0.1
1988	122,042	14.74	66,411	8.02	18,857	2.28	–	–	500	0.06	–	–
1989	277,147	14.05	453,322	22.99	42,581	2.20	–	–	865	0.04	–	–
1990	295,418	13.33	550,863	24.85	54,719	2.47	–	–	1,398	0.06	–	–
1991	329,229	13.89	607,456	25.63	60,174	2.54	2,532	0.11	1,895	0.08	115,935	0.43
1992	251,117	15.89	147,473	9.33	46,991	2.97	1,887	0.12	2,290	0.14	112,813	7.97
1993	301,848	18.67	103,248	6.39	50,644	3.13	1,355	0.08	3,422	0.21	134,634	8.33

Table 5.2 continues overleaf

Table 5.2 continued

Year	Grand Larceny		Theft of non-motor vehicle		Fraud		Smuggling		Counter-feiting		Others	
	Cases	%	Cases	%	Cases	%	Cases	%	Cases	%	Cases	%
1994	355,201	21.39	116,613	7.02	57,706	3.47	1,096	0.07	5,417	0.33	153,678	9.26
1995	412,418	24.40	98,001	5.80	64,047	3.79	1,119	0.07	5,237	0.31	170,629	10.10
1996	404,056	25.24	72,774	4.55	69,688	4.35	1,147	0.07	5,128	0.32	184,111	11.50
1997	448,917	27.82	56,607	3.51	78,284	4.85	1,133	0.07	5,422	0.34	186,901	11.58
1998	603,180	30.37	54,581	2.75	83,080	4.18	2,301	0.12	6,654	0.34	265,917	13.39
1999	659,725	29.33	49,539	2.20	93,192	4.14	1,205	0.05	10,047	0.45	331,988	14.75
2000	1,149,728	31.61	450,377	12.38	152,614	4.20	1,993	0.05	15,863	0.44	575,134	15.81
2001	1,433,058	32.15	496,339	11.13	190,854	4.28	1,784	0.04	11,204	0.25	763,800	17.13
2002	1,349,570	31.12	502,065	11.58	191,188	4.41	855	0.02	5,220	0.12	710,802	16.39
2003	1,288,879	29.33	556,871	12.67	193,665	4.41	1,178	0.03	3,132	0.07	701,556	15.97
2004	1,257,253	26.65	663,433	14.06	205,844	4.36	955	0.02	2,315	0.05	741,426	15.71
2005	1,126,919	24.24	682,680	14.69	203,083	4.37	925	0.02	1,858	0.05	744,924	16.03
2006	1,072,667	23.05	637,473	13.70	13,648	4.59	974	0.02	1,784	0.03	769,303	16.53

1 The classification of crime has changed over the years. In 1987, there were seven categories: homicide, injury, robbery, rape, larceny (including grand larceny), fraud, and counterfeiting. In 1991, four categories were added, including human trafficking, smuggling, manufacturing and trafficking of drugs, and others. In 1995, the categories increased to 10, including homicide, injury, robbery, rape, human trafficking, larceny (including grand larceny, theft of bicycle), fraud, smuggling, counterfeiting, and others.
2 'Others' in 1991 included 8,344 cases of drug trafficking.
3 Data are from *China Law Yearbook* (1987–2006).

Table 5.3 Proportion of young persons convicted of a crime in the People's Courts 1990–2006

Year	Total number of persons convicted of a crime[1]	Number of young persons convicted of a crime			Proportion of the number of young to total number of persons convicted of a crime[2]
		Under 25	Under 18	18–25	
1990	580,272	332,528	42,033	290,495	57.3
1991	507,238	268,206	33,392	234,814	52.9
1992	492,817	250,262	33,399	216,863	50.8
1993	449,920	228,311	32,408	195,903	50.7
1994	545,282	267,842	38,388	229,454	49.1
1995	543,276	247,391	35,832	211,559	45.5
1996	665,556	269,749	40,220	229,529	40.5
1997	526,312	199,212	30,446	168,766	37.9
1998	528,301	208,076	33,612	174,464	39.4
1999	602,380	221,153	40,004	181,139	36.7
2000	639,814	220,981	41,709	179,272	34.5
2001	746,328	253,465	49,883	203,582	34.0
2002	701,858	217,909	50,030	167,879	31.1
2003	730,355	231,715	58,870	172,845	31.7
2004	753,314	249,128	70,144	178,984	33.1
2005	829,238	285,970	82,721	203,249	34.5
2006	873,846	303,631	83,697	219,934	34.7

[1] The data here exclude public security offences and refer to criminal offences only.
[2] The proportion is derived by dividing the number of young persons convicted of a crime (under the age of 25) by the total number of persons convicted of a crime in a certain year.

Source: *China Law Yearbook* (1991–2007).

Table 5.4 Reported public security offences vs reported criminal offences 1986–2006

Year	Public security offences		Criminal offences		Ratio[1]
	No. of cases	Rate per 100,000	No. of cases	Rate per 100,000	
1986	1,115,858	105	547,115	52	2.0
1987	1,234,910	117	570,439	54	2.2
1988	1,410,044	132	827,706	75	1.8
1989	1,847,625	170	1,971,901	182	0.9
1990	1,965,663	178	2,216,987	201	0.9
1991	2,414,065	214	2,370,000	210	1.0
1992	2,956,737	259	1,580,000	135	1.9
1993	3,351,016	291	1,616,879	141	2.1
1994	3,300,972	284	1,660,734	142	2.0
1995	3,289,760	280	1,690,407	143	2.0
1996	3,363,636	284	1,600,716	134	2.2
1997	3,227,669	268	1,613,629	134	2.0
1998	3,232,113	259	1,986,068	159	1.6
1999	3,356,083	276	2,249,319	179	1.5
2000	4,437,417	362	3,637,307	287	1.3
2001	5,713,934	462	4,457,579	349	1.3
2002	6,232,350	517	4,336,712	338	1.5
2003	5,995,594	476	4,393,893	340	1.4
2004	6,647,724	527	4,718,122	363	1.5
2005	7,377,600	585	4,648,401	356	1.6
2006	7,197,200	563	4,653,265	354	1.6

[1]The ratio is derived by dividing the rate of public security offences by the rate of criminal offences.

Sources: *China Law Yearbook* (1986–2007).

Discourse on crime

It is important to understand how crime and especially the recent crime growth are perceived in Mainland China, both officially and by the public. I will review these perceptions by drawing on certain observations on crime in the West. Contrary to human intuition, Durkheim (see Vold and Bernard 1986) proposed the famous thesis 'crime as normal in mechanical societies'. The rationale underlying the thesis is less radical. Firstly, the classification of certain people as criminals and thus their identification as inferior allow the rest of society to feel superior and righteous. Likewise, the punishment of criminals serves to reinforce that very sense of superiority and righteousness. Thus, crime and punishment maintain social solidarity. Secondly, crime is normal because there is not always a clear and definite line to distinguish criminal behaviour from that considered morally reprehensible or merely in bad taste. Finally, for Durkheim, crime is the price society pays for the possibility of progress. Moreover, as reviewed previously, the representations of crime and the criminal oscillate between two different social attitudes since the inception of modernity and criminological thought in the nineteenth century: sympathy and antipathy (Melossi 2000). Or as Garland (2000) ascertained, in the wake of the crisis of the welfare state, there emerged 'high crime rates as a normal social fact', and the perception that criminals are different 'others' has been altered. The above brief review is to guide the discussions on the Chinese discourse on crime.

In China, crime is a fully morally charged phenomenon. Often official documents, media reports and academic research are replete with language of strong moral flavour, in line with the strongly moralistic quality of the whole society. For example, rising crime is seen to signal the moral decay of the whole society.[7] Tanner (1999: 133) observed that the criminal law, criminology, and the statement of the Communist Party leadership reflected a strong commitment to the principle that the individual, no matter what his or her social, economic, or family circumstances, is morally responsible for his or her own actions. He made the following observations on the moral outrage aroused by crime in China: 'From the central committee of the communist party's characterization of hooligans as "dregs of society" to a high-ranking procuratorial official's description of thieves as lazy, undisciplined persons whose personal hygiene leaves much to be desired to the remarks of criminologists that women engaged in prostitution because they lacked a sense of shame, had an unrestrained appetite for luxury, and were unable to control their sexual desires, one observes throughout the Chinese literature on crime *a strong sense of moral outrage*' (Tanner 1999: 133; emphasis added).

In China, criminals are regarded as both different and dangerous. The difference denotes that criminals are morally inferior; for example, they lack shame. The catchword in Chinese, *min-fen* ('public outrage'), reflects the public's perception of both the difference and the dangerousness of criminals. For example, Epstein and Wong (1996) explored the concept of 'dangerousness' in the PRC criminal justice system. They argued that it is a concept informed by certain political considerations necessary to maintain social order in a one-party socialist state, and that it forms an element in criminality, sentencing and prisoners' treatment. Often, morality, difference, dangerousness and traditional cultural prejudice (e.g. women are inferior to men) are entangled and conflated.

Notwithstanding the moral inferiority, difference and dangerousness ascribed to crime and criminals, there is in China a strong faith that criminals can be changed for the better due to the Confucian conviction that 'humans are born good'. So early interventions are stressed, as the metaphor goes, 'to nip crime in the bud'. On the other hand, the socialist ideology dictates that socialism does not produce crime. The mixture of all the elements, to a very great extent, shapes the landscape of crime and its control in China. For example, an academic made the following observations in the 1980s: 'In our socialist country, crime can be prevented. It is not a cancer; it can be cured'.[8] Accordingly, the official language always carries the words 'to eliminate crime' (*xiaomie fanzui*). In China, crime is supposed to bring shame not only to the criminal himself, but also to his family, his work unit, the neighbourhood, and other social organizations of which he is a member, such as the Youth League or the Communist Party. Thus, to control crime, all the social and state forces should 'join hands', constituting the basic nature of social control in China: the formal mixes with the informal, and the private blurs with the public. This is evidenced in successive, state-initiated social betterment campaigns such as, 'construction of spiritual civilization', 'comprehensive management of social order', 'strike hard' and finally the BLSCC programme, the latter being the focus of this study.

With the advent of the economic reform and its relentless reorientation of social relations, crime rose alarmingly. The rising crime simultaneously caused both panic and denial, typified in the launch of the 'strike hard' campaigns in the early 1980s. Issues such as the relationship between development and crime also aroused heated debate throughout the country. The ideological idealism that socialism did not produce crime ran counter to the harsh reality of incessantly soaring crime. With the translation of Shelley's book *Crime and Modernization* (1981) into Chinese, there emerged two theses in China positing the nexus between crime and development: the 'synchronism theory' (*tongbu lun*; crime grows at the same pace as economic development) and 'cost theory' (*daijia lun*; crime is the price society pays for its development). But, to a certain extent, those discussions are still confined to ideological and methodological inadequacies. For example, a large number of academic writings in this regard tend to be descriptive studies at best or theoretical speculations at worst. For example, in examining the rise of crime, most studies look at the change in the absolute figures (rather than age-sex specific rates or other devices of modern criminology), without any further statistical analysis. In this regard, Liu (2005, 2006) employed some sophisticated statistical techniques, such as time series, to examine in-depth any change in crime and its relationship to economic development. To a large extent, this evidence-based approach is something that native Chinese scholarship is yet to draw upon.

It is undeniable that with the overall social atmosphere loosened and relaxed, more open discussions of development and crime, juvenile delinquency, policing reform, etc., are published in academic journals and books. In certain respects, ideology gradually gives way to realism, and the official discourse on crime also changes. For example the official propaganda of 'crime elimination' has gradually shifted to crime reduction, and crime control. In the popular discourse, people increasingly regard crime as part of daily life rather than as an abnormality, and public tolerance of crime has increased (see Dutton and Lee 1993).

Social control in China

As discussed in the earlier section of this chapter, social control in China is a fusion of the present and the past, and of the imported Western and the indigenous Chinese approaches. More specifically, it is a blend of the formal and informal control mechanisms, epitomized in the 'mass line' and 'relying on the masses'. But this fusion appears remarkable in the eyes of Western observers. For example, Clark (1989: 57), when visiting China in the 1980s with a group of American criminologists and legal scholars, expressed this doubt: 'We are intrigued by the unfamiliar coexistence of such a highly centralized government supported by a legendary bureaucracy and hierarchical social structure, side by side with a world-renowned heavy reliance on informal or people's control of conflict and unacceptable behavior.'

It has become an unhelpful cliché that social control in China is the integration of the formal and the informal mechanisms. To make that statement more concrete, in this section I introduce several social control institutions, both formal and informal, with a focus on their structure, operation, and role in social control. In so doing, I sketch the basic structure of the social control system in China, and at the same time pave the way for the examination of their roles, whether retained or transformed, in the BLSCC programme in Shenzhen in the wake of the economic reform. The institutions include the household registration system, neighbourhood committees, work units, and the public security organs.[9]

Household registration

The Chinese *hukou*[10] system can be traced to as early as 2100 BC. But only in the Qin dynasty (475–221 BC) was it formally established. In 359 BC, Shang Yang was Employed by Emperor Qin Xiao-gong to implement a series of reform measures, among which is the *hukou* system. It stipulated that 10 households form a unit, within which joint liability is practised, meaning that anyone in that unit is responsible for the behaviour of the other residents. A uniform, nationwide household registration system was established to register births and deaths. Only one adult male may live in one household; otherwise, the household must be split. People who want to move must solicit official approval and endorsement; otherwise, they will be treated as fugitives and arrested. All migrants must hold some official documentation or certificates; going through any checkpoint requires a pass, and staying in any hotel requires valid documents. Regular and detailed household statistics nationwide were reported (Yu *et al.* 1997). The *hukou* system survived the vicissitudes of change throughout the long Chinese history, and in the PRC the *hukou* system was maintained and transformed. As Dutton (1992: 189) observed, this signified a transformation of the family-based household registration system from a mechanism of a patriarchal state to a general system of population registration based on a centrally planned, socialist economic model. More specifically, he argued, 'This transformation in the registration systems signifies a wholesale shift in strategies of social policing. It comprised a move away from the community-based self-help strategies of the traditional regime and the emergence of the professionalized welfare regimes of the state; it represented the shift from family to individual and then, later, to collective. It signified the emergence of a new concern for the "nation state" and, more importantly, the emergence of the centrally planned nation state' (1992: 190). What is reflected in the above argument is a rather basic proposition that generic forms of social control can be retooled or reformed irrespective of the power. In the case of transformed *hukou*, imperial forms of control are found as useful to the socialist system.

In January 1958, the 'Ordinance of *Hukou* Registration in the People's Republic of China' was promulgated, marking the official establishment of the *hukou* system in the PRC era. It registered the population on the basis of their birthplace or their fathers'/husbands' residence. It was first established in the cities, and then expanded to the countryside. The registration of *hukou* is under the jurisdiction of the local police station, with a registration policeman (*huji minjing*) taking direct charge. A registration form covers the following items: the household head or relation to household head, name, sex, birthplace, birth date, age, place of origin, nationality, religious faith, educational level, marital status, profession, work unit, moving records, and re-registration records. The *hukou* system is not just for population control, but it is also a welfare system. It is intimately related to systems of employment, personnel management, supply of grain and oil, housing allocations, medical services, compulsory education, and control of urban populations, and all other systems are centred on the household registration system (Kang *et al.* 1998). *Hukou* status is also inheritable, along with all the benefits associated with it.

One of the remarkable features of *hukou* in the PRC is that it differentiates between urban and rural registration status, but attaches rather different meanings, both material and symbolic. Under the *hukou* system, Chinese citizens are classified into those with agricultural *hukou* status and those with non-agricultural *hukou* status based on the location of their permanent residence. The former, mostly in the countryside, receive no state benefits, except the right to farm. The latter are entitled to various privileges and benefits, including coupons for obtaining heavily subsidized rice, oil, cloth, and sugar from state-operated shops; job placement; and housing, education, and medical benefits in their home city or town. The non-agricultural *hukou* system further assumes a hierarchy, with state benefits diminishing from major cities to small towns. Since the state finances those benefits, it discourages any transfer from agricultural to non-agricultural *hukou* status or any transfers or movement up the urban hierarchy (Woon 1999). The *hukou* system is contingent on the state-planned economy, and in turn it serves to strengthen the latter.

A citizen's *hukou* status is inheritable and the only opportunities for agricultural *hukou* holders to change their status are via marriage, college entrance, joining the army or other, unusual channels. If a class system in the customary sense was eliminated in the Chinese revolution, the *hukou* system actually set up a new class distinction between urban and rural dwellers, or at least constructed a new set of status categories, if not precisely a new class system, to replace the dismantled class hierarchy of the past (see Solinger 1999: 35–36). Therefore, as Dutton (1992: 250) argued, 'by functioning as the basis of welfare allocation, *hukou* registration was presented as something to be desired rather than as an onerous duty to be avoided. *Hukou*, then, far from being overtly repressive, became a regime of "positivities" under which "benefits" were allocated.' But the 'positivities' are reserved for the urban residents only.

The *hukou*'s emphasis on welfare and benefits should not be taken to mean that it is not concerned with moral policing and social control, an important feature of its traditional counterpart. As Kang *et al.* (1998) argued, apart from identification, urban population control, and providing demographic information, the *hukou* system plays an important role in 'protecting social stability'. *Hukou*, by and large, dictates 'immobility'; thus, it locks people into their native place, especially rural residents. This immobility enhances mutual surveillance and conformity. Moreover, the *hukou* system is closely related to other institutions of social control, such as the neighbourhood committees, the police, and *danwei*. For example, based on the registered information, the registration policeman identifies adults with criminal records, or those who pose a potential threat to social order. He also trains juveniles to obey social rules. With the cooperation of the grass-roots organizations, he seeks to eliminate any factors affecting social stability and to assist criminal investigations. He gets involved with the local residents and spends most of his time on local affairs such as sanitation, the welfare of the residents, and family visiting. Thus, order is preserved by the clear distinction between the outsiders and the insiders of a particular neighbourhood, by the control of social mobility, and by the exposure of the private life of the residents to the public (Fu 1990). The *hukou* system also helps maintain social order through managing the targeted people (*zhongdian renkou*; see Wang 2004). Thus, *hukou* and the information gathered through it serve as the basis of other forms of social control.

The *hukou* system and its associated functions are compatible with a planned economy under strict control of the state. In differentiating the urban from the rural residents, the *hukou* system creates and enforces the inequality between the cities and the countryside. With the advent of the reform era, the rigid *hukou* system came under tremendous pressure to reform, and this is to be presented in the next chapter.

Crime and social control in China

Neighbourhood committee

A neighbourhood in Chinese cities is not merely a residential location in its geographic sense. It is also a social organization managed by the grass-roots branch of the Chinese government, the 'street office', through the neighbourhood committee (*Juweihui*, also translated as residents' committee).[11] The neighbourhood committee is the lowest of the administrative hierarchy in China. As Figure 5.1 illustrates, below the district government level, the management structures are regarded as self-help-based and informal. Each street office manages 25,000 to 50,000 residents. Under the street office is the neighbourhood committee, each with 5 to 9 staff members managing 100 to 700 households. According to the Ministry of Civil Affairs of China, the functions of the neighbourhood committee include conflict mediation, law and order, environmental improvement, economic development, mutual help, neighbourhood service, political education, grass-roots feedback, assistance to families in need, and promotion of the material and mental well-being of the residents (cited in Wong 1999). As Wang (2002) observed, the neighbourhood has long acted as the government (or the 'leg' or errand servant of the government),

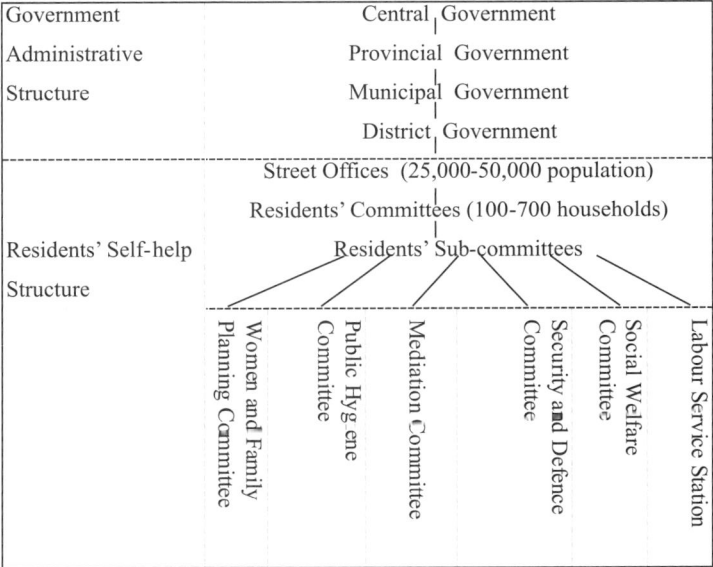

Source: this figure is combined from the two figures cited in Wong (1999).

Figure 5.1 The hierarchy of administrative structure in China.

115

fulfilling the functions of community management according to the instructions of the government.

Each neighbourhood committee normally contains six sub-committees: Women and Family Planning Committee, Public Hygiene Committee, Mediation Committee, Security and Defence Committee (also called Public Security Committee), Social Welfare Committee, and Labour Service Station (see Figure 5.1). Among the six subcommittees at the neighbourhood level, the Mediation Committee and the Security and Defence Committee perform local informal control functions. The Mediation Committee is responsible for resolving conflicts between groups, organizations and individuals in the neighbourhood. Since most crimes are triggered by unresolved civil conflicts over marriage or property, the Mediation Committee aims to prevent crime by mediating in those conflicts. It pursues the main goal of promoting public morality and a sense of neighbourliness among the residents. The functions of the Security and Defence Committee are to educate people in safety and legal matters, to maintain order, to report suspicious counter-revolutionaries and offenders in the neighbourhood, to provide assistance to the police for local defence and household registration, to re-educate juveniles who have committed mild offences, and to report major discontent among residents to appropriate local departments (Chan 1993, Wong 1999).

According to Fang (1988: 180), the relation between the neighbourhood subcommittees and the judicial organs 'consists in the former co-operating with the latter following its instructions'. More specifically, the former 'supplements' the latter in the following respects: (1) to compensate for the scarcity of judicial personnel (the socialist legal system is still imperfect); (2) to supplement the time limits within which judicial personnel work; (3) to avoid limitations of the scope and character of judicial responsibility; (4) to compensate for poorly informed judicial personnel (Fang 1988: 180). But Fang also identified certain problems with the neighbourhood subcommittees: (1) the members generally lack an understanding of legal concepts; (2) the subcommittees are always in financial difficulties; (3) the committees continue to be undermanned (Fang 1988: 185). In these respects, whether the situation improves, remains the same, or gets even worse will be addressed in the case of Shenzhen.

According to Troyer (1989: 30), the personnel at the local level are often retired people, the majority being women, and many are illiterate and have been handpicked by officials in the street office. Troyer (1989) also observed that they may not occupy a high status in the community and may even be seen as 'meddling busybodies'. In fact, most of them are volunteers, receiving little or very low pay. As Chan (1993) observed at the neighbourhood level, there are the traditions of mass mobilization and campaigns, articulated in the mass line. The residents' committee organizes 'mass activities' periodically, either to respond to the call of the higher government or the Party, or on its own initiative. For example, the residents' committee mobilizes the residents to 'do good deeds' (*zuo hao shi*), to 'learn from Leifeng' (*xue Leifeng*)[12] in March each year, 'to thoroughly clean the neighbourhood' (*da sao chu*), and to engage in other voluntary activities (see Chan 1993). Residents' committees also encourage mutual surveillance at the neighbourhood level, either of local residents or outsiders or strangers. This is an approach that is feasible and effective when the population is static under the *hukou* system.

At the neighbourhood level, the following factors, when taken together, should undoubtedly enhance local social control, and should have an impact on the local crime level: the two subcommittees (security and defence, and mediation) that take direct responsibilities in public security, the mass activities organized by the residents' committees, the mutual surveillance encouraged by the residents' committees and made feasible by the limited living space, and the geographic and residential immobility. But in the wake of the economic reform, there are changes at the grass-roots level that affect neighbourhood mutual help and volunteerism, as identified by Chan (1993: 23–27). These changes range from the development of the grass-roots economy, the increasing sense of consumer rights among residents, the changing patterns of neighbourhood relationships in city life, and the increasing mobility due to urban redevelopment and to Party control of street office decisions. More specifically, for example, residents can move in and out with ease, making mutual surveillance increasingly difficult. The replacement of two- or three-storey buildings by high-rise buildings has increased the social distance among formerly closely involved residents and thus decreases mutual surveillance (Situ and Liu 1996a). Moreover, the former, largely 'spiritual' incentives have gradually lost appeal (thus, people are less interested in voluntary mass-cleaning campaigns), and the low morale among grass-roots cadre is one of the major obstacles to further development, as, for example in the community-based welfare network (Chan 1993: 186). Thus, according to Chan (1993), because political education and propaganda on the 'superiority of socialism' yield diminished returns, a shift of approaches (for example, from direct indoctrination and propaganda to a more sophisticated programme of 'soft-sell' techniques) will have to be made to improve the quality of grass-roots cadres and to reactivate the mutual-help networks dormant since the beginnings of the economic reform. In Chapter 7, concrete changes of this kind, as evidenced in local neighbourhood committees in Shenzhen, especially their impact on grass-roots social control, will be presented.

The work unit

Shaw (1996: 3) defined the Chinese work unit as 'an officially established or registered organization. It owns property, occupies a plot of land, undertakes a type of enterprise, feeds a group of people, and builds up a wide range of vertical and horizontal relationships within the society.' Unlike in the West, the Chinese work unit is surely not a mere workplace. He observed that the organization of the work unit is different between rural and urban areas. In rural areas, a work unit is based on a production brigade or a village committee comprising several natural villages, while in cities or towns, a work unit is organized around a line of production, business, service, profession, or administrative function. In fact, the common use of *danwei* in China refers specifically to a workplace/organization in the cities with an urban *hukou* attached.[13] For example, as noted by Shaw (1996), in any first-time encounter, Chinese people always ask, 'what is your work unit?', instead of 'who are you?' or 'what is your name?' But this reflects encounters between urban people. Villagers usually ask, 'which village are you from?' or 'what is your family name?' Furthermore, in the countryside, the fact that someone has a 'work unit' underlies that he is working in the cities and possesses an urban *hukou*, something desirable and enviable for villagers, a legacy of the *hukou* system.

Although the internal structure and external connections of a work unit change by size, rank and line of business, Shaw (1996) observed that, internally, there are both a management network and a party system in parallel, each with a clear division of labour and a systematic structure and process of administration, discipline, and control. Externally, a work unit is engaged in both horizontal and vertical relationships, with its supervising agencies, local government, local community, its clientele, and the market or profession of its line of enterprise (see the previous discussion on *guanxi*'s cooperate and administrative uses).

Shaw (1996) argued that the work unit affects the individuals affiliated to it and the society at large. For individuals, it is where they work, live, establish a social network, and pursue their goals of career development and personal success, because the affiliation is always lifetime, and could even be transferred to their children.[14] For the society, on the other hand, it is the first and last organizational bastion where policy lines and programmes are executed. Interestingly, the benefits and services granted to individuals, along with the control exerted over them, are interdependent: 'You want the benefits so you should be under control.' In other words, 'Chinese firms have a wide variety of benefits that can be used as powerful tools in the exercise of authority' (Walder, cited in Bakken 2000: 35).

It is very important to note that a work unit provides its workers with housing at a peppercorn rate, which is literally called 'housing assignment' (*fen fang*). In each work unit, there is a special department taking direct charge of this task.[15] The work unit housing estates are usually constructed within large compounds surrounded by walls and are quite often guarded by work unit personnel. According to Dutton (1992: 231), symbolically, the walled-compound structure demarcates the power and jurisdiction of the work unit in much the same the way that the traditional Chinese compound house (*siheyuan*) demarcated the power and jurisdiction of the family head. That is, for Dutton, this transfer of the surrounding wall from household to work unit household compound indicates the transfer of power from home to work unit. Regardless of its seemingly traditional linkage, the work unit system and its special type of authority could be described as 'communist neo-traditionalism'. It is 'traditional' because it is associated with 'dependence, deference, and particularism', and it is 'modern' because it is associated with 'independence, contract, and universalism' (Walder, cited in Bakken 2000: 35).

More specifically, the kind of social control a work unit exerts upon individuals takes the following forms: control in the form of ideology through political study and self-criticism; control of behavior through residency; creation of enduring official identities through confidential records; and sanctioning of deviance through civil rewards or penalties, administrative discipline, quasi-justice, and para-security (Shaw 1996: 21). In this respect, according to Shaw (1996: 22), work units have actually incorporated family, neighbourhood, spiritual control, and other elements into an effective system of social and organizational control. He also identified the discretionary powers by which the work unit keeps its employees in line. First, it holds three 'magic weapons' over its workers: household registration (*hukou*), dossier keeping (*dang'an*) and administrative discipline (*Jilu chufa*).

Second, work units are allocated the responsibility of civil dispute mediation and the power of direct or indirect law enforcement.

In summary, Shaw (1996: 31–33) summarized the nature of social control in Chinese work units as having five characteristics. First, despite the fact that most work units apply modern technological and material facilities to standard lines of business, they are organized according to the East Asian mode of human relations and socialist political economy. Second, control in the Chinese work unit is of both a general and local nature. It is general because many of its practices are universal all over the country. It is local because it is executed within a specific unit's organizational authority and resources. Third, control in Chinese work unit is both formal and informal. It is formal because a work unit is primarily an official organization with authority granted directly from the state. It is informal because, unlike the criminal justice system, the control structure and processes inside a work unit are based upon work relations and remain largely suggestive and regulative. Fourth, control is patriarchal, inherently associated with provisions of care and support. Finally, underlying all the above characteristics is the fact that the Party oversees, reinforces and guides controls by the work unit administration.

However, as we are going to see later, with the reform gaining full speed – notably, for example, in the relaxing of population mobility, the marketization of the housing, the poor state of the State-Owned Enterprises (SOE), and the thriving private industry and joint industry – the work unit, especially its control system, is undergoing dramatic transformation.

Public security organs (the police)

In China, the police system consists of five components: the public security police, the state security police, the prison police, the judicial police in people's procuratorates, and the judicial police in the people's courts (Li 1998). The public security police account for about 86 per cent of the police force and shoulder the main duties of maintaining social order and controlling crime. Normally, in China, 'the police' refers to the public security police, and so no distinction will be made from here onwards between police and public security police. The central agency of the police is the Ministry of Public Security, which is accountable to the State Council. Corresponding to the levels of the government, there are levels of public security police. The lowest level is the *pai chu suo*, a local police station generally set up at the street office level in cities and at the township level in the countryside.

By February 2006, there were over 52,000 such local police stations with over 490,000 police officers, accounting for 27 per cent of the whole police force (He 2006). In the police system, a dual leadership is enforced, which means that, in terms of profession and operation, all the public security police fall under the leadership of the Ministry of Public Security, while in terms of administration they fall under the leadership of the corresponding levels of the government (Brewer *et al.* 1996; Du 1997; Li 1998; Wong 2002; Fu 2005b).

The public–police ratio in China is much lower than that in most Western jurisdictions. Table 5.5 shows the number of police officers from 1988 to 1993 (data subsequently were not published). In 1993, the police–public ratio was about 125/100,000.[16] In December 2007, a source from the police indicated that the total police force was around 1.8 million, a ratio of around 138/100,000 (the total population is 1.3 billion).

The guiding principle of the police, in fact of all the government agencies, is the 'mass line',[17] and serving the people. The public security organs at all levels are supposed to maintain a 'fish and water' relationship with the masses whereby the police are like fish and the masses are the water. According to Wong (2000: 18), 'mass line' formed the basis of 'people's policing' whereby the local people are supposed to be self-policed. He argued that it is more appropriate to refer to 'mass line' policing as 'people's policing' in the earlier days of the PRC when the whole of 'the people' as an exploited and oppressed class were mobilized to impose their political will. But in

Table 5.5 Number of People's Police (in units of 10,000) 1988–93

	1988	1989	1990	1992	1993
Total	135.0	135.0	138.0	148.4	147.7
1. Professional People's Police	76.9	76.9	76.9	82.5	85.4
Public security police	15.0	15.0	15.0	22.3	34.9
Household registration	15.7	15.7	15.7	11.0	–
Criminal	7.9	7.9	7.9	8.1	8.2
Traffic	10.0	10.0	10.0	11.7	12.2
2. Armed police	–	58.1	61.1	65.9	62.3
Fire control	8.5	8.5	9.3	9.5	9.8
Border control	7.0	7.0	8.3	7.7	8.3

Source: *China Law Yearbook* (1989–94).

the later years (since 1979), 'people's policing' became 'community policing' in which the local people are encouraged to take part in managing their own affairs. In some sense, the mass line is both a means and an end.

Guided by the mass line, the police shoulder a wide range of responsibilities. By Western standards, the 'uncle police' in China do much 'non-police' work (see Bracey 1989; Fu 1994), such as providing assistance to residents who are in trouble, such as the elderly and the sick; mediating neighbourhood and family disputes; cleaning the streets; helping to rehabilite and educate offenders; birth control; and collecting taxes in the countryside, to list just a few. Even according to the new standard of community policing in the West, police work in the West would pale compared with what Chinese police are supposed to do. This could be illustrated in the following example of 'garbage collection' cited in Bracey (1989: 138). In the 1980s during their visit to China, the American team used the following example to explain to their Chinese host what community policing is. In a US inner-city area, garbage collections were made rarely and sporadically, and so the local police officer helped residents there to identify the agency in charge of garbage collection, accompanied them to lodge a complaint, and was able to persuade a ranking official in the sanitation department to remedy the situation. The Chinese police suggested that a Chinese police officer would have removed the garbage himself. To some extent, Chinese policing comes very close to the ideal policing articulated by Sir Robert Peel in 1829.

Police powers are set out in the Police Law 1995 and the Criminal Procedure Law 1997. They include the power (1) to arrest, (2) to detain, (3) to interrogate suspects and (4) to impose administratively coercive and punitive measures on individuals or organizations who breach the Regulation on Public Administration Punishment (the predecessor of the public security law) (see Li 1998). Penalties under this fourth heading range from a warning, a fine, and detention, to re-education through labour for from one to three years. It is also stipulated that the police can detain an active criminal or a major suspect under any of the following circumstances: (1) he is in the process of preparing to commit a crime, is committing a crime, or is discovered immediately after committing a crime; (2) he is identified as having committed a crime by the victim or by any eyewitness on the scene; (3) he is discovered to have incriminating evidence on his person or at his dwelling; (4) after committing the crime, he attempts to commit suicide or to escape, or is a fugitive; (5) there is a possibility that he may destroy or falsify evidence or collude with others to devise a consistent story; (6) he does not reveal his true name and address, and his identity is unclear; and (7) he is strongly suspected of committing crimes, or of going from one place to another, and committing multiple crimes, or he is a member of a criminal gang (see Li 1998).

Bracey (1989: 139) observed that in order to analyse Chinese policing, we must struggle to understand a law enforcement organization that combines a community policing programme such as would be the envy of any Anglo-American police executive, with the far-reaching, comprehensive, and lightly supervised powers of security administration, punishment and re-education through labour. He argued that Chinese policing approaches entail the intensive use of all of Black's (1980) styles of policing: penal, compensatory, therapeutic and conciliatory. He made the following observations about the Chinese police: 'Both the extent and the diversity of police activity ensure that police will not only be a prime element in enforcing the criminal law, but that they will also play a major role in the elaborate system of informal social control – a role that defines the unique quality of policing in China' (1989: 139).

In the reform era, the police are under both internal and external pressures to adjust to the new social and economic environment. Crime is soaring, and public–police relations are worsening (see e.g. Fu 1990; Dutton and Lee 1993; Feng 1995; Du 1997). Wang (1999) examined 10 urgent problems facing the public security organs, such as leadership style, the distribution of the grass-roots police force, and the streamlining of the police structure. In particular, the mass line has been under severe challenge. For example, regarding the reform of the local police station initiated since the 1980s, the reform reports seldom mention 'mass line' or serving the people (Fu 1990). There are even suggestions from native scholars that the concept of 'the masses' should be replaced by 'the public' so as to get rid of its political flavour (Ma 1998).

Wong (2002) conducted a thorough examination of the police reform from the mid-1980s to the late 1990s, which he regarded as 'frame-breaking'. His investigation showed that in terms of the police mission, the reform has had the following results: (1) the police have become less concerned with political matters and more involved with law enforcement and order maintenance activities; (2) the police are less concerned with providing service and more focused on controlling crime; (3) the police are less concerned with serving the people in general and more committed to meeting the needs of economic development.

Network of control mechanisms

In this section on social control in China, I mainly introduced the several institutions that assume a wide range of control functions. The thrust of the Chinese control mechanism lies in the fact that all sorts of control institutions at all levels must cooperate with each other to form a control network. Among the institutions introduced above, there are complex interlinks, interdependence and cooperation. For example, the Security and Defence Committee and the Mediation Committee work closely with the police: the committees are under the guidance of the police and assist the police in social order maintenance and criminal investigation (Bracey 1989). Moreover, the neighbourhood committees and the work units are interrelated. As revealed above, most neighbourhood committees are set up in the residential areas of the work units. Since individuals and individual householders are so intimately tied to the work units, those neighbourhood committees, regardless of their connections with the street office, the police and the courts, are mostly under the direct supervision of the work units (Fang 1988; Shaw 1996). Further, in contrast to Western practice, the Chinese police are directly involved in corporate security management: a corporate policing model (Jiao 1997). A public security department (*bao wei ke*) is set up in each medium-sized or large work unit. The department is staffed with trained para-police personnel, equipped with law-enforcement instruments, and maintains direct contact with the state police force. Mostly the department supervises subcommittees and groups on public security (Fang 1988). In a small work unit, there is at least one person in charge of public security (Shaw 1996). The staff of the public security departments are appointed and/or dismissed by the leaders of the *danwei*.

Finally, *hukou* is related to the neighbourhood committee, the work unit and the police. In urban areas, individuals must obtain permission from their work units to register their households with the local police and food supply departments, and their *hukou* status is further monitored by the neighbourhood committees (Shaw 1996). Moreover, the interaction and negotiation between the institutions are not static. For example, Dutton (1992) charted the development of the relationship between the registration police and the neighbourhood committees. In the post-liberation period, efforts were made to separate the policing of the register from the moral and social policing of the neighbourhood committees. In the period leading to reform, one of the subsidiary duties of these neighbourhood committees was to aid in the work of the registration police. With economic reform and the increased demands upon the registration police, this divide could not be sustained. The police increasingly called upon the neighbourhood committees to shoulder more of the burden of registration work. In a word, all the control mechanisms are based on the *hukou* system and the planned economy. According to Dutton (1992), on the one hand *hukou* could be utilized to institute a planned economy, while, on the other hand, when coupled with other techniques such as the compound housing format in the work unit or the neighbourhood committee structure, *hukou* could be involved in the policing of labour discipline and in the moral and ethical concerns of the workers.

With cooperation and coordination by all the institutions, a series of community-based control mechanisms were established, such as *bangjiao* (help and education), *tiaojie* (mediation), and *qunfang qunzhi* (mass prevention and mass management). All of the above constitute important elements of the general crime policy *shehui zhi'an zonghe zhili* (comprehensive management of social order), which will be elaborated on in Chapter 6.

Conclusion

This chapter mainly covers crime and social control in China. During such a critical stage of modernization and development in Chinese society, it is even more important to examine crime for the purpose of enhancing economic construction and protecting social stability. Since the 1950s, crime has changed in terms of quantity, type, nature, and composition, and a particular ecological pattern of crime has formed. Meanwhile, the discourse of crime, both official and public, is also being transformed.

Regarding social control in China, several prominent institutions with a role in social control were introduced. With the partnership approach and multiagency cooperation, a tight web of social and crime control has been formed in China. To employ the definition of community crime prevention in Chapter 3, the Chinese control model is intrinsically community-based. As referred to above, it is a cliché that social control in China is the integration of formal and informal mechanisms. However, the above examination of control functions exercised by the several institutions also demonstrates that the formal blurs with the informal. For example, in the arena of social control, both formal and informal, the Party, through its nationwide, cell-like organization and policies, plays an important role. Troyer and Rojek observed, 'In order to understand the dynamics of social control in China, one must begin by examining its informal control network. This is where the pressure to conform is pervasive and intense. The existence of this informal network does not mean that the authorities are insignificant. Indeed, a basic argument... is that *what appears to be an informal social-control system is actually controlled by Chinese officials* (1989: 6; emphasis added). Thus Braithwaite (1999: 11–12) threw into the dustbin the section on Chinese community policing contained in an earlier draft of his book *Crime, Shame and Reintegration* (Braithwaite 1989), because Chinese informal justice seemed to involve so much more stigmatization and punitiveness than Japanese justice. But he noted that Chinese restorative justice, in both its positive and negative aspects, deserves more attention because China has by far the largest and most diverse programmes. So he admitted that it was 'an intellectual mistake' to scrap the China section of *Crime, Shame and Reintegration* partly 'because the study of Chinese history may hold one key to a macrosociology of restorative justice'.

Apart from its community-based nature, social control in China also reflects the rationality of social capital. As discussed in the previous chapter, prior to the advent of the 'webs of commerce', rural life was characterized by internal intimacy and external isolation; that is, strong bonding social capital and weak bridging social capital. In this regard, Chinese cities, to a large extent, display many similarities. Prior to the full-swing development of the economic reform, the basic urban entities, such as neighbourhoods and work units, were also internally intimate and externally isolated. In work units, individual workers were granted employment, health care, education, and pensions, covering all aspects of life. In the neighbourhoods, residents lived close to each other. Those co-workers or neighbours (in work unit housing areas, the two overlap) supported and controlled each other, a manifestation of close relationship internal to the neighbourhood or work unit. Also of foremost importance was that fellow residents or fellow workers were financially of equal status – 'equality' under socialism. Or, as the proverb goes, they 'eat from the same big pot' (*chi da guo fan*) with 'an iron rice bowl' (*tie fan wan*). In terms of relationship with external entities, work units and neighbourhoods were, to certain extent, isolated from each other. Work units provided all sorts of living necessities to support individual workers 'from the cradle to the grave', and the *hukou* system forbade mobility; thus, the work units in the cities became isolated enclaves. In the neighbourhood, the individual residents were assigned housing by their work units and they virtually could not move at will because of the rigid *hukou* system, thus, informal external exchanges with other neighbourhoods or outside entities were infrequent. In the island-like work units and neighbourhoods in Chinese cities, it is envisaged that crime mainly comes from without. Here I expect that the point of insufficient bridging social capital due to immobility and isolation will be regarded as rather unconventional, mainly due to the common understanding of some hallmarks of Chinese society, such as group orientation, mutual interaction, or simply *guanxi*. But as Fei (1992 [1948]) constantly stressed, the immobility, solitude and isolation characterized the groups, instead of individuals, as, for example, here in the case of neighbourhoods and work units. So the common and 'conventional' understanding of Chinese society is through the prism of the internal dynamics inside certain entities, not external dynamics. Without doubt, the internal dynamics or bonding social capital can reach the point of saturation in the Chinese context. As Dutton and Lee observed, prior to economic reform, China put in place a comprehensive form of public security management. This form of management depended on a 'closed system' of management (*fengbi guanli*) (see Dutton and Lee 1993). This 'closed system' is consistent with the internal closure of communities I observed above.

With the advent of the economic reform, all the old institutions are undergoing transformation, and hence their role in social control is simultaneously changing. To explore these changes and their impact on the levels of crime is one of the important tasks for the following chapters in the case of Shenzhen, a forerunner of reform and open-door policies.

Notes

1 In sketching the 'history of the present', I am fully aware of the difficulties in such an undertaking and thus try my best to be less ambitious. In the process, I also attempt to avoid the danger of producing simply 'a stew of elephant and rabbit', a metaphor used by Clifford Geertz (1990) to depict the tendency of mechanically arranged (or time-line driven) historical analysis in anthropology.
2 Ironically, it is revealed that during the period in France covered in Durkheim's anomie thesis, recorded crime actually declined. Formulating his theory of anomie in the context of a study of suicide rates, Durkheim simply assumed that crime was also increasing (see Vold and Bernard 1986).
3 Guo (1998) has a slightly different view of the crime waves and peak years. According to both the characteristics of crime and 'social and

historical background', he classified the whole period into three stages: 1950–65, 1966–87, and 1988–96, and he observed that there are four waves within these periods: early 1950s, early 1960s, late 1970s to early 1980s, and late 1980s to early 1990s. For both Guo (1998) and Cao (1997), the latest crime wave lasted for the longest time, with the most remarkable levels of seriousness, quantity and sophistication. They both discussed in detail the prevalent types of crime in each period.

4 See Fu (2005a) for the re-education through labour system in China.
5 The 'six-evils' campaign was initiated in late 1989 to fight against prostitution; producing, selling, and spreading pornography; kidnapping women and children; planting, gathering, and trafficking in drugs; gambling; and defrauding by superstitious means. In Guangdong province, triad activity is included to make 'seven evils'.
6 See C. Yang (1994) for a detailed discussion of the public security offences and their impact on crime rates in China.
7 Other Chinese terms in this regard include 'faith crisis' (*xinyang weiji*), 'spiritual slide' (*jingshen huapo*', 'loss of morality' (*daode lunsang*), etc.
8 The academic, Zang Liquan from the Beijing Institute of Juvenile Studies (China Academy of Social Sciences), made the argument when a team of American criminologists and legal scholars visited China in the 1980s. See Troyer *et al.* (1989: 41).
9 There are certainly other important entities, such as the family and the school, and criminal justice agencies such as the courts, procuratorates, and corrections. I exclude family-based social control out of two considerations. Firstly, the role the family plays in social control is not specific to any culture, although undoubtedly the Chinese family plays a rather different role in view of the emphasis put on family life in Chinese culture. Secondly, the role of the Chinese family has been undermined in modern times. Grant (1989) observed that in the communist era the Chinese family lost its once-exclusive ability to control and regulate its members' lives, and that it instead became the object of regulation by institutions of social control created by the PRC government. Dutton (1992) also described in detail how the power and autonomy of the family have been undermined in modern China.
10 In Chinese, *hu* literally means household, and *kou* mouth. Generally, *hukou* contains several meanings, such as household and number of people residing in the household, categories of residence status (e.g. non-agricultural vs agricultural in modern China) and registration of the residence and so on. In this context, *hukou* refers to either the system of household registration or the status of a registered residence. The discussion of *hukou* mainly focuses on its modern form. As for the course of its evolution in traditional China, see Dutton (1992).
11 The 'organic ordinance on urban neighbourhood committees' was promulgated in 1954, and it was replaced by the 'organic law on urban neighbourhood committees' promulgated in 1990.

12 Leifeng, a former peasant and soldier, earnestly served the people until his death in an accident. He was declared a national hero. The month of March is designated 'Month of Learning from Leifeng' when people from all walks of life are called on to do good deeds and help those in need.
13 In this respect, Bakken also made similar observations, 'the system (of work unit) is seldom found in the countryside, but entirely dominates the scene in the cities' (2000: 33).
14 The *jie ban* system stipulates that if the parent retires with an unemployed child, the child could take over the parent's former job in the work unit.
15 Understandably, this department is of paramount importance to every worker. There are many Chinese publications and films depicting corruption related to 'housing assignment'.
16 Dutton and Lee (1993) mentioned that in 1991 the ratio was about one police officer for every 1,400 people (equivalent to 71 per 100,000). According to Du (1997), at the end of 1994, the number of police was 1.24 million, and the police–public ratio was 74 per 100,000.
17 'Mass line' refers to 'for the masses, relying on the masses, from the masses and to the masses' (Yu *et al*. 1997: 152).

Chapter 6

Building little, safe and civilized communities in Shenzhen: community crime prevention with Chinese characteristics?

Part One: CMSO, and BLSCC development and outcome

From this chapter on, the focus of the book moves to Shenzhen, a prism through which to look at the reform unfolding and the consequences engendered for the whole country. This draws upon the approach recommended by Shue (1988) in current studies of the Chinese polity. It 'puts the analysis of *process* at the center of the research effort and traces the mutually conditioning interactions among elements in the polity that tend more commonly to be dichotomized into abstractions like "state and society", "structure and culture"' (Shue 1988: 4). That is, a static viewpoint and rigid dichotomization will not work, and, instead, sufficient attention should be paid to the developmental process and the interactions between seemingly dichotomized elements. He labelled this approach the study of the *social intertexture* of Chinese politics, and suggested that the analyst continually juxtaposes the finest of complex local detail with the most sweeping of discernible social trends and patterns. In the following chapters, I endeavour to capture the process of development and at the same time ascend from the local to the national level.

This chapter is the first part on BLSCC. It consists of three parts. First, it introduces the general crime policy, 'Comprehensive Management of Social Order' (CMSO). Particularly, it discusses the prevention prong of CMSO: the strike-hard campaign. Second, based on the official reports, it outlines the features of BLSCC and its developmental process, showing that BLSCC is moralistic and politically driven. Third, it briefly discusses the outcome of BLSCC, as assessed by the local authority. It should be pointed out that this chapter and the next one draw heavily on the official reports and academic output in Chinese. At certain points, I particularly keep the original flavour by literal translation. Notwithstanding my great efforts to convey the original meaning of certain terms, slogans, and jargon, some of those translations still sound a bit awkward in English.

CMSO: a duality

With the economy developing and living standards improving in the early 1980s, the Chinese leadership increasingly and anxiously perceived the threat of 'spiritual pollution'. Thus, there was a need to avoid the traps supposedly experienced by advanced Western societies, a high material standard in tandem with a low spiritual level, as demonstrated, for example, by a high crime level. This heralds the inception of the theory of 'two civilizations' in 1982. The theory dictates that socialist construction should consist of two interdependent parts: construction of material civilization and construction of spiritual civilization. While 'material civilization' represents economic growth and its concomitant material manifestations, 'spiritual civilization' consists of two aspects, 'the cultural and the ideological permeating and promoting each other' (see Bakken 2000). It is precisely under this atmosphere of the construction of spiritual civilization that there emerged the general crime control policy 'Comprehensive Management of Social Order' (*Shehui Zhi'an Zhonghe Zhili*, hereafter CMSO)[1] and the *yanda* (strike-hard) campaign.

CMSO, as a general policy for fighting crime and maintaining public order, emerged in the early 1980s when the Party and central government were stricken by anxiety over rising crime. It was initiated in a forum, 'Public Security of the Five Cities of Beijing, Tianjin, Shanghai, Guangzhou, and Wuhan', convened by the CCP Political and Legal Committee in 1981. Later, in June 1981, the CCP Central Committee endorsed the minutes of the forum, and it was explicitly stressed that, 'to fundamentally improve public security necessitates the engagement of the Party Committees at all levels and the full implementation of "comprehensive management"'. In January 1982, 'The CCP Directive on Strengthening Political and Legal Work' was promulgated, which further stipulated, 'to fundamentally improve public security entails the strengthening of the Party leadership, the involvement of the whole Party, and the earnest implementation of the "comprehensive management"'. In January 1991, with the approval of the CCP Central Committee, a meeting on the national comprehensive management of social order was held in Yantai, Shandong. In the meeting, the 'work guideline', 'guiding principle', 'work scope', 'leadership system', and 'work system' were endorsed. After the meeting, the CCP Central Committee and the State Council promulgated 'the Resolution on Comprehensive Management of Social Order'. On 2 March 1991, the National People's Congress (NPC) Standing Committee passed 'the Resolution on Comprehensive Management of Social Order'. According to a *Legal Daily* editorial by Zhong (1999), the two resolutions marked a milestone in the development of CMSO. On 21 March 1991, the Committee on Comprehensive Management of Social Order under the CCP Central Committee was established, with the responsibility of 'assisting the CCP Central Committee and the State Council to lead the national work on comprehensive management of social order'. A series of regulations and laws on CMSO was then promulgated by the Committee, the CCP Central Committee and the government at various levels (Lu and Zhao 1999; Zhong 1999).

For example, in Shenzhen, the Municipal Committee on CMSO was established in May 1991, with the Municipal Deputy Party Secretary and Chairman of the Municipal People's Congress Li Youwei as its director. Later in 1991, the Committee on CMSO at the district level was established. On 16 September 1994, 'the Shenzhen SEZ Ordinance on CMSO' was endorsed by the Shenzhen People's Congress and took effect on 1 November 1994. On 23 January 1995, 'the Implementation Measures on the Leadership Responsibility System of CMSO in Shenzhen' was promulgated, and on 1 December 1995, 'the Assessment Measures on the Leadership Responsibility System of CMSO in Shenzhen' was issued, which was further revised on 4 November 1996 (see SZPLY 1996–7).

According to Lu and Zhao (1999), three problems remain, although a substantial number of laws and regulations have been made following the two resolutions in 1991. First, with the pace of social and economic development accelerating, the two 'resolutions' are outdated, as they fail to reflect the new social and economic characteristics and to take into account the advances in criminological research. Second, at the national level, most of the by-laws on CMSO were made by the Committee on CMSO at various levels, but it is hard to implement the by-laws because the Committee on CMSO has no legislative authority. Third, by-laws on CMSO at the local level are simply repetitions of those at the national level and thus do not cater for the local situation of public security. There has also been a heated debate around the issue of CMSO legislation at both the central level and the local level (see Wang *et al.* 1998: Chapter 6).

As discussed above, CMSO was launched in tandem with the launch of the construction of spiritual civilization, and, more accurately, it was supposed to serve the interest of the latter, especially, given the holistic nature of CMSO. Ever since, the intimate connection between the two has persisted. For example, according to Gui (1998: 35), in practice, there was an inverse relationship between the level of the construction of spiritual civilization and the amount of crime. Thus, for him, the construction of spiritual civilization plays an important role in crime prevention, and strengthening the former will improve the latter.

Bakken observed that the word 'comprehensive' is often used in the campaigns for spiritual civilization, and that CMSO reflects a wish to coordinate and systematize old approaches to control in a comprehensive, modern, organized way (Bakken 2000: 254). As noted by Tanner (1999), the Chinese theorization and conceptualization of CMSO reflects 'an eclectic combination' of a series of theories, including Marxism, Mao Zedong's theory of contradictions, concepts of disease drawn from Chinese medicine, systems theory, information theory, and management theory. According to him, a certain logic underlies the apparent eclecticism. First, crime is a systemic problem that warrants strategies addressing the offenders' whole life circumstances and whole social milieu. That means all social forces should be mobilized to tackle crime. Second, CMSO has to be rationalized by the 'national status quo' (*guo qing*); that is, China is still in the preliminary stage of socialism.

Wang *et al.* (1998) deployed systems theory to argue that CMSO is a 'social systematic project' and its long-term goal is to create a sound social environment for the reform and opening up, and the construction of socialist modernization. Its essence is that under the leadership of the CCP and government, all social forces should be mobilized to enhance public security. This is to prevent and reduce lawbreaking and crime and to maintain social stability, by combining the speciality of the police and other criminal justice agencies with the contribution of the masses, and by employing political, economic, administrative, educational, cultural and legal means (see e.g. SZPLY 1996–9; Wang *et al.* 1998).

CMSO has been in effect for nearly two decades, surviving and attesting to several 'waves' of crime and crime policies in China. According to Wang *et al.* (1998), the basic experiences of CMSO lie in the following four aspects: (1) to uphold the leadership of CCP and government; (2) to adhere to the responsibility system of 'whoever is in charge is held responsible'; (3) to stick to the principle of 'treating both the causes (*biao*) and the symptoms (*ben*) but emphasizing the treatment of the symptoms';[2] and (4) to follow the credo of 'incorporating the specialty (of the criminal justice system) and the mass line'.

Lu and Zhao (1999) identified certain problems in the implementation of the CMSO. First, it does not cover the prevention and punishment of 'economic crime of misconduct in office' (*zhiwu jingji fanzui*) and 'crime of misconduct in office' (*zhiwu fanzui*). They pointed out that the target of the strike-hard campaign was 'street crime'. For example, the first strike-hard campaign in 1983 targeted such criminal offences as homicide, injury (aggravated assault), explosion, arson, hooliganism, trafficking in human beings, robbery, manufacturing and trafficking of drugs, highway robbery, larceny, smuggling, and other such offences. However, 'economic crimes of misconduct in office' (such as corruption, bribery, misappropriation of public funds, etc.) and 'crimes of misconduct in office' (such as embezzlement, dereliction of duty, and false confession by force) are dealt with by the 'anticorruption' campaign. Thus, they proposed that these types of crime should be included in CMSO. Second, in practice, CMSO did not balance the relationship between 'social prevention' and 'general prevention by criminal justice', and tended to prioritize the latter by launching strike-hard campaigns one after another. In other words, they are strongly opposed to the overemphasis of crime prevention through law enforcement.

Regarding the second point, they are not alone. The guiding principle of CMSO was summarized in six words 'strike, prevent, educate, manage, construct, and reform'. Basically, the six aspects could be put under a duality of 'punitive' (strike and reform) and 'preventive' (prevent, educate, manage, and construct) approaches. Regarding the relationship between the get-tough prong of 'punishment' and the soft prong of 'prevention', the policy is supposed to be 'combining both punishment and prevention with the focus placed on prevention' (*da fang bingju, yi fang wei zhu*).[3] However, in reality, the punitive aspect overwhelms the preventive one and even predominates, primarily because of the abrupt increase of crime. The following discussion seeks to sketch briefly the strike-hard campaign in China, as a stark contrast to the preventive aspect, epitomized in BLSCC to be introduced in the next section.

Strike-hard

In the West, the Chinese anticrime campaign *'yanda'* (strike hard) might conjure up a grisly picture of violation of human rights, wide use of the death penalty, and inadequacies of the criminal justice system (see e.g. Stern 1997; Tanner 1999; Hood and Hoyle 2008). Here the focus is on its punitive nature in contrast to the preventive aspect of CMSO. The first national strike-hard campaign was launched in China in 1983. However, as noted by Tanner (1999), the initiation of the two campaigns ('severe and rapid punishment' in 1981 and 'strike severe blows against serious economic crime' in 1982) set the stage for the launch of the first *yanda*. To facilitate or legalize the two campaigns, altogether four decisions by the NPC Standing Committee were introduced to revise the criminal law and the criminal procedure law.[4]

The first *yanda* started in late July and early August 1983 and lasted until around late 1986 and early 1987. Altogether, three battles were launched to 'swiftly and severely'[5] punish criminals. Again the NPC Standing Committee promulgated two 'decisions' as its legal basis,[6] albeit not until over a month into the campaign, as noted by Tanner (1999).

The main targets of the strike-hard campaign included: (1) hooligan gang elements (*liumang tuanhuo fenzi*); (2) serial offenders; (3) murderers, arsonists, bombers, poisoners, drug traffickers, rapists, robbers and persons guilty of serious theft; (4) traffickers in women and children; criminals who force, lure or shelter women in prostitution; or criminals who produce, reproduce, or sell publications, pictures or recordings of reactionary or pornographic content; (5) members of reactionary secret societies currently engaged in wrecking activities; (6) persons escaped from labour reform camps, persons released from labour reform or labour re-education who commit new crimes, and other persons under warrant of arrest for criminal activities; (7) active counter-revolutionary elements who write counter-revolutionary slogans and pamphlets, letters of counter-revolutionary content or anonymous letters, and other remnants of Lin Biao and the Gang of Four currently engaged in wrecking activities (see Tanner 1999: 90). According to Yang (1996), apart from criminal offences, it also covered some public security offences such as undermining public security and fraud by superstitious means.

The second national strike-hard campaign was launched in April 1996, with the major task of 'catching active criminals, clearing big cases, catching fugitives, and ferreting out gangs'. It comprised of three sequential 'battles' (28 April, 15 May and 30 June). By the end of the year 1996, it was still under way and the CCP Central Committee ordered that in areas with the strike-hard targets basically achieved, the next step should focus on regular strike-hard battles (Liu and Tang 1997: 163). The targeted crimes include serious robbery; theft; prostitution and patronage prostitution; manufacture and trafficking of pornography; manufacturing, consuming and trafficking drugs; trafficking women and children; homicide, illegal manufacture of guns and ammunition, explosives, and controlled knives; gambling, secret-society-type gangs, and hooliganism (Yang 1996).

The third national 'strike-hard' campaign was started in April 2001, and lasted for two years. It targeted criminal gangs of 'secret society nature' and hooliganism; serious violent crimes such as causing explosions, homicide, robbery, and kidnapping; and serial crime which affects the public's feeling of safety such as theft (see Zhang 2002). Trevaskes (2003) finds that although operations are more sophisticated and specialized, the broad strategies of the first months of the third strike-hard campaign did not differ significantly in approach from those employed in the first campaign.

It would be misleading to think that the strike-hard campaign is limited to the three national ones. As the then Premier Li Peng declared in the 1997 National Political and Legal Work Meeting, *yanda* should adopt three forms: (1) 'central and uniform action', (2) 'special battles', and (3) 'regular *yanda*' (see SZPLY 1998: 205). Every year sees one or more 'special battles' (*zhuanxiang douzheng*) or seasonal 'offensives' (*gongshi*), at the behest of the Ministry of Public Security, the State Council, or the CCP Central Committee. To take Shenzhen as an illustrative example, there were five 'special battles' and 'uniformed actions' in 1995. These are described as the winter crime-eliminating battle; the spring *yanda* offensive (March–May); uniformed action to ban drugs (March-September); strike hard at crime involving guns and special battles of confiscating illegal weapons and ammunition (20 August to end of the year); and strike hard at prostitution and patrons of prostitution, and clear up entertainment venues. In 1996, there were three battles, including strike hard at 'gangs and bandits'; the strike-hard 'great war'; and the winter action of 'welcome 1997 and secure peace'. The year 1997 saw the following battles: winter action of 'welcome 1997 and secure peace'; 'one-hundred-day' strike hard and clear-up action; 'great patrolling by an alliance of ten thousand police and public'; 'double-celebration' clear-up uniformed action, 'three-greats' (great patrolling, great inspection, and clearing serious cases), 'welcome spring action', and 'nine-month special battle to ban drugs'. In 1998, there were 'uniformed action to strike hard at robbers and bandits on the highway; anti-'three-theft' special battle; summer offensive of fighting secret societies and evil forces, and strike hard at robbery and snatching; and special battle of striking hard at smuggling, theft, and robbery of automobiles' (SZPLY 1996–9). Since 1999, at the national level, there have been 'Pursuit Targeted at Criminal Fugitives across China' and 'Nationwide Combat against Abduction' in 1999, 'Wipe Out Pornography and Strike Hard at Illegal Publications' in 2000, and 'Strike Hard at Economic Crime' in 2001. During the first half of 2002, a battle of 'Strike Hard at Secret Society and Wipe Out Evil Forces' was launched, in which 229 police officers died on duty and 2,826 were injured nationwide.[7] On 17 July 2002, the Ministry of Public Security called upon the PSBs nationwide to 'Strike hard at Robbery and Snatching'.

The first national strike-hard campaign was under the auspices of Deng Xiaoping. According to Gong (1998), the concept of *yanda* constitutes one of the main points of 'Deng Xiaoping Thoughts' in that it is closely related to the People's Democratic Dictatorship in the new era (to treat serious criminal offenders as the targets of the People's Democratic Dictatorship). Hence, it is intrinsically related to the construction of the legal system, both aspects reflecting Deng's 'socialism with Chinese characteristics'. *Yanda* articulates Deng's 'two hands' policy: one hand with material civilization, and the other with spiritual civilization; one hand with reform and opening-up, and the other with striking at crime. The mooring of *yanda* with 'the People's Democratic Dictatorship' and the official endorsement of *yanda* by the Party demonstrate that *yanda* is fundamentally political in nature, although it is regarded by most academics and criminal justice researchers in China as a criminal justice policy (see Traveskes 2007).

Native Chinese scholars have engaged in research and debates on the *yanda* campaign. For example, three reports from the 'Research Team on *Yanda* Theory and Practice' were published in the 1998 *Journal of the Chinese People's Public Security University*. One of the reports analysed *yanda*'s 'social background' (Tian 1998), and declared that *yanda* is warranted and justified because crime is unavoidable and will possibly increase further. The 'historical background' of *yanda* is determined by socialism at its preliminary stage. The 'economic background' of *yanda* includes the coexistence of multiple economic elements, the distribution system of coexistence of multiple individual income distribution methods, the unbalanced economic development between regions, and the difficulties facing state-owned-enterprises. The 'social-political background' comprises numerous threats such as infiltration, subversion, sabotage by both internal and external hostile forces, the emergence and spreading of corruption in society, increases in 'group incidents' triggered by various internal contradictions among the people, the influence of religious and nationalist splitting activities, the backwardness of the democratic and legal systems, and the inadequacies of the social system in the transition from the planned economy to the market economy. The 'social cultural background' covers the changes in the people's value system and the influences of new social thinking, influences from feudalism and capitalist corrupted thoughts, and influences from the thought of bourgeois liberalization. The 'social security background' mainly lies in the dramatic increase of criminal offences, including serious felony, homicide, and criminals' deliberate revenge against society (e.g. through bombing, rampant gang crime and hooliganism); economic crime; and 'pornography, gambling and drugs'. This acceptance of the existence of crime in a socialist society signifies a significant shift in the discourse about crime in China, apart from justifying the strike-hard approach to crime.

Throughout the years, the formula for *yanda* goes according to the following script: at a certain point of time crime becomes intolerable and public outrage becomes aroused. This leads to an appeal for an anticrime campaign from the Party or government, which in turn causes all government agencies, departments, the media and the masses to be mobilized against crime, with 'command centres', targets and tasks established. This is followed by all-out actions, including reporting crime by the public, large-scale arrests, mass trials and executions justified under the rubric of the idiom 'killing the chickens to scare the monkeys'. In turn, this finally leads to the end of the campaign with the great effects publicized and 'model' units and individuals commended. Then everything returns to normal to await yet another cycle of *yanda* battles.

Wang *et al.* (1998) identified the main problem of *yanda* practice. Principally, it lies in a simplistic understanding of *yanda*. They argued that the guidelines for *yanda* as a long-term strategy, as stipulated in the CCP Central Committee 'decision' in 1983, were simply understood as regularly organizing *yanda* campaigns. Thus, *yanda* became 'simple strike' and 'strike for the sake of strike', with little or no 'comprehensive effects'. Moreover, the misunderstanding of *yanda* action led to a lack of any feasibility study on *yanda* strategy and over-expectations of *yanda*'s impact (to quote the authors, 'with the intention of striking everything but striking nothing'), which the authors regarded as a passive response to crime. In other words, *yanda* is a reactive rather than proactive strategy. According to them, the *yanda* strategy was established under special circumstances, including an 'abnormal situation of public security' during a period of public outrage over crime and a strong appeal for a crack down because of the chaos caused by weak 'dictatorship organs'.

Second, they critique the actual formulization of *yanda* plans. On one hand, centralized uniform battles become the fixed and only formula of *yanda* strategy, leading to lack of creativeness and flexibility and an inability to adjust to current complex and new situations and problems, especially as manifested at different local circumstances. *Yanda* thus became fitful and superficial, and as a result it 'cast the net wide but caught only the minnows'. Its emphasis on 'swift battle and swift victory' caused it to be detached from other public security strategies, and thus it only had short-term effects at best. The fitful *yanda* campaigns also caused vicious circles, which led to local police officers' inattentiveness to grass-roots work. In addition, the implementation of *yanda* plans became a formality. This was because the process became rigid and predictable from following established plans: from holding assignment meetings, to mobilizing the masses, to investigating and solving cases, to sudden efforts of clearing up and arrest, and finally public trials. Predictably, criminals are called to surrender, and these efforts always occurred around the time of festivals or holidays. Criminals could readily grasp this formality and came up with their own countermeasures such as escaping or hiding out for a temporary period and then coming back to commit crime again.

Third, *yanda* was governed by an excessive singularity of goals. To strike at crime became the only goal of *yanda*, and this weakened the preventive and managerial aspect of public security management. Moreover, the number of criminals caught became the only criteria of measuring the success of *yanda*. This led to three problems: (1) criminals from routine actions are accumulated and included in the *yanda* statistics, leading to the odd result that the number of criminals caught in one single 'battle' exceeded the total number apprehended over several months or even a year; (2) the inattentiveness to deep-rooted criminal conditions and the sweeping actions against the most obvious 'illegal elements' led to the arrest of a large number of public security offenders with little or no criminal guilt, litigants of economic disputes and civil cases, thus only inflating the numbers of criminal elements caught; (3) the single pursuit of the number of suspects caught caused the neglect of investigation, interrogation and corroboration of evidence.

The above criticisms focus on the formality, inefficiency, and local-level manipulation in the process of *yanda*. But, in terms of inefficiency, the local scholarship focuses, it seems, upon the problems in implementing *yanda*, with little challenge to the fundamental question of whether *yanda* could really deter and prevent crime. To use the terminology of programme evaluation, these evaluations focus on 'implementation failures', not 'theoretical failures'. As revealed by the state-compiled criminal statistics, crime did not recede regardless of the successive waves of strike-hard campaigns. This is consistent with the findings in the Western literature regarding the effectiveness of aggressive, deterrent enforcement, such as the 'three strikes and you are out' policy. One of the main targets in the first *yanda* campaign was the newly emerging gang crimes and gang leaders, with the aim of preventing further recruitment of juveniles and wiping out gangs by removing the most active gang members. But the operation of criminal networks is not clearly known: whether the void left by the removed gang leaders later would be filled by other members or gangs was seldom considered. It turned out that the criminal networks survived, the gangs multiplied, and there was a fall in the age of the youths involved. In 1986, a record-high figure of 93.3 per cent of all gang members were at the age of 25 and under, almost half of them under the age of 18, and in the late 1980s gang crime accounted for 60–70 per cent of all criminal offences in China (see Bakken 2000: 392). Bakken argued that the high proportion of criminal youth perhaps was due to the fact that their actions are generally more publicly accessible and observable than those of adults and that they are less experienced and more easily caught. In spite of the officially claimed successes, the decomposition of aggregate crime data reveals that 'the decreasing crime rate over the short run was due entirely to a fall in theft and petty crime… serious theft tripled from 1982 to 1986 and violent crime increased' (Bakken 2000: 393). All of these prompted Bakken to conclude that *yanda* 'started as a political campaign, motivated not by increasing crime rates but by the need to do something about the prevailing general social disorder and the public's loss of confidence in the police force' (2000: 392).[8]

Although the range of *yanda* targets by and large reflects the new development of crime in the new era, the *yanda* campaign, just like CMSO generally (see Lu and Zhao 1999 above), did not cover corruption and other misconduct committed by Party and state officials, such as illegal detention and interrogation under torture (see Tanner 1999: 90). Besides, one of the hallmarks of *yanda* is to 'jointly handle cases' (*lianhe ban'an*), whereby the police, prosecution, and courts, which are supposedly independent, work together to render 'severe and swift' punishment. This greatly damages the integrity of the laws and the criminal justice system, and exposes them to the possibility of miscarriage of justice. This is one of the most vehement protests against *yanda* by critics outside the PRC (Tanner 1999; Tanner 2000; Trevaskes 2003, 2007; Bakken 2004).

Native commentators also pointed out that *yanda* leads to an overemphasis on punishment at the expense of prevention in CMSO. Sometimes, it went so far that the community-based prevention in China, which once fascinated Western observers, was pre-empted by *yanda*. Thus, grass-roots work, and mass organizations are neglected, which makes the public security work like 'water without source, and trees without roots' (Wang *et al.* 1998). This runs counter to the CMSO guideline of 'combining both punitive and preventive methods with the focus on the latter'. There is a suggestion from a semiotic point of view that 'combining *da* (punishment) and *fang* (prevention) should be changed to 'combining *fang* (prevention) and *da* (punishment)', with the argument that this change is not simply reversing the sequence of the two terms but reflects the relationship between dealing with crime's root causes and dealing with crime per se (Lu and Zhao 1998). While rhetorical debate is one thing, practice is another thing. The Chinese government has been caught in the quagmire of balancing the two aspects of CMSO in the aim of handling rising crime.

In contrast to *yanda*, the prevention side of CMSO, in essence, entails an all-encompassing control net, composed of both formal and informal institutions. This is in line with the characteristics of social control in China presented in the last chapter. While the conclusion drawn in the last chapter on the intrinsically community-based social control in China is premised on a state-planned economy and its corresponding social institutions such as *hukou, danwei,* etc., the general policy of CMSO emerged during a different social circumstance of dramatic economic reconstruction, greater population mobility, and changing social relationships in the wake of the reform and opening up. Thus, to be 'comprehensive', CMSO sounds 'ambitious' and 'unrealistic'. The BLSCC programme in Shenzhen, with a focus on prevention, has been claimed to be 'the carrier of CMSO' (SZPLY 1996–9) and 'a community prevention program with Chinese characteristics' (e.g. Cao 1997: 180). The next section moves to BLSCC in Shenzhen to investigate how crime prevention operates in Shenzhen, the forefront city of economic reform and opening-up.

BLSCC and its development in Shenzhen

Shenzhen's rapid development runs parallel to an increasingly serious crime problem. The solution is premised on the consensus reached by the Party committee and government in Shenzhen that 'from an objective point of view the increase in social order problems is unavoidable, and no one can reverse this inexorable trend. What can and should be done is keep the degree of increase under control, so as not to endanger social development and stability. This is the throes of social progress' (Huang and Luo 1997: 5). To manifest this understanding of crime on one hand, and to respond to the call from the central government to apply the CMSO approach to crime on the other, the BLSCC programme gradually took shape in Shenzhen. As Chan (1993: 2) observed, the 'small is beautiful' and 'small and complete' approaches to development in China were regarded as great successes. To a certain degree, this amounts to a reversal of the 'big' 'collective' approach widely adopted in the Mao period, in which the collective's responsibility was interpreted, consciously or unconsciously, as holding little individual responsibility and hence low individual incentive. The division of the collective into small entities, epitomized in the 'household responsibility system' in the rural reform in the early 1980s, clearly designates individual responsibilities that are in turn directly linked to individual rewards. This greatly motivated individual incentives, as demonstrated in practice.

In Shenzhen, the demarcation of little communities is based on convenience or original geographic boundaries. There are eight types of little communities in Shenzhen: (1) multistorey residential areas; (2) natural villages; (3) industrial areas; (4) blocks of high-rise buildings; (5) warehouse areas; (6) tourist areas; (7) multiple-function areas; and (8) schools, hospitals and government offices (SZPLY 1999). A 'little, safe and civilized community' (LSCC) apparently is two-pronged: safety and civilization. In terms of safety, residents have feelings of safety, very few serious public security cases occur, and general public security cases may be kept under timely control. In terms of civilization, it includes politics, economy, culture, education, a hygiene and health service, etc. The two prongs are interdependent, and neither may be overemphasized at the expense of the other (Wang *et al*. 1998). To be more specific, in a LSCC in Shenzhen, there is strong conformity to law and regulation, the public order is good, the degree of civilization is high, the social morale is high, the environment is beautiful, and the neighbourhood relationship is harmonious (Huang and Luo 1997). For a little community to be eligible to be an LSCC, it must meet certain criteria and go through a complicated rating process by designated agencies. The rating classifies the communities into model, advanced, pass or failure, on a yearly, instead of a one-off, basis. If a community fails to meet the standards in the second year, it is stripped of the original level. It can also strive to upgrade to a higher level in the subsequent years.

The BLSCC programme underwent a gradual process of development over several years. Table 6.1 summarizes its development from 1992 to 1998. It was a process from planting the seeds, to budding, to blossoming and to bearing fruit. For the second three-year plan, the guiding principle is to enhance 'large area stability' through maintaining 'little community peace'; that is, to ascend from building 'little communities' into 'large areas' and even the whole city. This is hailed as a significant step forward in further maintaining 'safety' and 'civilization' by keeping the momentum of BLSCC.

Table 6.1 Development of BLSCC in Shenzhen 1992–1998

'Seed'	1992	pilot study in Xianxi village and Nanshan village
	1993	essential concepts of 'little', 'safety' and 'civilization' emerged
'Bud'	1994	decision on the first three-year plan was made in June
'Blossom'	1995	'Five Standards on LSCC', including 'Eight Subjects and Forty-five Measurement Indicators', was promulgated
First three-year plan	1996	the above regulation was revised
	1997	the Notice on BLSCC Funding, the principle of 'four ones'
		By the end of 1997, 1,499 LSCCs, coverage of 972.1 km^2 and 3.35 million people, coverage rates of 50% and 92%, respectively
'Fruit'	1998	Three regulations on management of floating population were promulgated
Start of the second three-year plan		By the end of 1998, 1,699 LSCCs, coverage of 1,042 km^2 and 3.58 million people, coverage rates of 53% and 94%, respectively.

Officially claimed outcome of BLSCC in Shenzhen

Whenever a campaign was completed, the government would report, via the mass media, success stories in rather general terms such as 'greatly improved', 'markedly decreased', 'substantial achievement', and 'our investigation shows that the masses are very satisfied with the campaign', etc. Occasionally, surveys were conducted, although their methodological integrity was not clear and the results always corroborated the success stories. For example, as Bakken (2000: 392) discussed, in the *yanda* campaign a 1984 investigation of neighbourhoods all over China gave Chinese criminologists and politicians a reassurance of success. Turning to BLSCC in Shenzhen, the official documents are full of yearly achievements with concrete numbers, such as how many communities were rated 'pass' or 'model', how much money was invested, how much hardware was installed, and how many people were organized, among other things.

Two surveys were also conducted by the government. The first was conducted in 1995, and I tried to obtain the detailed methodology, to no avail. The original texts read as follows:

> In 1995, the city Party Committee and government investigated the LSCCs twice. 2,100 residents were interviewed and over 80 group interviews were held. The public reported that since the initiation of the program, neighbor relationships became smoothened, the association between the military, the police and the public became closer, residents' awareness of the legal system was increased, and quality of civilization was improved. Statistics showed that disputes of various kinds decreased over 80%, compared with that of the same period prior to the initiation of the program. (Huang and Luo 1997: 6; verbatim translation)

The second appeared in the speech by Deputy City Party Secretary Li Ronggeng at the summary meeting for the first three-year plan in April 1998.

> One of the achievements lies in the marked improvement of public security. In all the little communities built so far, all kinds of cases decreased 50% compared with the same period prior to their building. Inside 848 little communities, no criminal cases occurred. All these built a foundation for the stability and betterment of public security citywide. The masses' feeling

of safety has greatly increased. We conducted a survey with a sample of over 30,000 people, and 95% of the masses and foreign businessmen answered that they have feeling of safety. (SZPLY 1999: 225)

The yearly achievements are based on the information submitted by the local communities. Given the 'responsibility system', it is obvious that the local leaders have a strong desire to portray a positive picture. The surveys were conducted by the official agencies, and no independent parties were involved.

Notes

1 It is variously translated as 'a comprehensive approach towards public security' (Fang 1988), or 'comprehensive improvement of public order' (Jiang and Dai 1990), or 'comprehensive management of public security' (Tanner 1999).
2 Both *biao* and *ben* are frequently used in the Chinese literature. But it is difficult to find English equivalents to convey accurately the meaning of the two terms. *Biao* literally refers to the tips of branches of a tree, and *ben* the roots of a tree. I find that normally they are translated into the 'symptoms' and 'causes', respectively, inadvertently relating them to the 'disease' model (of crime and crime prevention in this context). In discussing the social control perspective contained in the discourse of moral education in China, Bakken (2000: 86) provided a succinct observation of *biao* and *ben*, together with his way of translating the two words, 'Courts and prisons are the outward signs (*biao*) of control, while moral or ideological education is the basis (*ben*) of social control'.
3 While I consider the preventive and punitive aspects as two components of CMSO, Tanner (1999) contrasted CMSO with *yanda*, with the former being preventive and the latter punitive. If at the early stage of CMSO more focus is put on prevention, CMSO tended to combine the two aspects of *'da'* (punishment) and *'fang'* (prevention) since 1991, when the two provisions clarified certain important aspects of CMSO. My review of the Chinese literature seems to confirm this.
4 Three decisions were introduced for the first campaign: (1) the 'decision regarding the question of approval of cases involving death sentences' transferred the power to approve death sentences in cases other than counter-revolution and corruption from the Supreme People's Court in Beijing to the higher (provincial level) people's courts; (2) the 'decision regarding the handling of offenders undergoing labour reform or labour re-education who escape or commit new crimes' provided that escaped inmates might have their sentences increased by up to seven years and

allowed 'increased punishment' (*jiazhong chufa*) for escaped inmates found guilty of new offences; and (3) the 'decision regarding the question of time limits for handling of criminal cases' allowed the extension of time limits for investigation, prosecution and adjudication of criminal cases 'in remote areas for which transportation is inconvenient'. One decision was introduced for the second campaign: 'decisions regarding the severe punishment of criminals who seriously undermine the economy' increased the range of punishment for certain economic crimes (see Tanner 1999: 72–79).

5 Yang (1996) noted that in the first *yanda* the slogan was *according to law 'swiftly and severely'*, but in the second *yanda* it was *'according to law swiftly and severely'*. Yang (1996) interprets the shift of the inverted comma as reflecting more legal and regulative nature in the second *yanda*.

6 Firstly, the 'decision regarding the severe punishment of criminal elements who seriously endanger public security' revised the criminal law to allow punishment up to and including death for the offences of leading a hooligan group; causing intentional injury; injuring state personnel or civilians who expose or arrest criminals; leading a group engaging in the abduction and sale of people; illegal manufacture, trade, transport or theft of weapons or explosives; organization of sects or secret societies; the use of superstition to carry out counter-revolutionary activities; and luring or forcing women into prostitution or sheltering prostitutes. It also created a new offence of imparting knowledge of criminal methods, to be punished, depending to the circumstances, from less than five years of imprisonment to life imprisonment or death. Secondly, the 'decision regarding the procedure for rapid adjudication of cases involving criminal elements who seriously endanger public security' stated that in serious criminal cases the people's courts need not be bound by the requirements of Article 110 of the Criminal Procedure Law, which stipulated that the defendant must be notified of the charges made against him seven days prior to trial, and that defendants, witnesses, defence lawyers and interpreters be summoned or subpoenaed at least three days prior to trial. It also shortened the time limit for filing an appeal from ten to three days (see Tanner 1999: 92–93).

7 See a report stating '229 police officers died on duty during the first half of this year' at http://jczs.sina.com.cn, visited on 25 July 2002.

8 Contrary to the common understanding that the first *yanda* campaign was launched to combat rising crime, Bakken (2000) noted that in September 1983, the crime rate was in fact the lowest since 1979. Tanner (1999) concurred with him in this point. Interestingly, Bakken (2000) drew heavily on the approaches of social construction and symbolism in his analysis of *yanda*. For him, rising crime is officially constructed, and *yanda*'s symbolic meaning lies in the fact that 'the criminal and his destruction become a symbol of both transgression and defence of social and cultural boundaries' (2000: 397).

Chapter 7

Building little, safe and civilized communities in Shenzhen: community crime prevention with Chinese characteristics?

Part Two: BLSCC measures

This chapter is the second part on BLSCC. It mainly introduces BLSCC measures, including organizational features, safety measures, civilization measures, and the rating system. The grouping of measures is convenient for understanding the nature of BLSCC. The categories are not mutually exclusive. Instead, some of them are interlinked, as indicated below. Second, based on Chapters 6 and 7, it discusses BLSCC's officially claimed 'Chinese characteristics', identifies the differences from and similarities to the social control mechanisms in effect prior to the full-swing development of the market economy, and examines the role social capital plays in BLSCC.

BLSCC measures

Organizational features

Organizational features of BLSCC mainly include ideological mooring, the leadership responsibility system, and mass prevention and mass management.

Ideological mooring
At the outset, BLSCC emerged from the broader perspectives of the construction of spiritual civilization and the general crime policy of CMSO. In fact, it gained legitimacy and momentum by anchoring itself to the latter two doctrines in the socialist system. For example, on 25 March 1997, Deputy Secretary of the City Party Committee Li Ronggeng declared,

In 1996, BLSCC in Shenzhen has achieved great effects, which enhanced the improvement of public security, promoted the development of the construction of socialist spiritual civilization, and provided a stable social and political environment for the reform and opening-up, and the economic construction. (SZPLY 1998: 208)

Therefore, BLSCC bears distinctive marks of the popular political ideology. Its slogans and methods are directly transplanted from the larger perspective, ranging from the leadership responsibility system, the principle of 'whoever takes charge is held responsible', 'learning from models', the setting of BLSCC yearly quotas, and the strategy of 'mass prevention and mass management', to the complicated rating system. As Gui (1998) argued, there is an inverse relationship between the construction of spiritual civilization and the level of crime. Empirical studies also support the above statement. In one survey, a normal group of young people is compared with a group of criminal youths in their answers to the question, 'Has the street or village where you live developed the building of civilized street or village activities?' Four times as many (44 per cent versus 10 per cent) from the normal group identified the existence of 'civilized street' or 'civilized village' activities (see Bakken 2000). As Bakken (2000: 345) pointed out, 'Unfortunately, the data do not permit us to look for spurious findings or flaws in the methodology used.'

Leadership responsibility system
The leadership responsibility system is regarded as the key to CMSO and the maintenance of stability. In the official reports on BLSCC, it was always listed as the first contributing factor to the successful implementation of BLSCC. It was made into law and is directly associated with the leaders' year-end assessment, eligibility for 'model' titles, and promotion.

The leadership responsibility system was stated as one of the important guarantees to strengthen CMSO in 1995. Its core is listed as follows: 'to maintain public security is one of the official goals for the No.1 leaders of the Party and the Government at all levels and for the leaders who take direct charge of public security. It is one of the important parts of their assessment, and is one of the important conditions for their promotion, reappointment, and eligibility for "models" and "rewards"' (SZPLY 1996: 120).

The system was implemented according to the following steps. First, there was the formulation of regulations. In 1995, two regulations were formulated: 'Shenzhen City Implementation Measures on the Leadership Responsibility System of CMSO' and 'Shenzhen City Assessment Measures on the Leadership Responsibility System of CMSO'. Second, there was the determination of persons responsible for public security. The top leaders of the Party and the government at all levels are the first responsible persons, who take *general* responsibility for public security of their jurisdictions, and the leaders who take charge of public security at the equivalent levels are the second responsible persons, who take *direct* responsibility for public security of their jurisdictions. Third, there was the signing of contracts. On 1 March 1995, a mobilization meeting was held on 'social and environmental comprehensive management'. At the meeting, the City Party Secretary signed contracts on CMSO with the responsible persons from the districts and those from the departments directly affiliated to the City Party Committee and Government. By the end of April 1995, all the levels of the Party Committee and Government had signed contracts with their lower levels. Fourth, there was inspection and assessment. All the assessment work followed the steps stipulated in the above second regulation on 'assessment measures'. Every higher level assessed the performance of its lower level. To ensure the smooth running of the assessment, at the city level an assessment team led by the Deputy Party Secretary was formed, and those units that shoulder major responsibilities for CMSO were designated as key assessment targets. During the same year, the principle of 'whoever takes charge is held responsible' was followed to manage the 'special professions and public entertainment venues' (SZPLY 1996: 43).

During the first and second half of 1996, respectively, two assessments were conducted on the districts and those departments and units directly affiliated to the city government. For the second assessment, the 'assessment measures' and 'the scoring standards' were reformulated. The findings from the assessments emphasized the following five aspects. Firstly, leaders at all levels had placed great emphasis on the work of CMSO, and worked out general plans, yearly plans and implementation arrangement, and had come up with timely solutions to the difficulties and problems emerging during the process of CMSO and BLSCC. Secondly, relevant offices and personnel on CMSO had been set up. Thirdly, internal security systems and organizations of 'mass prevention and mass management' had been strengthened, and the crime rate of the work unit employees had fallen. Fourthly, great efforts had been put into BLSCC. Fifthly, all forces had formed a synergy to support the 'strike-hard' campaign and placed foremost importance on stability. Meanwhile problems had been identified. In addition, 'model' individuals, units and collectives had been rewarded (SZPLY 1997: 113).

The strengthening of the leadership responsibility system had direct bearing on BLSCC. The implementation of BLSCC was one of the important items by which to assess the leaders. The city Party committee and government announced 'suggestions on further strengthening BLSCC' and the leading structure and personnel for BLSCC were further substantiated. In May alone, two meetings were held on BLSCC to further strengthen the leadership responsibility system for BLSCC. Fifteen major leaders from the city Party committee and government each took responsibilities for two little communities' BLSCC work. Leaders at various levels followed suit and altogether over 200 little communities were taken up (SZPLY 1997: 115).

Here it is worthwhile to briefly introduce the reformulated 'Shenzhen City Assessment Measures on Leadership Responsibility System for CMSO'. This included six chapters and 23 clauses. The six chapters were as follows: general principle; assessment organs; assessment scope; assessment criteria; assessment measures and requirements; and assessment scoring, rewarding and penalty. Three forms for assessment and scoring criteria were attached, respectively, for officials responsible for the public security of the districts, of the city organizations, and of the administrative institutions and enterprises of the first and second categories. In every form there were four items: 'leaders' emphasis', 'good organization', 'implementation of measures' and 'social effects'. There were slight differences between the three forms in the content of each item and the distribution of the scores (see SZPLY 1997: 224–232). A close examination of the third item of implementation measures in all three forms reveals that the content is mainly about BLSCC.

In 1997 and 1998, the leadership responsibility system was further implemented, yearly contracts were signed between leaders of various levels of the administrative hierarchy, assessments of the leaders were made according to the 'assessment measures', and model individuals and units were designated. In 1997, the assessment was in three steps: (1) on-site inspection, with such methods of 'listening, observing, asking, and discussing'; (2) leaders' presentations on CMSO at a special meeting; (3) comprehensive assessment according to the assessment criteria to determine model leaders and their units (SZPLY 1998: 135–136).

In 1998, President Jiang Zemin declared that 'whether the public security situation is good or bad in a particular place first and foremost hinges on the Party and government leaders of that place, especially the No. 1 leaders of the Party and government'. Thus, the Shenzhen leadership made great efforts to 'protect peace in a place'. At the eighth plenum of the second congress of the Shenzhen CCP, the effort 'to further improve public security' was made the goal for the next two years. After the plenum, on 20 August 1998, the Party committee and government promulgated 'the decision on strengthening CMSO and further improving public security'. Mobilization meetings were then organized, and more contracts were signed by leaders of various levels. In mid-1998, a large-scale inspection was conducted citywide. Of the 8,735 units inspected, 4,938 were good, 3,452 average, and 345 bad. Notices of rectification and revision were sent to the 'bad' units, with the areas for rectification and revision pointed out and a deadline set. At the end of the year, another around of assessment was carried out with a focus on the units for rectification and revision. From the assessment, three units (the Yida electronic factory, the New Yijia department store, and the Shungang branch of the Shenzhen Quarantine Bureau) were singled out for criticism and the responsible persons of the units were given 'one vote negating all'.[1] This was hailed as a major breakthrough for the CMSO assessment work (SZPLY 1999: 135). Besides, a series of local level leaders were reassigned because of their inadequacy in CMSO. Among them, a CMSO responsible person at the township level was deprived of his eligibility for provincial CMSO model individual, a local police chief was dismissed from office, and a local deputy police chief was given a reprimand and warning as a penalty.

To carry out the second three-year plan of the BLSCC, the Party and government leaders continued to take responsibility for the BLSCC programme in one, or more than one, little community. I obtained from the City Office of BLSCC a detailed booklet listing for the year 1998 the major leaders (at the city level and district level), the corresponding little communities in which they were willing to take responsibility for BLSCC, and the basic information on the little communities. Some of the little communities were in the process of building toward LSCC status, while others were striving for an upgrade along the four grades.

As acknowledged by Wang *et al.* (1998: 352), it is not easy to implement the leadership responsibility system, especially the 'one vote negating all' principle in practice. Firstly, it was easier to 'negate' the small units than the large units. For those small-scale factories or enterprises, if significant public security problems occurred, and all the 'negating' conditions were met, it was generally easy to apply the 'negating' principle. But for those large or medium-sized SOEs, it became very difficult. There was substantial local and senior intervention and resistance to assessment. Secondly, it was easier to 'negate' the units than the unit leaders. It was easier to cancel the eligibility of a work unit for CMSO model awards than to deprive the main leaders of a work unit, especially top party or government leaders of a large area, of the opportunity for model status, rewards, and promotion. These difficulties were corroborated in the interview with the Shenzhen officials. It is likely that it was more difficult in the private and joint enterprises because the negating system mainly relied on administrative disciplining. Thus, the difficulties became more acute in Shenzhen considering its large proportion of private or joint enterprises. This was evident in the regulation of 'assessment measures'. The three attached forms for assessment and scoring criteria targetted the governmental officials and the leaders of the enterprises of the first and second categories directly affiliated to the city government. In the regulation of 'assessment measures', clause 20 specifically states: 'If the leaders responsible for public security in foreign enterprises or private enterprises fail in the assessment, they are handled accordingly by the City or District CMSO committee in cooperation with relevant departments.' This is rather vague compared with the explicit penalty spelled out for the leaders by the three appended forms.

Another problem of the leadership responsibility system is that there is insufficient coordination and cooperation between different organs and agencies; that is, 'lack of synergy', as pointed out by the city mayor, Li Zibin, in 1997 (SZPLY 1998: 2006).

Mass prevention and mass management
'Mass prevention and mass management', literally means that the masses, all social forces, and all government agencies are mobilized to control and prevent crime. This is one of the important principles of CMSO, and is followed everywhere in China. For example, J. Yang (1998) reported that in Shanghai the mass prevention and mass management involved a force of 300,000 people, among whom there were over 7,800 workers' picket members, 14,300 'social order joint protection team' (*lianfang dui*)[2] members, and 7,000 service members for migrants' public security management. Citywide there were 3,460 neighbourhood committees, 3,001 village committees, 7,900 public security cadres affiliated to the enterprises or administrative institutions, 191,400 public security protection activists, and 27,000 security guards. Further, there was a 'social order joint protection'

force mainly comprised of over 300,000 retired people, with the cooperation of 80,000 employees and Party members. The task for this force was to voluntarily protect buildings, villages, and sentry posts. All of them contributed to a 'multilayered, all-weather and rural-urban network' of mass prevention and mass management.

In the BLSCC programme in Shenzhen, a similar network was formed involving all strata of the society. In Shenzhen, BLSCC in essence is mass work and grass-roots level work (Huang and Luo 1997). Although the popular understanding of the approach of mass prevention and mass management seems to emphasize the mobilization of all forces for joint action, a review of the literature reveals that in fact there is another dimension to this approach. This is to mobilize the individuals or work units to employ crime-prevention measures inside either households or work units, as represented by one of the BLSCC slogans, 'Manage well your own matters and watch your own doors.' This dimension constitutes one important part of the 'crime prevention is everyone's business' slogan and is also reflected in the situational measures to be introduced below.

As pointed out above, LSCC includes eight types and is not limited to residential areas. Thus, those little communities become the locus for people to organize together to tackle crime and disorder in that very location. In the process, the 'special organs' (police and other criminal justice agencies, neighbourhood committees, 'social order joint protection teams', mediation committees, public legal education teams, *bangjiao* teams, and internal public security agencies) combined forces with the public (residents, work unit employees, and students) in a concerted way. Meanwhile, the mass media, such as newspapers, and TV and radio stations, also joined in by publicizing the launch and progress of BLSCC, reporting model individuals or work units, and even covering certain problems, albeit less often. The media also played an important role in BLSCC activities. At both the district and city level, all the media channels were utilized to cover and publicize BLSCC. It is reported that by April 1998, 608 issues of the *BLSCC Special Newsletter* had been published by BLSCC offices at the city and district level, and 6,000 pieces of news coverage had been produced by the mass media channels at the city level, and over 30,000 pieces at the district level (SZPLY 1999: 227). That I was able to collect a substantial number of newspaper articles on the model community is clear evidence of the role of the mass media.

In 1995, the force of mass prevention and mass management reached 120,000. In implementing BLSCC, great efforts were made to link BLSCC with the routine running of local organizations and in the process the local organizations were further strengthened. By the end of 1997, '67 local Party Committees and 131 neighborhood committees were regulated; 6 neighborhood committees, 86 public security committees, 409 mediation teams, and 36 public security teams were newly established. There was an increase of 3,100 public security personnel and private guards' (SZPLY 1998: 14). But as acknowledged by city party secretary Zhang Gaoli in 1998, 'Shenzhen developed very rapidly, and the construction of local organizations lagged behind. In particular, in the local police stations and neighborhood committees, generally there is a lack of personnel and funding but the workload is very heavy' (SZPLY 1999: 220).

The approach of mass prevention and mass management was also manifested in raising funding for BLSCC. In the West, community crime-prevention programmes are always hampered by lack of funding. In Shenzhen, the funding was specified in the 'notice on the issue of BLSCC funding' since 1997. The principle of 'four ones' was adopted; that is, one part from city government finance, one part from the beneficial units, one part from residents and households, and one part from charges on 'convenience services' extended to the public. For example, in 1997, the government invested 30,000 yuan in every newly built BLSCC (SZPLY 1998: 205). During the first three-year plan, a total of 1.25 billion yuan was raised (30.18 million from the city government, 42.23 million from the district governments, 130.81 million from the townships (street offices), and 844.175 billion from the work units and the public) (SZPLY 1999: 226). As for donations from the public, for example, every household in Futian New Village donated 10,000 yuan for BLSCC, and the total reached 860,000 yuan. In Longgang District, Ye Xuequan, at the age of 78, donated 10,000 yuan for BLSCC, vacated his own house so that it could become the BLSCC office, and paid the salaries for three security guards (SZPLY 1999: 226). This model citizen was widely publicized in Shenzhen.

Apart from this optimism coming from the *Yearbook*'s reporting on raising funding for BLSCC, there was always an upbeat message that funding for BLSCC had been achieved by great effort in the ten-odd written presentations submitted by individual communities to the municipal office of BLSCC, which I obtained. However, my fieldwork shows a rather different story. In community A, the government invested heavily to establish it as a national model. Wanxia Housing Company, the property company in charge, also invested heavily to make it an advertisement for itself. All the service industries, such as shops and restaurants situated inside the community, paid management fees. Its residents are relatively better off, so it was no problem for the residents and households to pay the management fees on time. The Office of Housing Management actively participated in all sorts of 'income creating' (*Chuangshou*) activities. For example, it organized student study camps in summer holidays. Because of its fame, many companies organized promotion activities in the community, for which the Office of Housing Management charged a fixed fee. Moreover, since all the housing units are fully fitted with anticrime devices prior to residents moving in, such as iron doors and windows, the residents need not purchase them. Thus, community A found it easy to raise funds for BLSCC.

Community B faired worse. The government funding to the neighbourhood committee was fixed. Since it was not designated as a key BLSCC target, no extra funding was provided. But it could gather funding from the large number of factories and enterprises situated inside the community. The community cadre told me that although the residents there were wealthy, they were not so eager to pay extra fees for BLSCC.[3] But the cadre could charge for certain kinds of services, such as street cleaning and sanitation. Also as revealed earlier, this community is based on a shareholder-ownership; thus, funds could be obtained from the enterprises. Moreover, for certain fees, if the residents refused to pay, the amount could be debited from their dividends from the shareholding enterprises. So, basically, community B fared reasonably, although the cadres expressed frustration in this regard.

The most disadvantaged was community C. The community cadre kept complaining that 'their feet were tied' and that the community was on the verge of dysfunction because of a lack of funding. The amount of 20 million yuan for the neighbourhood committee to run was fixed. Since the income of the residents is not high (a large number of the residents were employees in SOEs) and some residents were laid off, it was very difficult to collect the management fee of 0.35 yuan per square metre. It is a residential community, so there were no 'beneficial work units' inside for the neighbourhood committee to charge fees. The cadre said that they were rather eager to 'create income' by offering certain beneficial services, such as charging for car parking, and opening a number of small convenience stores inside the community. But they could not get approval from the higher-level government. During half of the three-hour interview, the cadre explained at length why and how those 'income-creating' measures would benefit the community and pleaded with us to convey the message to their higher-level superiors. So, based on the experience of the three communities, how and whether funding for BLSCC could be provided depended on the community's resources, both internal and external. It could not be raised by simply publishing certain rules.

The approach of mass prevention and mass management was in line with the long-cherished tradition of 'combining special organs with the mass line'. It was also directly responding to the inadequate police force and financial sources in the communities, as admitted by Wang and Chen (1998). In this regard, perhaps it was not particularly different from the context of and rationale for the emergence of community crime prevention in the West. But in the West, one of the significant challenges is how to organize the public. In today's China, as Wang and Chen (1998) claimed, the market economy has heavily impinged on the foundation of traditional approaches to community prevention, the public-ownership economy. Thus, it becomes more and more difficult to organize the public in this respect, regardless of all the rhetoric. Based on the Shanghai experience, Yang (1998) identified a series of problems in implementing mass prevention and mass management, such as the lack of legal basis and law enforcement authority, the quantity and quality of the personnel for mass prevention and mass management, and the lack of funding and equipment.

Multiagency cooperation, as an essential part of the mass approach, seemed to be problematic. In the West, this is acknowledged widely in crime-prevention programmes. For example, Sampson *et al.* (1988) pointed out that regardless of its popularity, the multiagency approach should not be uncritically considered as a panacea for crime and other problems in the inner cities. Instead of an overblown, all-encompassing, multiagency approach, what they advocate is 'a more narrowly focused approach, with specific forms of interagency relationships, on specific themes and problems, provided that they seek to minimize the problematic consequences of the multiagency approach' (1988: 491). Crawford (1998b) also identified the important tensions between managerialist preoccupations of policy and the rhetoric of multiagency partnerships, both being important dynamics of community crime prevention. The Shenzhen mayor's reflection on the 'lack of synergy' between the related organs and agencies seems to offer an inkling of the counteractive effects of the multiagency approach in BLSCC.

In fact, the ideological basis of mass prevention and mass management, such as free service and ready-to-help voluntarism, seemed to be fragile and collapsing. Sometimes, actions of 'learning from Leifeng', or free service simply became a source of ridicule.

This was evident in two examples provided by Bakken (2000).[4] Such examples abound throughout Chinese society. But in terms of BLSCC, measures have been adopted to accommodate the transformation of the society at large, such as the deployment of hired security guards in the communities, which will be introduced below.

Measures for safety
Measures for safety in BLSCC mainly include police as the main force, private security services, situational measures, and management of the floating population.

Police as the main force
The Shenzhen Public Security Bureau (PSB) was established in March 1979. In 1980, the total police in Shenzhen numbered 932, with 19 university graduates, just over 2 per cent. By 1995, the force had risen to 9,532, with 1,139 university graduates (11.9 per cent) (Bian 1997). Tan and Xue (1997) reported that generally among the police force, college or university graduates accounted for 33.72 per cent; those with professional diplomas, 25.07 per cent; senior high school graduates, 38.8 per cent; and those below junior high school, 2.41 per cent. The police–public ratio in 1995 was 244 per 100,000, much higher than the national rate of 117 per 100,000 in the early 1990s. In 1992, Shenzhen PSB adopted a patrolling model for the main roads and streets. After the Ministry of Public Security issued the 'Regulation on Patrolling by City People's Police' in 1994[5] (see Shi and Meng 1996 for the detailed regulation), Shenzhen formally established the patrolling police team in 1995 (SZPLY 1996). In 1997, the 110 telephone hotline number for crime reporting became operational in Shenzhen in accord with the reform and professionalization of the PSB.

From the beginning, the police actively took the lead in the BLSCC programme. They were involved in installing target-hardening crime-prevention measures, such as 'three preventions' (prevention by people, by techniques, and by products) and 'three irons' (iron windows, iron doors, and iron cabinets). Since the police have taken charge of the *hukou* system, they play an important role in managing the floating population. To control and prevent public security offences, one important measure is to manage the 'special professions', such as entertainment venues (e.g. dance halls, and sauna and massage parlors), the hotel industry, the market in second-hand products, and the publishing industry. The police also link BLSCC with wiping out 'pornography, gambling and drugs'. For example, they participated in public education on drug abuse and made sure one of the important criteria for BLSCC is 'no drug addicts, no drug abuse dens and no drug abuse network' (SZPLY 1999: 140).

To better adapt to the tasks of BLSCC and CMSO, the police actively adopted a series of adjustment tactics. For example, 'Ten Service Promises of the Shenzhen PSB' were made in 1997. These promises covered the following areas: faster response to crime, fire alarms and traffic accidents; improvement of services such as processing ID card, driver's licence and passport applications; stating beat, traffic and patrolling officers' proper behaviour; and other anticorruption commitments. The aim was to increase efficiency and improve the police–public relationship. For example, it was stipulated that a beat officer should spend no less than two-thirds of his working day on the beat, so as to guarantee that the public could see the officer regularly, and to strengthen the public's feeling of safety. A police–public communication card was introduced, so as to ensure that the public, when encountering difficulties, could get timely help from the officer (SZPLY 1998: 30).

The general goal for the local PSB was established as 'few cases, good order and public satisfaction'. In the local PSB, officers even worked at weekends to ensure service would be available around the clock. The beat officers engaged in 'four a's' activity: 'to have *a* walk household by household; to have *a* meeting with the male, the female, the old and the young; to say *a* hello when everything is under control; and to have *a* thorough handling when problems are detected' (SZPLY 1998: 12). The beat officers also conducted the 'four-haves' activity: 'to *have* a thorough understanding of the beat situation, to *have* a good relationship with the beat public, to *have* a stable team for the management of beat public security, and to *have* a fundamental improvement of beat public security' (SZPLY 1998: 136).

In fact, the beat police officers are one of the important assessment targets of BLSCC. The following is stipulated in Appendix 2 to the 'Five Standards for Shenzhen BLSCC': the Operational Directions of the Eight Subjects and Forty-five Measurement Indicators of BLSCC, which will be introduced later.

> Item 1 of Clause 6: (1) A beat officer who within one year gets to 'know four aspects'[6] of 60% of the permanent residents in his beat with less than 700 households gains 15 points, otherwise 5 points will be deducted for every 10%; (2) A beat officer who within one year gets to 'know four aspects' of 50% of the permanent residents in his beat with 700–900 households gains

15 points, otherwise 5 points will be deducted for every 10% less; (3) A beat officer who within one year gets to 'know four aspects' of 40 per cent of the permanent residents in his beat with over 900 households gains 15 points, otherwise 5 points will be deducted for every 10% less; and (4) A beat officer who within three months gets to know 100% of the 'key population' and his targets for 'help and education' in his beat gains 15 points, otherwise 5 points will be deducted for every 10% less.

Private security service
The PSB, unlike its Western counterparts, became directly involved in maintaining security in enterprises and companies in China (Jiao 1997). But with the establishment of foreign-owned enterprises and joint ventures in China, especially in the eastern coastal areas, the old policing style became increasingly problematic: on the one hand, such companies found it difficult to accept the police's involvement in their internal security maintenance, and, on the other hand, the police could not accept the Western-style private security in those companies. Finally, a compromise was reached between the companies and the police that led to the establishment of the first 'security service company' (SSC; *bao'an fuwu gongsi*) in 1985 in the Shekou Industrial Zone of Shenzhen. It was client-oriented and based on fee-for-service. However, it was placed under the tight control of the police, ranging from approval, through recruitment, to organization and profit.

Emerging with the nascent market economy, the SSCs, albeit with such a compromise, caused substantial concern and debate at the outset. But the market demands in a transitional economy attested to their importance in maintaining public order and reducing theft. The first SSC started to be accepted by the public and new ones were set up in other cities, such as Dalian, Guangzhou, Shanghai and Beijing. In 1988, the State Council approved the 'Report on the Establishment of SSC' submitted by the Ministry of Public Security, and a year later the Ministry of Public Security promulgated a 'Notice on Strengthening the Management of SSC'. Afterwards, further similar notices were issued by the Ministry of Public Security. On 27 June 1994, the Chinese Association of SSC was established (see Fu 1993; Yu *et al.* 1997). Apart from the SSCs, local companies, organizations and communities employ a large number of security guards. For example, there were 220,000 security guards in Guangdong province in 1999. Sixty-six security companies approved by the Guangdong PSB employed more than 30,000 security guards. Other companies and work units employed a total of 190,000 (*South China Morning Post* 1999).

In its birthplace of Shenzhen, the SSC and the security guards play an important part in mass prevention and mass management. In BLSCC, security guards contribute greatly to the 'safety' and 'civilization' of the communities. For example, it was reported:

> In 1997, there were 585 guarding posts and personnel of 3,213 under the Shenzhen Security Service Company. The security guards in assuming their duties caught and turned over 423 criminals of all kinds and assisted the PSB in 108 cases, and stopped 170 disasters, rectified 575 cases of internal irregularity, mediated 476 civil disputes, did 1,982 good deeds, received 835 praises and 71 awards, was featured 23 times in mass media, and created a rate of 98% for three-nos (*no* infringement of the discipline or law, *no* public security and disaster cases, and *no* criminal cases). (SZPLY 1998: 18)

All the communities in this study employed security guards. Community A had about 30,000 residents and employed 150 security guards; community B, 10,500 residents and 41 security guards; community C, 4,078 residents and 10 security guards. The cadre in community C complained that the number was inadequate, but they could not afford to employ more. It is interesting to note that in all the communities the cadres always stressed that most of the security guards were demobilized soldiers. Presumably this preference is related to the job nature of the security guards and the need to find work for former People's Liberation Army (PLA) soldiers.

Regardless of the importance placed on security guards, there is concern that the whole SSC industry is not regulated by law, and the security guards are often of a low calibre and lack training. Both the flourishing and 'weed-like' nature of the industry is illustrated by the following case of Guangdong.

There were 220,000 security guards in the province in 1999. But many of them were poorly trained. Less than 17 per cent of them had training in areas such as law and professional ethics. These security guards came from very different and complicated social backgrounds and their standards varied. A large majority were recruited without review and examinations. In some areas, even ex-convicts were hired as security guards. Some security companies engaged in illegal trading and commercial activities. Thus, legislation was proposed to strengthen administration of the industry. Under the proposed regulation, security guards would be clearly defined as professionals who offered security services to their clients and were not part of the law enforcement agencies. They did not have the legal power of arrest, and they were prohibited from using force when performing their duties. It also included a provision under which police approval would be required in the setting up of security units.

Shenzhen was no exception to this scenario. For example, measures were adopted to 'rectify' the industry:

> The rectification work was carried out on both the security service force and the neighborhood committees' security protection force. 320 teams with 4,213 members were handed over to the municipal or district security service companies, 1,383 teams with 7,288 members were disbanded. With the rectification, 175 teams with 3,194 members were shifted to the management by the neighborhood committees' security protection force, 2,057 teams with 33,509 members were put under jurisdiction of the local police stations or security service companies. (SZPLY 1998: 136).

However, the emphasis was put on strengthening control by the PSB. In the 'Decision on Strengthening CMSO and Further Improving Public Security', promulgated by the Shenzhen Party committee and government on 20 August 1998, it is clearly stipulated that:

> PSB organs should strengthen the leading and professional guidance of the force of security guards and make them a backbone force in maintaining local level public security. Management ordinance on security service should be made as soon as possible, and the security service industry should be rectified and regulated. Security guards should undergo intensive education and training by the municipal or district PSB before they are posted. Work units who employ security guards should improve regulations and manage them properly. Any work unit which establishes a force of security guards or employs any security guards should seek approval from the PSB, and no private employment or abusive recruitment is allowed. Security guards should abide by the regulations and law, should not abuse their authority or bully the mass, and should not obstruct the entry of on-duty PSB officers into any village or factory. (SZPLY 1999: 235)

Situational measures

As in Western practice, situational measures were adopted to minimize the opportunities for crime. Among the eight types of communities, some were in the 'closure' style, others in the 'half-closure' style, and still others in the 'open' style, according to their geography and functions. Thus, during the process of BLSCC, measures similar to 'defensible space' and 'crime prevention through environmental design' were implemented. In some communities, fences were established; community entries and exits were redesigned, and even separated in some cases. The so-called 'illegal structures'[7] were demolished, as in community B, also an important means for managing the migrants and a useful measure to make the community more 'civilized'. This was to 'design out' crime, as in the initiatives in the West.

In Shenzhen, substantial emphasis was put on promoting residents' 'prevention awareness', as a kind of self-protection. Individual households and work units were encouraged to install more 'target-hardening' measures. There were activities aimed at 'creating security in three kinds of houses' (residential houses, warehouses, and banks and other financial agencies); 'three kinds of prevention' (prevention by people, by techniques and products); and 'three irons' (iron doors, iron windows, and iron cabinets). To control the entry and exit of outsiders, gates were installed at all building exits and intercoms were set up. More advanced devices such as electronically controlled, antiburglary doors, infrared detectors, and CCTV became increasingly popular. Personnel, mostly retired residents, were organized as superintendents of individual staircases, buildings, and blocks. Regular patrolling by both 'security defence teams' and security guards was arranged. However, such seemingly common-sense measures should be understood in the historical context. In the 'golden age' of the 1950s, 'doors were unbolted at night and no one pocketed anything found on the road'. Previously, in the traditional compound house (*siheyuan*), several families lived side by side, and there was no need even to close the doors. In the low-rise buildings, the staircases inside the buildings were open to all, giving potential criminals easier access to the households. Now, open buildings of this kind are still very common in the inland areas. As noted by Cao (1997), in Beijing, for example, only after one household was burgled would all the other households be forced to install iron doors or windows, or iron gates to the buildings.

Such high-rise, closing and hardening came at a price. The communication and interactions between neighbours became much less frequent, if not rare. As the traditional Chinese saying goes,

'Although they can hear their neighbour's chickens and dogs, people grow and die without ever visiting their neighbours.' In community A, some old people complained that they hated the iron doors because they imposed a distance between neighbours. People seemed to become more ego-oriented. As another traditional Chinese saying goes, 'Each person should sweep the snow from his own doorstep and should not fret about the frost on his neighbour's roof.' When witnessing a crime, such as a pocket being picked on a bus, no one would intervene. Moralists and educationalists claimed that this kind of indifference and apathy had made criminals more aggressive (see e.g. Cao 1997).

Management of floating population
Since the floating population accounted for a large proportion of people living in Shenzhen, the problems allegedly related to them were more acute. Migrants in China reportedly commit a disproportionately high amount of crime in their destination cities. In Shenzhen, that proportion was said to be exceptionally high, as indicated in the official reports below:

> Those who committed crime in Shenzhen are mostly itinerant criminals among the migrants, accounting for 95%. Within Guangdong province, they are mainly from areas such as Heyuan, Maodong, Maoming, and Chaoshan. Outside Guangdong province, they are mainly from Sichuan, Hunan, Hubei, Henan, and Guangxi, with those from Sichuan (2,790) and Hunan (2,190) accounting for 37.4% of all itinerant criminals. (SZPLY 1997: 40)

> In 1998, 9,501 suspects were caught citywide, with migrants accounting for 95.7%. According to the statistics, people from Sichuan accounted for the highest proportion of 21.5%, people from other parts of Guangdong province the second highest of 21.2%, and people from Hunan the third highest of 15.7%. (SZPLY 1999: 18)

> Among the criminals caught throughout the years, migrants accounted for over 95%, and 'three-no' people accounted for over 70%. (SZPLY 1999: 133)

> Based on the reality of Shenzhen, homicide and other serious criminal cases all occurred in the rented housing units. In terms

of the proportion of criminals, crime by migrants accounted for about 95% of all crime. (SZPLY 1999: 211)

In contrast, in the official reports or the yearbooks available to me, no other references were made about crime committed by indigenous people, apart from the following:

> Crime committed by indigenous residents especially indigenous youth has risen: some of them took drugs, some of them committed crime at the control of secret society members. Crime by school students increasingly became prominent. (SZPLY 1997: 40)

There is no way to verify the above reports on migrants' crime. But apart from the general aspect that migrants committed a high proportion of crime in Shenzhen, there are at least three other points contained in the above quotations: (1) migrants from certain places are more prone to committing crime in Shenzhen; (2) among the migrants, the 'three-no' population committed most of the crime; (3) migrants committed a disproportionately high amount of crime in the 'rented housing units'. The above aspects of migrants' crime to a very large extent determine the government policies on their management. Migration is closely related to the *hukou* system, and thus the management of migrants simultaneously shows how the *hukou* system was maintained and adjusted in Shenzhen, one of the front lines of the reform in China.

In fact, during the whole process of Shenzhen's development, the Shenzhen government treated the management of migrants as one of its top priorities. The former Shenzhen mayor, Li Zibin, declared on 31 January 1997 that 'the management of floating population is not only related to the social and political stability, it is also related to the reform and opening-up and the smooth progressing of the economic construction, and the nurturing of a new generation of "four-have" citizens' (SZPLY 1998: 206). When BLSCC was launched, the management of migrants was put on its agenda. The Secretary of the Party Committee, Zhang Gaoli, announced on 30 March 1998, 'If you want to know whether BLSCC in a community is successful or not, you can most probably get the answer by inspecting its management of floating population' (SZPLY 1999: 224).

The following measures were gradually adopted to manage the migrant population: (1) 'second-border' management; (2) management through 'temporary residence permits'; (3) management of rented housing units; (4) management of the 'three-no' population; (5) public legal education; (6) seeking cooperation from the original provinces of the floating population.

Second-border management
As revealed previously, Shenzhen City includes the Shenzhen SEZ and two other districts of Bao'an and Longgang. In 1986, Shenzhen clearly demarcated the SEZ proper by introducing the 'regulation on population exchange between Shenzhen SEZ and the inland areas'. The government spent 200 million yuan on setting up a barbed wire fence 89.2 km long with eight checkpoints, which was later further extended to 126.6 km. Special personnel were dispatched to maintain the border. This is the so-called 'second border'. To pass through the checkpoints along the second border, a person must produce a Shenzhen ID card (for permanent residents) and temporary residence permit (for temporary residents) or border pass (for migrants who enter the SEZ for the first time prior to their application for the temporary residence permits in Shenzhen) (see Liang and Yang 1994).

Thus, migrants were supposed to apply for a border pass from the local PSB of their home province before they actually started the journey of migration. Strict guidelines were spelled out by the Ministry of Public Security on local PSBs issuing the border pass. So the first step for managing the floating population was to control the second border. Those without a valid border pass were refused entry. But this policy inadvertently gave rise to the problems of trafficking in human beings and counterfeiting of border passes. Migrants could pay 50–100 yuan to 'snakeheads' to pass the border through gaps in the barbed wire. They could pay a taxi driver to hide in the taxi, or pay for a fake border pass. It was reported that criminals coordinated the whole process involving the fake border passes, from manufacturing to wholesale and retail. So the government sent special personnel to patrol the border, regularly repaired the damaged parts of the barbed wire, cracked down on criminals engaged in producing or selling fake border passes, and strengthened the checks on anyone entering Shenzhen.

Management via temporary hukou and temporary residence permits
Once migrants entered Shenzhen with the border passes, they were expected to register with the Shenzhen PSB. According to the revised 'Shenzhen SEZ ordinance on managing temporary population's *hukou*',[8] those who wished to stay more than 7 days had to register

for 'temporary *hukou*' in the local PSB, and those who wanted to stay more than two months had to apply for 'temporary residence permits'. Starting from 1995, labour migrants were separated from non-labour migrants. For labour migrants to stay for more than seven days, either their employers or they themselves had to register for their temporary *hukou*. For non-labour migrants to stay for more than seven days, if they stayed in rented housing units, the owner of the rented housing units had to register for the migrants' temporary *hukou*; if they stayed in non-rented housing, either the owner or the migrants themselves had to register for the temporary *hukou*; if they stayed in hotels, they had to register for residence according to the relevant regulations.[9]

For labour migrants to stay for more than two months, either their work units or they themselves had to apply for the temporary residence permits valid for two years. The temporary residence permits must list the following: (1) name and sex; (2) ID card number; (3) temporary residence address; (4) other necessary items. There were also specifications on the charge of the permits, renewal, notification of the PSB in the event of changing addresses, and transfer from temporary residence *hukou* to temporary residence permits.

Thus, for labour migrants to apply for the permits, they must have employment documents. It is noteworthy that the *danwei*, unlike before, has been less involved in the process of *hukou* registration of migrants. The regulation specifically stipulates that 'any temporary resident who does not hold valid documents for entry or for temporary residence but stays in the SEZ should be turned over by the PSB to the civil affairs departments to be deported according to relevant regulations' (Clause 45).

Therefore, the temporary population has been managed by issuing temporary residence permits, considering that most of them stay for more than two months. For example, in 1997, management of the population via the permits was further strengthened by reinforcing the renewal system for temporary residence permits. The management information was computerized at all three levels of the PSB: from the local police station to the public security subbureau at the district level to the public security bureau at the city level. Throughout the year, 3.45 million temporary residence permits were issued. By strengthening management and containing crime and disorder occurring in the rented housing units, the criminal cases occurring in the rented housing units declined by 43 per cent, compared with the previous year (SZPLY 1998: 18). It was reported that in all the 871 LSCCs built until 1997, the management of residents and rented housing units was achieved by issuing a card for every resident and keeping a file for every household. In 500 of the 871 LSCCs, the management of such information has been basically computerized. The proportions of registration for temporary *hukou* and application for a temporary residence permit reached over 80 per cent and 90 per cent respectively (SZPLY 1998: 207).

Managing the temporary population via the rented housing units
For example, in 1997, there were 354,357 rented housing units (among them, 192,895 were inside the SEZ and 161,462 outside). There were 134,806 owners of rented housing where 1,310,644 temporary migrants stayed (SZPLY 1998: 18). All owners of the rented housing were required to sign 'one approval and two contracts' (approval for housing renting, public security contract and family planning contract) with the local police station or the local office of CMSO. By the end of the year 1997, 437,610 'public security contracts' had been signed – 90 per cent (SZPLY 1998: 18). In Luohu district alone, the proportion of 'one card for every resident and one file for every household' was as high as 97.8 per cent, and the proportion for 'one approval and two contracts' reached 80.8 per cent, with all the information computerized (SZPLY 1998: 153).

As in the assessment of the beat police officers discussed previously, in Appendix 2 to the 'Five Standards of BLSCC', there have also been clear stipulations, with merit and demerit points, for compliance with the above management measures (such as proportions for registration for temporary *hukou* and temporary residence permits, proportions for 'one card for every resident and one file for every household', and information on the rented housing), for a community to be eligible for LSCC (see SZPLY 1997: 223 for the details).

By signing the contracts with the authorities, the owners of the rented housing were expected to keep a keen eye on their tenants and report anything suspicious. But as the cadres in community B admitted, some landlords just focused on the rentals. Quite often, they were well aware of their tenant's crime, but did not report it.

Management of the 'three-no population'
This was accomplished by establishing the temporary settlement areas and by regular sweeps and deportation.

As revealed previously, the 'three-no population', 'the three-no tribes', and 'the illegal structures' placed a substantial amount of pressures on public health and law and order maintenance. Regular sweeps and strike-hard campaigns were launched to reverse the situation, but it seemed to make little difference: illegal structures were rebuilt, the three-no population returned, and three-no tribes were restored (see Liang and Yang 1994). Certainly, it is misleading to regard all the migrants residing in the illegal structures as three-no population. Some of them simply could not afford rental for more decent rented housing units. Thus, starting from the early 1990s, the government issued 'the Shenzhen SEZ provisional plan on the construction and management of settlement areas for the temporary population' (see Liang and Yang 1994: 286–288). With this plan, settlement areas in every district were assigned to build temporary housing units for migrants to rent at a subsidized rate. The 'provisional plan' provided guidelines on the location of the settlement areas, the standards of the buildings, the principles for rental charges, the eligibility for application, the setting up of the management office, and the rules for residents to follow. It is noteworthy that the location of these settlement areas had to be 'far way from the downtown and residential areas, but with sewage system and convenient transportation' (ibid.). The applicants for residence had to hold temporary residence permits, and documents for employment in the work units or self-employment.

Community E was such a housing block; it used to be the location of a 'three-no tribe'. At the entrance, there was a big board, with a map, an outline of the community, and the address and telephone number of the renting office. The outline listed the following:

> The little community XXX is one of the LSCCs in Shenzhen. It covers land of 40,000 square meters, with 65 buildings and 1,500 single flats. Inside the little community, there is a hospital, a wet market, a food street, a car park, and shopping centers and other facilities. Inside this little community, the management is good, the service is satisfactory, security guards patrol twenty-four hours a day, and there are four clean-ups a day. Throughout the years, it has been praised by the higher-level relevant departments regarding the public security, greenery, and hygiene. It is a comfortable, safe and happy place for temporary residents.

Inside, there was a stark difference between this community and other communities, especially community A. The main road was lined with three-storey buildings. There was very limited space between the buildings. With little greenery, it seemed to exude a colour of grey regardless of the upbeat message on the board at the entrance. There was a local police station and an office of family planning for the outside population. But no one was working because it was Sunday. All the notices on the boards were about management of the 'outside' population and rented housing, and family planning policies. There was an urgent notice from the housing management department about application for temporary residence permits. The main content of the notice was as follows:

> Notice from the local police station states that the Municipal PSB will conduct an inspection on the application for temporary residence permits before July 27. In the inspection, all those without temporary residence permits will be treated as 'three-no population'. Upon contact with the *hukou* division of the local police station, we will set up a processing desk on temporary residence permits in the community office on public security in the afternoon of July 25. All those without the permits should come to the office to apply in the afternoon of July 25 with 300 dollars, 3 photos, and one photocopy of the ID card (no surcharge will be imposed).

Why did migrants generally resist applying for the permits? One important reason is that if they had not already found a job, they could not present the employment documents, one of the essentials for an application. Another reason perhaps lies in the application charge of 300 yuan, which, for a migrant with a monthly wage as low as several hundred yuan,[10] would be a burden. Since the 'provisional plan' specified that their location would be 'far way from the downtown and residential areas', they would find themselves in the kind of settlement area where there would be a concentration of the marginally employed, the 'underclass', and the 'undesirable'. These are the slums of the modern Chinese cities, where migrants are excluded socially and economically, although the authorities tend to reject the existence of slums.

In fact, the settlement areas are not for the 'three-no population' in its real sense of being '*no* valid legal documents, *no* legal occupation and *no* legal residence'. For the 'three-no population' in its real sense, the measures are sweeps and deportation. In the sweeps, the illegal structures where they stay are demolished. For example, in 1997, over 30,000 units of illegal structures were removed citywide (SZPLY 1998: 137). In the Luohu district bordering Hong Kong, in the sweeps, 'vagrants such as beggars, flower girls, squeegee-men, scavengers, those who set up temporary stalls for gambling, other jobless, "blind migrants" [transient workers], and "three-no" people were deported from the SEZ. To welcome the handover of Hong Kong, five large-scale clean-ups were conducted. Throughout the year, 53,860 "three-no" population were cleaned up, and 26,875 "three-no" population and 121 "three-no" foreigners were deported. In the clean-ups, 382 criminal clues were found and 556 suspects of *breaking the law and committing crime* were caught' (SZPLY 1998: 153).[11]

Public legal education
Public legal education was organized to enhance migrants' awareness of law. For example, starting from April 1996, at the initiation of the city office of CMSO and in coordination with departments such as labour and legal education, a large-scale systematic legal education programme was conducted to spread legal basics to the 'outside workers' within half a year (SZPLY 1997: 115).

In his speech on 31 January 1997, former Mayor Li Zibin stressed the contribution of those 'outside workers', urged local government agencies to attend to their needs, and then outlined a plan for their legal education:

> Party committees at all levels, political and legal departments, labor departments, youth departments, workers' unions, and women's associations should look after them. Special personnel should be sent to those factories or enterprises with a large number of outsider workers to conduct regular legal education activities, to reduce crime rates, to actively find and nurture the model individuals among them, to praise and publicize them with a timely manner, and to create a good atmosphere of abiding by the law and regulations. Last year, a large-scale legal education program was provided to the outside workers and good results were achieved. Citywide 1.43 million outside workers participated in the legal education activities. Among them, 0.63 million have obtained the qualification certificates. This year this kind of activities should continue, and we should strive for an across-the-board education for all the outside workers within three years. (SZPLY 1998: 206)

Seeking cooperation from the origin provinces of the floating population
As indicated above, migrants from certain provinces, such as Sichuan and Hunan, committed a high proportion of crime. It was said that Uygur migrants from Xinjiang were specialized pickpockets working

in highly coordinated groups. Indeed, I witnessed this on a bus.[12] In light of the disproportional amount of crime based on geographical origins, the Shenzhen government strengthened communication with the authorities of those provinces to seek their cooperation (e.g. by tightening up the issuing of border passes) (SZPLY 1998: 206). But considering the huge economic disparity between Shenzhen and those inland areas, a reluctance to assist was envisaged.

In the process of adopting the measures to manage the floating population, relevant legislation was passed. Stress was put on the coordination between different departments and divisions of the government. In May 1996, the 'leading team on managing the floating population' was established, with one of the deputy governors as the team leader. Special budgets were earmarked to employ more assistants of *hukou* management at the local police stations for the floating population. Thus, a multilayered managing network was formed with the police (from the local police station to the subbureau to the bureau) as the leader enlisting the forces and sources at the neighbourhood level and other government agencies such as the labour department. As referred to earlier, the holistic approach also targeted migrants who had violated the family planning policy; in fact, implementation of the family planning policy constituted one of the important aspects in the management of the floating population. The community cadres we interviewed all mentioned this issue and the strategies they adopted.

Measures for civilization

As discussed earlier, the prong of civilization is as important as that of safety in BLSCC. It is officially claimed that if safety is overemphasized at the expense of spiritual civilization, there will be no long-lasting public security and stability. In BLSCC, the measures in this regard include moral education, harmonizing the relationships between community 'stakeholders', the building of community culture, and 'purification' of the community environment. Some of these measures are interlinked with each other or with those discussed earlier.

Moral education

Moral education was focused on enhancing awareness of and, more importantly, compliance with the socialist moral rules and Party/government policies. Consistent with the wider agenda, this kind of moral education was done through launching campaigns or organizing activities. Its driving force was to 'evaluate and select' 'model' or 'civilized' individuals or units. It was also a seasonal activity. For example, periodically, model individuals were selected for awards and praise: 8 March every year (Women's Day) was for model women and 1 May every year (Labour Day) was for model workers. At half-year or year-end, model workers or leaders were 'evaluated and selected'.

Moral education is also event-driven. For example, after the National Congress of the Chinese Communist Party holds a meeting, activities will be organized to study the meeting documents. If an important government/Party policy is announced, similar activities will be organized to study the policy, and discuss how to implement it locally. As Bakken (2000: 416) observed, 'the problem of Chinese education has always been to make the individual live according to accepted customs and rules of conduct, not how to enable him to rise above them'. In moral education in China, compliance is the golden rule, at least verbally or through overt behaviour. But whether individuals internalize the indoctrination of rules or policies is unknown. Bakken's (2000: 91) thesis of 'ways of lying' in the exemplary society of China argues that showing proper conduct without necessarily internalizing the rules guiding that very conduct is also acceptable, and in most circumstances becomes the measuring rod in various evaluations in China.

A story in the *Shenzhen Legal Daily* (1999) illustrates this well. It was about a 'drama' of 'sending warm', directed and performed by cadres of a neighbourhood committee.

> Around 3 pm August 6... four to five cadres from X neighborhood committee came to Y's home. They pulled a tricycle with a jar of gas for cooking and a bag of rice. The neighborhood committee cadres said they came to 'give loving hearts and send warm'. They moved the jar of gas to the kitchen and put the bag of rice on the rice container. Several of them started sweeping the floor. One of them with a video camera started shooting the scene. About 10 minutes later, the shooting finished, and the group moved the bottle of gas and rice back to the tricycle and left.

The editor commented, 'the more such kind of "warm" is sent, the colder the masses' hearts become'.

Crime is a fully morally charged problem in China. The policy on the phenomena of *'huang, du,* and *du'* (pornography, gambling and drugs) reflects it. *Huang* (literally 'yellow') is a generic term for anything obscene, such as pornography, prostitution and visiting prostitutes. Regarding *'huang'*, in January 1997, Mayor Li Zibin urged the leaders at all levels to judge *'huang'* with an attitude of 'right and wrong'. He declared that reform and opening-up and the construction of modernization should proceed in the socialist direction, and at no time would it be possible to exchange it for temporary economic interest at the expense of spiritual civilization (SZPLY 1998: 205). Similarly, in August 1998, the Party Secretary Zhang Gaoli stated:

> Underlying the lingering phenomena of *'huang, du* and *du'* are complicated social and economical reasons. Some comrades hold ideologically wrong conceptions. Some of them think that to promote economic prosperity cannot avoid the phenomena of *'huang, du,* and *du'*. Others think that the phenomena in some other places are even more serious than that in Shenzhen. Still others think that crackdown on them will affect the economy. This kind of conception is very wrong and very harmful. They should rectify the guiding ideology of economic construction. To rely on evil means or wicked channels cannot develop the economy. Even if the economy develops, it will collapse in the end. (SZPLY 1999: 220)

In the field, I heard of similarly 'wrong' and 'harmful' comments on *'huang'*. Some business operators in the areas of entertainment in the city complained that with the launch of the crackdown on those phenomena, especially *'huang'*, their business was badly affected. Others even noticed that at those times, the streets became desolate and that much fewer people crossed the Louhu border linking Shenzhen with Hong Kong.

It was reported that certain villages had a concentration of prostitutes ('second wife', concubine, or mistress). The women were migrants from the inland areas. Community D was notoriously known for this and gained much unwanted publicity in Hong Kong. The cadre in the adjacent community C accidentally mentioned that residents in that village had become very angry about this notoriety because it affected the value of their property. Interestingly, in July and August 2002, several Hong Kong newspapers ran the story of that village (*Mingpao Daily* 2002, *South China Morning Post* 2002a, 2002c). The main theme of the reports was that the economic doldrums in Hong Kong had led many Hong Kong men to abandon their second wives, leaving them to a miserable life. In all the reports, those migrant second-wives were depicted as lazy, greedy and hedonistic. Given that this village was also an LSCC, we cannot resist casting doubt on its residents' zeal and model activity.

In community C, the cadre said they were very aggressive in enforcing measures against the phenomena of *huang, du* and *du*. The beat police officer and the beat *hukou* management assistant were both very responsible in this respect. Single women or single men residing in the community would be visited every three days to make sure that they are not prostitutes or second wives, or drug abusers, drug traffickers, or members of the triads, respectively. But he admitted that it was relatively difficult to determine whether a woman is a 'second wife'.

Promoting harmonious relationships
BLSCC also aimed to promote good relationships and mutual help between neighbours. For example, on the grass in front of the Office of Housing Management in community A stood an elegant board with the 'village pact' inscribed. The part on 'neighbours' mutual help' read, 'strict with oneself and lenient towards others; mutual love and harmony between families and neighbours; respect the elderly and love the young and be ready to help others; take the interests of the whole into account and cherish the reputation'. In the gates to the buildings in communities A and B, there were such warnings as 'mass prevention and mass management, ensure peace and security, watch out for each other, close the door upon entry or exit, and watch out for each other and be aware of strangers'.

In BLSCC, residents are encouraged to actively fight crime and other social evils. For example, in community A the village pacts also contained such proverbs as 'never hesitate to do what is righteous to uphold stability'. In community D, there were such slogans on the walls of the buildings as 'everyone is prepared to catch criminals', and 'firmly crack down on thieves'. But in community B, the cadre complained about the 'backward' ideology of people in the current times. In the cadre's words, 'They fear death, they are afraid of "stirring a fire only to burn themselves"'. When the authorities are chasing criminals, the bystanders are just indifferent.'

As claimed, one of the results of BLSCC was that the relationship between the military, the government, the police, the cadre and the public had been improved. Thus, the harmonious relationship was not limited to that between neighbours. As noted earlier, the police conducted activities such as 'four-haves' and 'four-ones' to improve their relationship with the public.

Building community culture
Building community culture seemed to be an all-encompassing concept as regards civilization. On certain occasions, it seemed to overlap with the above aspect of moral education in BLSCC. Roughly put, it aimed to enrich community social life and enhance residents' knowledge by organizing various recreational, sports and educational activities. For example, in community A, there was a special 'department of community culture' in charge of all the cultural activities. In fact, community A was famous for the activities organized. In communities B and C, all the cadre mentioned some activities either for the youth or elderly. At a special meeting on BLSCC in 1998, Party Secretary Zhang Gaoli emphasized the importance of building community culture:

> Every little community is a battlefield. If socialist culture, which advocates and extols 'the true, the good and the beautiful', does not occupy it, ugly and corrupted ideology, and unhealthy trends and evil practices will get a chance to get in. So in BLSCC, we should vigorously develop community culture, regulate the management of venues of community culture activities, ensure the construction of corresponding facilities, organize recreational and sports teams for the masses' own enjoyment, integrate patriotic education, legal and moral education, and education on the awareness of safety and civilization into the lively and active mass activities, so as to enhance the masses' awareness of civilization and self-defense ability, and to ensure that BLSCC is long lasting and finally forms a virtuous cycle. (SZPLY 1999: 225)

But the attendance rate at the activities was not as high as expected. In community A, when a shopkeeper's mother was asked whether she participated in any of the various activities for the elderly, the shopkeeper said that her mother did not participate because she was busy. Another old woman said she did not join the dancing team or *qigong* team because she was busy taking care of her grandson. She said that those who participated had grandchildren who had mostly reached school age. Almost all the participants in exercise activities were the very elderly. I once asked a group of three women whether they participated in any of the activities. They said that they did not because they were very busy, and they needed to sleep after work. The leader of community A remarked that it would be perfect if one-third of the residents participated in the activities.

Purification of the environment

The civilization of the community is also embodied in its physical environment. In BLSCC, measures were adopted to clean, improve and 'purify' the environment. For example, one of the achievements in BLSCC in 1997 was the improvement of the environment in creating green belts of more than 3 million square metres; building or paving 400 km of road, cleaning up dirty ditches of more than 460,000 m, and removing of 550,000 tonnes of rubbish (SZPLY 1998).

The stress on the improvement of the physical environment is based on the strong belief that the physical environment has a great impact on individuals' moral and mental aspects. According to Bakken (2000: 159), this reflects a kind of 'environmentalism'. Indeed, this practice has a long history in China. The story that the ancient philosopher Mencius' mother moved three times to find a proper educational environment for her son still resonates in modern China.

Rating system

As revealed above, the complicated rating system was introduced in 1995 and revised in 1996. The 'Five Standards of BLSCC in Shenzhen' refers to the following five aspects: (1) political stability, stability and unity in the community, and good ideological and political quality of the residents; (2) adoption of good public security, and security and prevention measures; (3) standard management of public facilities, clean and hygienic public places, and responsibility system implemented to ensure 'hygienic streets, orderly environment, and purification and green belts'; (4) sound grass-roots level organization; good grass-roots level work; close relationship between the cadres, the public, the military, and the police; normal relationship between the management and the workers; amiable relationship between neighbours; and harmonious relationships between family members; (5) good standards in community spiritual civilization, and measures of ideological construction and cultural construction carried out (SZPLY 1997: 217).

Appendix 1, 'The Eight Subjects of BLSCC', listed the standards in detail, and they were further classified into 45 items, with scores for every subject and item assigned.[13] Appendix 2, 'The Operational Directions of the Eight Subjects and 45 Measurement Indicators of BLSCC', explains in detail how to enact Appendix 1, with merit points and demerit points designated. Appendix 3, 'The Rating Criteria for Eligible LSCC', explains how to calculate the points and the penalties for any misconduct in the evaluation process. The total score is 1,000.

A score over 940 is a pass and a score below 799 is referred to as 'in the process of building'.

Bakken (2000) discussed in detail the Chinese evaluation system: the organization of the evaluation process, the objectivity of the evaluation, the bureaucratic logic of over-measurement, and the evaluation's role of surveillance. The complicated BLSCC rating system aims to achieve objectivity, and force the individual communities to meet the standards.

Conclusion

I have quoted extensively (and perhaps irritatingly) from the official documents and native academic commentary for the sake of providing an original flavour to those who are unfamiliar with the Chinese ideology and discourse on social control and crime prevention. Interestingly enough, the text is full of numbers and slogans. It seems that in the Chinese context no new policy or propaganda campaign is complete without a number or slogan attached.

BLSCC emerged in a particular political and ideological context. With the economic success achieved, the government emphasized that material civilization and spiritual civilization should be pursued simultaneously. Crime was escalating with economic development, so it was decided that the approach of CMSO should be adopted. But the 'get-tough' aspect of punishment of the CMSO did not produce the results desired. Thus, it was decided to pursue a comprehensive approach to emphasize both the punishment and prevention aspects. BLSCC, with its focus on prevention, was in a stark contrast to the 'get-tough' approach of 'strike hard'.

In terms of the measures adopted, BLSCC, to a large degree, was in line with community crime prevention in the West, such as the situational measures. But considering its special social, political and cultural context, it did indeed have 'Chinese characteristics'. For example, the wide range of aspects and strategies, such as ideological underpinnings, mass prevention and mass management, the responsibility system, various kinds of contracts and pacts, heavy government investment (both administrative and financial), and the rating system, made BLSCC distinctive from community crime-prevention approaches in the West.

However, the control measures associated with BLSCC could only be well grasped by fully acknowledging both the differences from and similarities to the traditional social control mechanisms prior to the full-swing development of the socialist market economy. All the basic institutions, including *hukou*, neighbourhood committee, *danwei*, and the police, still played a role in social control and crime prevention. But they had undergone changes. *Hukou*, together with its registration and all its associated social welfare, had been impinged upon in the process of economic reform, but it still functioned to identify migrants as 'outside workers', although their contribution to economic development was undeniable, as the authorities acknowledged. In fact, their identification as outsiders led to their exclusion, in all its three levels, as suggested by Young (1999): economic exclusion from labour markets, social exclusion of people in civil society, and the ever-expanding exclusionary activities of the criminal justice system and private security.

Neighbourhood committees still functioned as one of the important grass-roots organizations, but were under budget strain. At the same time, their staff, structure, and accountability were in the process of adaptation. They also were challenged by other, newly emerging organizations that were perceived to be more efficient by the local residents, such as the office of housing management in community A. Thus, the role of neighbourhood committees had been downgraded and discounted.

The *dawei* system underwent the most marked change. Previously, *dawei*, as a social welfare provider, played an essential role in social control. But with the opening of the labour market, the state-controlled job assignment structure collapsed. *Danwei*, such as the foreign-owned, private and joint enterprises, did not have to shoulder such a heavy 'iron rice bowl' burden (i.e. taking responsibilities for the employee's social welfare) as before. Even the SOEs, if they still survived, were starting to shrug off the heavy burden of expensive staff health and welfare. Previously, in *danwei*, social welfare and social control depended on each other. Now this kind of interdependence had been broken. Thus, *danwei*'s role in social control was substantially diminished. Perhaps it is justifiable to say that in the foreign-owned, private, and joint enterprises its role was undermined and was even disappearing. Thus, to take neighbourhood committees and *danwei* together, Troyer *et al.* (1989: 32) were right in saying that 'neighborhood-level structures appear to be losing their influences'. But their prediction that 'future social control efforts will be directed through work units rather than neighborhoods ... the workplace appears to have become the locus of social control' was clearly misplaced (1989: 32).

The PSB still upholds the mass line, and still puts great emphasis on a good relationship with the masses. This is embodied in the 'four-ones', 'four-haves' and other similar slogans. But it has actively tried to adapt to the new environment and the new tasks. Its role of maintaining social order has been partly undertaken by private security, although the latter is under its control and is at most a junior partner.

Given social control's cultural embedding and social adaptability in the wake of the economic reform, all the above differences and similarities were to be expected. Taking together all the measures and institutions, BLSCC exemplified the role of social capital in community crime prevention. It incorporated all the forces and sources inside the community: the bonding social capital. Meanwhile, it tapped into the energy and input from outside the community: the bridging social capital. Especially in the second three-year plan, the guiding principle was to link 'little communities' into several 'large areas' citywide, so as to enhance 'large area stability' through maintaining 'little community peace'. This clearly aimed to use both internal and external sources of communities, and further manifested the essence of bridging social capital. In this process, the state, through all the levels of the Party and the government, played an important role. The community organizations worked with the police and other government agencies, in concerted effort to achieve the goal of 'safety' and 'civilization' of the individual communities. This concurs with the concept of 'new parochialism' proposed by Carr (2003).

Thus, social capital, in this sense, echoes Woolcock's (1998) comprehensive framework with four dimensions: strong ties between family members and neighbours; weak ties with outside community and between communities; formal institutions (including law and norms); and state–community interactions, as reviewed earlier. Particularly, in contrast to Western conceptualization (at least the mainstream one), the state could bond with social capital. In terms of 'transferability' (Crawford and Jones 1996), to 'transplant' such a programme to Western society would undoubtedly encounter substantial difficulties. Fortunately or unfortunately, this is congruent with the observations made by Brogden (1999) and Skogan (1990), on the difficulties in implementing community policing in Western societies due to cultural and value differences.

The presentation of BLSCC in this chapter was based on the official reports and my own fieldwork in five communities. As I have often pointed out, there is a gap between the two sources. Moreover, as noted, the rating system differentiated between four kinds of little communities, but the official reports were based on the communities with a higher grade. So it would be worthwhile to examine to what extent the communities could be distinguished. Although social capital generally underlies the rationale of BLSCC, there seemed to be some discord on the essence of social capital: for example, neighbours' indifference to ongoing crime, and a heavy reliance on security hardware. So the next chapter turns to the microcosm of the two communities A and B, with the aim of exploring in more depth the BLSCC programme, the differences between the two communities, and the role of social capital.

Notes

1 It is *yi piao fou jue* in Chinese, referring to the principle that if a leader fails in CMSO, he/she fails everything. To draw on 'three strikes and you are out', it is 'one strike and you are out'.
2 As a self-help force at the grass-roots level, the social order joint protection teams are established through collaboration among several districts, work units or organizations in order jointly to prevent crime and deviance and safeguard social order (see Yu *et al.* 1997 for more details).
3 The cadre gave me an example. An amount of 500 yuan per household for an alarm was refunded because most of the residents were not willing to install it.
4 The two stories are summarized as follows: one young man who tried to do good things became an eccentric in others' eyes, and another young man was harassed when he offered a free service repairing electrical appliances for the purpose of 'learning from Leifeng in serving the people and fostering unselfishness'.
5 The establishment of the patrolling police is of relative novelty in the Chinese context. It constitutes an important landmark of the police professionalization.
6 The four aspects an officer has to know include the resident's name; his original and current address; his practical performance; and his work unit's title, number of workers, and kind of work.
7 These so-called 'illegal structures' partly result from the *hukou* system. When migrants first enter cities, they tend to stay in the suburban areas. There some villagers-turned-landlords build temporary shacks to accommodate the migrants at a rate both sides accept. Some migrants also build shacks or similar structures in those unoccupied 'wild hills' or 'wild fields', thus becoming true squatters. Occasionally, as noted by Solinger (1999: 250), some settled migrants buy land from the local authority, albeit without consent from the higher level, to build some comfortable buildings. Those structures, either shacks or proper buildings, are defined as 'illegal structures'.
8 The ordinance was issued on 15 September 1995, and was revised on 9 April 1997. See SZPLY (1998: 231–233) for the regulation.

9 The temporary *hukou* registration must cover the following: (1) name and sex; (2) ID card number; (3) permanent resident address; (4) temporary resident address; (5) temporary residence duration; (6) reason for temporary residence; (7) any other necessary items.

10 In the first half of 2002, the average monthly disposable income of urban residents in China was 657 yuan (*South China Morning Post* 2002b).

11 These sweeps of the three-no population are reminiscent of the aggressive policing to restore order and the 'zero-tolerance' policing in New York City. Broadhurst (2002: 18–20) regards the 'celebrated success of New York's declining crime rate' as an epitome of the 'pro-active intelligence-led policing' and provides a succinct review of the elements underlying the success. One of the contributing factors to New York's success was the expanded use of the civil law by the Civil Enforcement Unit (CEI) to attack civic disorder and crime (Broadhurst 2002), but civil rights activists launched a series of lawsuits to challenge the practice of excessive, intrusive policing (Kelling and Coles 1997). In Shenzhen, challenges of that sort did not occur.

12 I took the bus back to the place I was staying. Since it was rush hour, it was very crowded on the bus and some people had to stand. Suddenly, I heard a man repeatedly shouting, 'My mobile phone has been stolen. Please return it to me. Otherwise I will ask the driver to drive the bus to the police station.' Then he asked those with mobile phones to dial his number. The mobile phone was then handed back to him. The bus driver opened the door and several men got off. Afterwards I learned from other passengers that in that group there were several men from Xinjiang and a woman with a little baby. The baby was used as a cover for them. A female passenger standing next to me said she noticed them the moment they got on the bus. It was also said that even before they actually boarded the bus, the driver had shouted, 'The woman with the little baby, please do not get on.' They always stayed at that particular bus stop and the driver was well aware of their behaviour. I got off with the man who recovered his mobile phone. He told me that when he realized his phone was stolen, he immediately informed the driver and asked him to drive the bus to the local police station. But the driver asked him to shout first. So the pickpockets returned the phone, but its battery had been removed. So even if someone had helped him by dialling the number, it would not have worked.

13 The eight subjects were as follows: (1) good organization (90 points); (2) good facilities (130 points); (3) good public security (210 points); (4) good observance of law and discipline (110 points); (5) good team (70 points); (6) good management of population (120 points); (7) good organization of activities; (8) good environment.

Chapter 8

BLSCC in two Shenzhen communities

This chapter presents in depth the implementation of the BLSCC programme in the two communities: a model versus a non-model. More specifically, the first section reports the qualitative data collected on community A: order and peace; the second section reports the qualitative data collected on community B: disorder and fear. Then the third section presents the data from the community survey in detail by contrasting the two communities in terms of three aspects of community life: (1) mutual help, social networks and interaction; (2) crime, fear of crime and attitudes to the security guards and the police; (3) awareness and perceived effectiveness of BLSCC. The chapter concludes by discussing both the qualitative and quantitative results in terms of the manifestation of the two aspects of social capital – bonding and bridging social capital – in the two communities.

Community A: order and peace

As noted above, community A is managed by an estate company, Wanxia. The company obtained the right to manage community A by bidding in 1994, an action that was claimed as 'an important landmark for property management in Shenzhen and even China at large'. Specifically, it was 'a turning point for a state-owned property management company to transit from planned economy to market economy'. At the outset, all the necessary target-hardening facilities, such as iron doors, iron windows and an intercom system, were installed in flats and buildings inside the community. Thus, there was no need for the residents to invest in crime-prevention hardware of this kind. There were three exit-entry points to the community with security guards on duty around the clock.

Community A started to take residents in May 1994. A team to lead BLSCC was established, with the chief of the local police station as team leader, the deputy chief of the local police station and the director of the office of housing management as its deputy team leaders, and the beat police officer and two employees from the office of housing management as its team members. The team took charge of an office of BLSCC. The general target for BLSCC was set as follows: 'to strive to be a LSCC nationwide within one to two years ... to prioritize public security prevention, to regulate population management, and try to control the rates of criminal cases, public security cases and fire cases under 2 per 1000 population'.

At the outset, BLSCC employed a team of 39 'semi-military' security guards, who were demobilized soldiers specifically recruited from the army stationed in Shenzhen. I was told that they had high political and ideological standards, and high military quality. Among them, 21 were Communist Party members. They underwent rigorous on-the-job training. They were divided into one traffic management group and three patrolling groups. Within half a year of its inception, the team caught 'in the act' two robbers in two separate robberies, caught 30 bicycle thieves in 24 robberies, and mediated and handled 24 fighting incidents involving 35 people. At the time of my fieldwork, I was told the team had grown to 150 members.

Apart from the team of security guards, there was a voluntary 'social order joint protection team' to play a role in 'mass prevention and mass management'. The team included 135 healthy older people chosen from the community residents. They were further divided into six groups, with a group leader elected. They were given lessons on their duties, key prevention tactics, and any precautions they should take when assuming their duties. Every group took responsibility for a particular area and the buildings within by performing prevention, patrolling and inspection work.

The achievement from September to December 1994 was reported as follows:

> There were only three criminal cases with two cleared. The rate decreased 72.7 per cent compared with that for the four months before BLSCC's initiation. No car or motorcycle was stolen. Seventeen public security cases occurred and 89 criminals of all kinds were caught.

Due to its good performance, it was given the first place in the citywide evaluation of 'safe and civilized residential areas' in 1994, and was rated as an LSCC in the first BLSCC evaluation in March 1995.[1]

The community gained widespread publicity, and, as noted above, I was able to collect a substantial number of newspaper reports. By scanning all of them, I found that the reports basically covered three aspects: (1) community service; (2) the prizes and awards it received and occasions of VIP visits; (3) examples of individual models/heroes in the community. Community service covered issues of two kinds. The positive side covered the activities held in the community, such as film screenings, programmes for residents to learn English, the 'evaluating and selecting' of civilized or model individuals or households, organizing of 'mass prevention and mass management' teams, voluntary services performed by fellow residents, and other competitions organized to 'enrich the residents' cultural and social life'. The negative side included residents' grievances such as a too high telephone billing rate and the office of housing management's response; lack of news-stands when the community was first opened; and fellow citizens' 'uncivilized' behaviour such as graffiti on walls, damage to trees and plants in the community, and noise pollution. The news reports on these issues further attest to the extraordinary publicity community A had gained and the emphasis by government on learning from models. The prizes, awards and VIP visits were mostly about, or as a result of, its achievements in BLSCC and in the construction of spiritual civilization.

As for the individual models/heroes, it is worth mentioning some cases that were more related to fighting crime and disorder. The beat police officer sent every household in community A his business card with his address, and telephone and pager numbers, and the following message, 'I am the beat police officer of community A. My duties are to manage social order by mobilizing and relying on the masses, to maintain public security, to protect public property, to prevent and stop crime, to manage *hukou*, to provide guidance to the social order joint protection teams, and to defuse worries and solve problems for the masses. I sincerely hope to seek your support and cooperation! If you have any difficulty, find the people's policeman.' Altogether he sent over 3,000 cards. All the follow-up coverage about him reported a wide range of good deeds he did for the residents.[2]

One case concerned a man who lost his life when trying to stop a robber. A disgruntled former worker in an entertainment centre in community A returned to take revenge by robbing its cashier of

19,700 yuan. When the robber was about to flee, an alert electronics worker started to give chase. But the robber stabbed him to death and also injured a security guard who joined the chase. Finally, he was caught in an adjacent community by several security guards. When he was put into the car, he threw out all the money through the window. The passers-by seized the money, ignoring warnings from the security guards. It turned out later that only 3,715 yuan was retrieved. One passer-by that was caught escaping with about 900 yuan was detained for 15 days for 'public security offences'. Later the robber was sentenced to death. The hero who 'sacrificed gracefully at the age of 23' was decorated, and his family was awarded some monetary compensation. The hero's other good deeds were reported after the incident and the citizens were called upon to learn from him. Apart from commending the hero and condemning the robber murderer, the newspapers also covered a series of editorials and readers' comments on the disgraceful bystanders' behaviour. One of my informants residing in community A commented that the hero was given such a high honour partly because the case occurred in the well-known community A. According to another resident, people breathed a sigh of relief that the disgrace of the bystanders' behaviour occurred outside community A.

There were other 'civilized' cases in community A. Two security guards bravely arrested two men who were escaping immediately after killing their former boss in a construction company. A security guard returned a mobile phone that he picked up in the community to the owner. Another two security guards guarded over the whole night a car whose owner had left a large amount of cash and valuables inside with one of its windows open. A resident turned over to the office of housing management a suitcase with cash and valuables, which later turned out to belong to a fellow resident's overseas Chinese relative. Regarding these 'model' and 'civilized' residents doing 'good deeds' inside community A, I could not resist asking how many people or cases of similar nature emerged in other communities. Perhaps what really matters is that in the other communities they were not reported, or more accurately, 'uncovered'.

Apart from the above impressive achievements and model behaviour by residents and security guards contained in both the reports submitted to the city office of BLSCC and the newspaper coverage, my observation and interviews with residents also showed that the residents were very satisfied with the community. One informant told me that she and her family were unwilling to move to another community, although the new flat available there was more spacious. An old lady told me that she and her son's family moved in just because of its order and security, although the rent was a bit higher. Residents' airing of grievances against community services in the local newspapers showed that they cared about their community, and residents' relief that the disgraceful bystanders' behaviour did not occur in their community demonstrated that they cared about their community's reputation. Without doubt, the community's publicity also exerted a great amount of pressure on both the management team and the residents to perform even better or at least to maintain the high level already achieved.

Community B: disorder and fear

Community B used to be a rural village and was now under the management of a popular grass-roots organization: the neighbourhood committee. In contrast, community B did not enjoy the wide positive publicity of community A, and I heard from my informants that it was once given some negative coverage because of its troubled public security. I was not able to obtain newspaper reports except one that I collected during my fieldwork, which will be referred to below. In the following, I will focus on its crime problems and certain measures taken by the local neighbourhood committee when BLSCC was initiated.

Crime problems

This community used to be under the jurisdiction of Shentian police station in Shenzhen. Its crime rate was the most serious of all the seven beats controlled by Shentian police station. In 1988, its criminal cases accounted for half of those reported to the Shentian police station and in 1989 one-third.[3] The severe crime and disorder of this community once attracted the attention of the then mayor, Li Bin, and the then Party secretary, Zhang Gaoli, who visited the community on different occasions. In 1993, a separate police station had been established inside the community in the hope that problems would be handled more swiftly and efficiently. The public security problem had two aspects based on the population composition: the permanent residents and the temporary residents.

The 1960s and 1970s saw wave after wave of illegal emigration to Hong Kong. In the wake of the economic reform, there also emerged waves of 'home return' of those former illegal emigrants. Some of them had joined the triads in Hong Kong, and were coming back to recruit new members in the village. The local and Hong Kong triad members formed gangs to commit crime in Shenzhen. Frequently, a Hong Kong triad (crime syndicate) 'big brother' (*dai lao*) used the village as a base or stronghold: after instigating his Hong Kong followers (*sai lao*) to commit crimes, the triad boss himself crossed the border to the village where his Shenzhen followers provided him with shelter, food and security. Sometimes, triad members in the two areas committed cross-border crimes such as trafficking of human beings, property smuggling, organizing vice rings, or drug trafficking. In the later 1980s, a village resident was recruited into the Hong Kong triad. At the behest of his Hong Kong 'big brother', he recruited several followers.[4] Thereafter, they formed a gang to commit various crimes in Shenzhen. The group of nine members (including three Hong Kong residents) eventually were arrested during a robbery.

Apart from the above historical and external reasons, the sudden and swift transition overwhelmed some local residents. As former farmers, the indigenous residents had limited education and inadequate skills; therefore, they could not compete in the Shenzhen labour market. Moreover, many of them could live a comfortable life on the income from their rented property, dividends from shares in the village enterprises, or remittances from overseas relatives, substantially reducing their motivation for job hunting. For example, an investigation of the local young people in 1990 revealed that 37 of all the 86 young people over 16 years old (the legal age of employment) were unemployed, accounting for 43.2 per cent. Among them, 48.7 per cent (18) were men, and 51.4 per cent (19) women; 67.6 per cent (25) were aged 16–22, and 32.4 per cent (12) were aged 23–28. For most of these unemployed people, the daily routine of the men was mainly playing mah-jong, watching TV entertainment programmes, or going to clubs or dance halls: for women, it was watching TV or doing housework. Moreover, most of them did not try to retrain themselves to (re)enter the job market. Thus, this group of local residents posed a potential risk to local social order. As shown above, they were also easy targets of triad recruiting. Since official reports seldom covered crime by indigenous residents, the information concerning crime by indigenous residents from community B is valuable in order to gain a fuller and especially unbiased understanding of crime in Shenzhen.

The most prominent threat to village order was assumed to be from the disproportionately large number of migrants (some of whom were workers in the enterprises, while others were jobless).

As host of a large number of migrants, community B was confronted with the huge task of maintaining order. In the process of dramatic development, the village failed to plan its structure reasonably; thus, large factory accommodation buildings were mixed up with residents' villas of several storeys and old clan temples. This disorganized layout hampered efficient informal social control and effective 'defensible space'. Inside the community there was once an area of over 10,000 makeshift huts for migrants, causing extra difficulty for the community in controlling those migrants.

Cleaning up of the environment

Community B started the BLSCC programme in September 1996, and was rated a 'pass' in 1998. During the process of implementing BLSCC, apart from the methods such as publicizing BLSCC by sending every household a letter which spelled out the words and deeds of 'civilization' in public, and strengthened the management of the temporary population, I found the most aggressive strategy lay in the cleaning up of the environment. According to the 'Community B work plan on BLSCC' made in April 1997, a campaign of 'comprehensive management of the environment' was conducted. The aim was listed as follows: 'battle for three months, completely clean up the "three-no" population, control various advertisements put outside buildings, demolish all the "illegal structure", give the streets and shops a new good appearance, deal with the unhygienic "hidden spots", forbid illegal hawking and unsightly public display of laundry and other items, and put the emphasis on the north part of the village, with the goal of cleaning up and reforming the working and living environment of the community, of promoting the economic development and of welcoming the 1997 handover of Hong Kong to China with a new village face.'

For that purpose, a leading team of BLSCC was set up and personnel were assigned. The schedule included two stages, and the first stage was for publication and mobilization. On 11 March 1997, the leaders of both the neighborhood committee and the share-holding enterprises attended a mobilization meeting convened by the higher-level street office. A mass rally was organized in the northern part of the village to announce the decision to demolish the illegal structures. Notices of cleaning up the environment were sent to all household heads and shopkeepers whose houses or shops needed rectification, and a deadline was set for the cleaning up.

The second stage was the 'concrete action of comprehensive management' from 11 March to 30 March 1997. As the first step, the eastern and western parts of the village started clearing up the illegal structures, and beautifying the environment. In the second step, the focus was on the northern part. The deadlines were set as follows: before 17 March all those with illegal structures should demolish those structures themselves, after 17 March coercive demolition would be done, and by 30 March all the illegal structures should have been removed.

From its initiation of BLSCC in September 1996 to May 1997, over one million yuan was invested. More than 5,000 illegal structures were demolished and 2000 tonnes of rubbish was removed. A report dated November 1997, stated that, 'with more than one year's effort, the appearance of the village has greatly improved, and cases concerning social stability declined. Since the start of BLSCC, no serious criminal cases occurred, the number of public security cases decreased.... But compared with other advanced units, the gap still remains large. Notwithstanding all the support given to us from all levels of the government, there are still some difficult problems for us to tackle.'

At the time of my fieldwork, in the north of the village where illegal buildings for migrants used to be concentrated, a new park was opened to the public. In the interview with the neighbourhood committee cadres, I was told that the Party secretary had taken the lead in demolishing the only cinema in the village, in which he had invested over 200,000 yuan, but, it had been classified as an illegal structure. Therefore, he was praised by the city government, and this was covered by several local newspapers. The northern part now looked quite neat and clean. But other parts of the village were still very disorderly and dirty. In the process of conducting the survey, all of the interviewers felt that the migrant respondents' fear level was rather high, even when they stayed in their own communities. It was also said that some mistresses resided in the community. According to the aforementioned news report, on the footbridge linking the village with the adjacent industrial zones, there were all kinds of problems, including solicitation by 'three-company' (bar) girls.[5] I also met a woman by chance who was there looking for her 'lost' husband.[6]

Comparison between the two communities in the survey

In the following discussion, the survey results are presented. In each part for each question, there is a general description of the results when the two communities are taken as a whole, followed by a comparison of the two communities.

Area one

Help for neighbours

As shown in Table 8.1, only 24.3 per cent of the respondents reported that in the last year their neighbours had asked them for help with watching their home or looking after their children when they were away. Respondents in community B more frequently reported help of this kind, but the difference between the two communities was not significant.

Help from neighbours

Similarly, only 27.0 per cent of the respondents had themselves asked their neighbours for such help in the last year. Again, respondents from community B reported more of help, but the difference was not significant.

The lack of such mutual help can possibly be attributed to two factors: either such help is uncommon or unnecessary in China, or neighbours are less willing to help each other.

Tongxiang *relationship*

When asked whether they had any *tongxiang* (people from the same village or province) living in the same community, altogether 79.5 per cent of them answered 'yes', and the rest (19.9 per cent) answered 'no'. Among those who answered 'yes', most of them (79.1 per cent) would ask their *tongxiang* for help if they had trouble. When the two communities are compared with each other, significantly more respondents from community B reported they had *tongxiang* in the same community (91.2 per cent versus 70.2 per cent, $P \leq 0.0005$; chi-square test) and more of them would turn to their *tongxiang* for help (86.7 per cent versus 71.3 per cent, $P \leq 0.015$). The results show that *tongxiang* is a very important kind of interpersonal relationship in Shenzhen, and more so among the migrants.

Community activities

Among all the respondents, 67.6 per cent recalled that there were cultural activities, clean-up campaigns or recreational programmes held in their communities. In community A, 82.8 per cent reported the existence of such activities, while in community B less than half (48.9 per cent) did so. The difference between the two communities was significant ($P \leq 0.0005$). As far as participation is concerned, among those who knew of such activities only one-third (31.2 per cent) had participated in them. There was no significant difference between the

Table 8.1 Cross-tabulation of area one by community

Variable	Responses			χ^2
Help for neighbours	Yes	No	Total	1.82
A (n/%)	24/20.7	92/79.3	116	
B (n/%)	27/28.7	67/71.3	94	
n/%	51/24.3	159/75.7	210	
Help from neighbours	Yes	No	Total	1.96
A (n/%)	27/23.3	89/76.7	116	
B (n/%	30/31.9	64/68.1	94	
n/%	57/27.1	153/72.9	210	
Tongxiang **relationship**				
Existence	Yes	No	Total	13.75***
A (n/%)	80/70.2	34/29.8	114	
B (n/%)	83/91.2	8/8.8	91	
n/%	163/79.5	42/20.5	205	
Ask for help	Yes	No	Total	5.93*
A	57/71.3	23/28.8	80	
B	72/86.7	11/13.3	83	
n/%	129/79.1	34/20.9	163	
Community activities	Yes	No	Total	27.13***
Existence				
A (n/%)	96/82.8	20/17.2	116	
B (n/%)	46/48.9	48/51.1	94	
n/%	142/67.6%	68/32.4	210	
Participation	Yes	No	Total	1.59
A (n/%)	33/34.7	62/65.3	95	
B (n/%)	11/23.9	35/76.1	46	
n/%	44/31.2	97/68.8	141	
Perception of neighbours' intervention behaviour	Yes	No	Total	1.68
A (n/%)	75/64.1	42/35.9	117	
B (n/%)	52/55.3	42/44.7	94	
n/%	127/60.2	84/39.8	211	
Intervention in pickpocketing (inside communities)	Yes	No	Total	21.15***
A (n/%)	106/92.2	9/7.8	115	
B (n/%)	63/67.7	30/32.3	93	
n/%	169/81.3	39/18.8	208	
Intervention in pickpocketing (outside communities)	Yes	No	Total	1.76
A (n/%)	84/73.0	31/27.0	115	
B (n/%)	60/64.5	33/35.5	93	
n/%	144/69.2	64/30.8	208	

*$P < 0.05$; **$P < 0.01$; ***$P < 0.001$.

two communities, although more in the model community indicated that they did participate (34.7 per cent versus 23.9 per cent). The results are consistent with the qualitative data. Indeed, community A organized all sorts of activities. In terms of participation, the findings are congruous with the remarks made by the cadre in community A. Further, they show that having more activities does not guarantee a higher participation rate. It is also consistent with the findings in many Western studies that it is very difficult to organize community residents.

Perception of neighbours' intervention
This question addressed the respondents' perception of their neighbours' possible response to their victimization. If they were being attacked or robbed, 60.2 per cent of respondents thought that their neighbours would either call the police or come to their aid, or both. About one in six (14.7 per cent) respondents predicted that their neighbours would just show their sympathy and support after the event. The remaining (25 per cent) respondents either thought their neighbours would avoid getting involved or had no idea how their neighbours would react. There was, however, no significant difference in various intervention responses between the two communities. When the responses are recategorized into the forms of intervention (come to victim's assistance, call the police, or both) and non-intervention (show sympathy and support after the event, avoid being involved, or no idea), the difference remained non-significant.

As shown by the data, the proportion of neighbours who called the police or came to help can be regarded as high. That means residents' perception of their fellow residents is not so 'indifferent' as many moralists and educationalists suggest. The lack of substantial differences between the two communities further demonstrates the difficulties of strengthening informal social control through interventions such as BLSCC, and appears to be similar to the practices in the West.

Intervention in a 'hypothetical' pickpocketing
This question examined the respondents' own possible response when witnessing a pickpocketing in the community. For the two versions of the vignette – migrant and non-migrant images of the offender – there was no significant difference found for intervention either inside or outside the community (Table 8.2). Thus, the two versions of the vignette are combined. Inside the communities, 28.4 per cent

Table 8.2 Perception of intervention in a pickpocketing case

	Vignette	Community	Sex	Age	Hukou
Intervention in pickpocketing (inside communities)	1.13	17.22***	3.90*	0.17	4.19*
Intervention in pickpocketing (outside communities)	0.44	1.35	24.80***	4.08	0.22

*$P < 0.05$; **$P < 0.01$; ***$P < .001$.

would stop the pickpocket directly, 15.4 per cent would cry out to scare away the offender, 33.2 per cent would call the police, 6.3 per cent would just show sympathy and support after the event, and 16.8 per cent would do nothing. In other words, 76.9 per cent would intervene in some form at the crime scene, while 23.1 per cent would not. Inside the communities, respondents from community A were significantly more likely to say they would intervene than those from community B (87.8 per cent versus 63.4 per cent).

Then the respondents were asked what they would do in the same crime scene if it occurred outside their own communities. Overall, 68.6 per cent of respondents said they would intervene and 31.4 per cent said they would not. Although outside the communities still more respondents from community A would intervene (73.0 per cent versus 65.6 per cent), the difference is not significant. It is noteworthy that notwithstanding a lesser likelihood of intervention outside communities, a number of respondents chose the more risky form of intervention outside than inside communities. Five respondents from community A and 14 from community B did so. Some respondents from community B explained that the reason behind their unusual reaction (i.e. a more risky intervention outside their own community) was their fear of retaliation inside their own community.

When comparing these results with the findings in the literature, it should always be noted that the question measured perception or attitudes, not actual behaviour. Even so, the rate of intervention based on the data is quite high compared with some simulated studies in the West. For example, in a simulated auto burglary, Formby and Smykla (1981) found that out of 16 simulated instances, only two instances were marked by any overt citizen awareness, neither of which produced interventions that would have been sufficient to stop the crime.

Despite an assumption that the migrant status of the offender would provoke a difference, no difference was found between the two versions of the vignette: the pickpocket as a migrant and as a non-migrant. This is contrary to studies of bystanders' behaviour in the West. For example, in a simulated study of bystanders' intervention in an act of theft by a worker, a businessman or a priest, Stewart and Cannon (1977) showed that the perpetrator's status played a key role.

The difference in willingness between citizens of the two communities to intervene in crime is consistent with the findings in the West. The social disorganization theory and 'broken windows' thesis both predict that in disorganized communities residents are less likely to implement informal social control. The disappearance of any difference between the two communities when an event took place outside communities further demonstrates the importance of community as a locale.

Although the emphasis is put on the difference between the communities, the impact of other control variables – age, sex, and *hukou*, on the intervention behaviour was also examined (Table 8.2). Sex differentiated intervention behaviour both inside and outside communities. The difference between males and females was significant inside communities, and highly significant outside communities, with males more likely to say they would intervene in both locations. Age played no significant role in intervention behaviour both inside and outside communities. In terms of *hukou* status, the difference was mixed. Inside the communities, the difference between permanent and temporary residents was significant, with the former more likely to say they would intervene. However, the difference disappeared when the event took place outside the communities.

The difference between males and females was most likely due to physical strength. By the same token, when taking physical strength as a factor, senior citizens would be less likely to intervene. But in China retired people are organized into teams of mass prevention and mass management, which perhaps explains why age played no role in intervention behaviour.

The fact that *hukou* status had an influence on intervention inside but not outside communities perhaps can be attributed to the two groups having different feelings of belongingness in Shenzhen. Permanent residents tended to have a stake inside the communities and have more feeling of belongingness. However, in the whole alienated environment of Shenzhen, migrants had no feeling of belongingness, and thus it made no difference either inside or outside communities.

In a nutshell, in terms of the first hypothesis, the results are mixed. Mutual help between neighbours in the form of watching the home or looking after children was not frequent in either community, and there was no significant difference between them. *Tongxiang* relationships were very prevalent and important for respondents from both communities, although more prevalent in community B. When in trouble, respondents from community B were more likely to have recourse to their *tongxiang*. Community activities were held in both communities, and residents' participation did not differ between them, although in model community A more respondents reported the existence of those activities. Regarding perception of neighbours' response to victimization, there was no significant difference between the two communities. Respondents from the model community were more likely to say they would intervene in a pickpocketing case as bystanders inside the community, while the difference disappeared outside the community. Thus the first hypothesis is only partly supported.

Area two

Major community problems

As reported in Table 8.3, in terms of the major problems in their own communities, 35.5 per cent of respondents were concerned with problems of public security. But there was a significant difference between the two communities: in community A, only 7.7 per cent regarded public security as the major problem, while, in community B, 70.2 per cent did. This is consistent with my observation and reports of the relevant cadres.

Crime prevalence inside communities

With respect to the 13 types of crime listed, 30.3 per cent of respondents thought none of them was a real crime problem in their community, 26.5 per cent of respondents chose one type from the list, and 14.7 per cent of them chose two. The majority (80.6 per cent) chose fewer than four types of crime. When the number of crimes perceived as problematic increased, the percentage of respondents decreased (see Table 8.4).

When the two communities were compared, the perception of crime prevalence inside individual communities was very different. In community A, over half (52.1 per cent) perceived no crime threat inside their community and only one respondent (0.9 per cent) chose three offences from the list. Yet, in community B, the majority (84 per cent) chose more than one, and two respondents (2.1 per cent) took all of the 13 crimes in the list as problems in their community (see Table 8.4). If the number of the crimes for every respondent is taken as a value earned for this question, and then the t-test is applied, the t value is 11.10, significantly different at the 0.001 level. That means that the two communities were very different in terms of perceived crime prevalence.

In terms of different types of crime (Table 8.5), the highest percentage was that of bicycle theft (32.2 per cent), followed by robbery (30.8 per cent) and 'violence and fighting' (29.4 per cent). The lowest was that of hooliganism (2.4 per cent). The difference between the two communities was more pronounced: for all types of crime, the percentages in community B were much higher than those in community A. In community A, the top three crimes were bicycle theft (17.9 per cent), gambling (15.4 per cent), and burglary (6.0 per cent), but in community B, the top six were robbery (63.8 per cent), violence and fighting (60.6 per cent), bicycle theft (50 per cent), burglary (39.4 per cent), gambling (38.3) and prostitution (29.8 per cent).

Migrants' criminality
Of respondents from the two communities, 37.4 per cent agreed that migrants were more likely to commit crime or other illegal activities, 10.4 per cent gave an answer of 'no', and just over a half (52.1 per cent) chose 'it depends' and 'don't know'. The difference between the two communities was not significant. In community B, where the majority of the population were migrants, more respondents answered 'yes' (42.6 per cent versus 33.3 per cent in A) and fewer answered 'no' (5.3 per cent versus 14.5 per cent). It is important to note the difference between the two types of *hukou* status. A chi-square test showed that there was no significant difference between permanent and temporary residents, although more permanent residents agreed with the statement (43.1 per cent versus 32.7 per cent) and more temporary residents chose 'it depends' (51.9 per cent versus 39.2 per cent).

The fact that only 37.4 per cent of the respondents chose 'it depends' and 'don't know' as regards migrant criminality is contrary to the official reports that in Shenzhen and in the whole country the majority of crimes are committed by migrants. *Hukou* status played no role in the perception of migrant criminality, and more respondents from community B (where the majority of the population are migrants) agreed with the statement. That means migrants themselves also

BLSCC in two Shenzhen communities

Table 8.3 Cross-tablulation of area two by community

Variable	Responses			χ^2
Major community problems	Crime	Non-crime	Total	88.93***
A	9/7.7	108/92.3	117	
B	66/70.2	28/29.8	94	
n/%	75/35.5	136/64.5	211	
Community crime prevalence	t-test			$t = 11.10$***
Migrants' Criminality	Yes	It depends or no opinion	No	Total	5.43
Community				117	
A	39/33.3	61/52.1	17/14.5	117	
B	40/42.6	49/52.1	5/5.3	94	
n/%	79/37.4	110/52.1	22/10.4	211	
Hukou					2.89
Permanent	44/43.1	47/46.1	11/10.8		
Temporary	34/32.7	60/57.7	10/9.6		
n/%	78/37.9	107/51.9	21/10.2		
Feeling of safety	Safe	Not safe	(No opinion)	Total	51.23***
A	111/94.9	1/.9	(5/4.3)	117	
B	57/60.6	36/38.3	(1/1.1)	94	
n/%	168/79.6	37/17.5	(6/2.8)	211	
Personal victimization	High	Low	(No opinion)	Total	17.91***
A	54/46	58/49.6	(5/4.3)	117	
B	68/73.1	20/21.5	(5/5.4)	93	
n/%	122/58	78/37.1	(10/4.8)	210	
Property victimization	High	Low	(No opinion)	Total	17.21***
A	46/39.3	68/58.1	(3/2.6)	117	
B	60/63.8	28/29.8	(6/6.4)	94	
n/%	106/50.2	96/45	(9/4.3)	211	

Table 8.3 continues overleaf

Table 8.3 continued

Variable	Responses			χ^2
Victimization experience	Yes	No	Total	9.45**
A	5/4.3	112/95.7	117	
B	16/17.0	78/83.0	94	
n/%	21/10.0	190/90.0	211	
Security guards				
Existence	Yes	No	Total	9.01***
A	117/100	0/0	117	
B	87/92.6	7/7.4	94	
n/%	204/96.7	7/3.3	211	
Importance	Important	Not important	(No opinion)	Total	24.33***
A	98/86.0	13/11.4	(3/2.6)	114	
B	31/37.3	49/59.1	(3/3.6)	83	
n/%	129/65.5	62/31.5	(6/3.0)	197	
Police				
Presence	Very often	Often	Sometimes	Total	6.80*
A	47/40.2	25/21.4	45/38.5	117	
B	36/38.3	34/36.2	24/25.5	94	
n/%	83/39.3	59/28.0	69/32.7	211	
Satisfaction	Satisfied	No opinion	Dissatisfied	Total	42.82***
A	79/78.2	11/10.9	11/10.9	101	
B	32/34.8	12/13.0	48/52.2	92	
n/%	111/57.5	23/11.9	59/30.6	193	

*$P < 0.05$; **$P < 0.01$; ***$P < 0.001$.

Table 8.4 Frequency of crime within the two communities

Number of crimes	Frequency			Percentage			Cumulative Percentage for A and B
	A and B	A	B	A and B	A	B	
0	64	61	3	30.3	52.1	3.2	30.3
1	56	44	12	26.5	37.6	12.8	56.9
2	31	11	20	14.7	9.4	21.3	71.6
3	19	1	18	9.0	0.9	19.1	80.6
4	14		14	6.6		14.9	87.2
5	10		10	4.7		10.6	91.9
6	5		5	2.4		5.3	94.3
7	4		4	1.9		4.3	96.2
8	2		2	0.9		2.1	97.2
9	1		1	0.5		1.1	97.6
11	2		2	0.9		2.1	98.6
12	1		1	0.5		1.1	99.1
13	2		2	0.9		2.1	100
Total	211	117	94	100	100	100	

Table 8.5 Percentages for 13 types of crime in the two communities

	Percentage		
	A and B	A	B
Burglary	20.9	6.0	39.4
Bicycle theft	32.2	17.9	50
Auto theft	9.0	3.4	16
Violence and fighting	29.4	4.3	60.6
Gambling	25.6	15.4	38.3
Drunkenness	16.1	6.0	28.7
Robbery	30.8	4.3	63.8
Sale or use of drugs	8.1	0	18.1
Prostitution	13.7	0.9	29.8
Hooliganism against women (sexual assault against women)	2.4	0	5.3
Swindling	4.3	0.9	8.5
Gang activity	3.3	0	7.4
Triads	4.7	0	10.6

agreed that their group was more likely to commit crime. Perhaps this is because, as in disorganized communities in the West, migrants have a higher risk of being both victims and offenders.

Feeling of safety
Overall, 79.6 per cent felt very safe or somewhat safe when walking alone at night in their community, and only 17.5 per cent felt unsafe or very unsafe. However, the difference between the two communities was highly significant: 94.9 per cent felt safe or somewhat safe in community A, while only 60.6 per cent in community B had the same feeling.

So, generally speaking, residents' level of feeling of safety was still high in both communities. Wang *et al.* (1998: 636) reported a 1992 survey conducted in Tengzhou, Shandong Province, which showed that the average assessment of the local public security was 0.894, that of the national public security was 0.781, and the respondents' feeling of safety was 0.863 (where 1.0 was very good, 0.75 was good, 0.50 was average; and 0.25 was bad). A 1991 study involving 15 provinces sponsored by the Ministry of Public Security included the following question: 'Under the current situation of public security, what is your feeling of personal safety?' Among the 14,860 respondents, 7.3 per cent reported that they felt safe, 43.7 per cent somewhat safe, 17.9 per cent average, and 23 per cent not safe (see Research Team of the Ministry of Public Security Project on 'Research and Evaluation on Public Feelings of Safety in 1991', 1991). Although it is not appropriate to compare the results from these different sources, the findings from the current survey at least shed some light on feelings of safety in China.

Chance of personal victimization
When asked about the possibility of personal victimization (violent assault and hooliganism), 58.1 per cent of respondents perceived it as very high or high, and 37.1 per cent as low or very low. Across the communities, a larger proportion in community B than in community A regarded it as very high or high (73.1 per cent versus 46.2 per cent). Consequently, a much smaller percentage in community B regarded it as low or very low (21.5 per cent versus 49.6 per cent). The difference is highly significant. Moreover, it is noteworthy that in community A no one chose 'very high', while 8.5 per cent in community B did so.

Chance of property victimization
As far as the possibility of property victimization (theft or burglary)

was concerned, the percentages of 'very high or high' and 'low or very low' were nearly equal (50.2 per cent versus 45.5 per cent). Again, the difference between the two communities was highly significant. In community A, the percentages for 'very high or high' and 'low or very low' were 39.3 per cent and 58.1 per cent, respectively, while in community B they were 63.8 per cent and 29.8 per cent, respectively. In community A, only 1.7 per cent respondents thought it was very high, while in the other community, nearly one-third (29.8 per cent) regarded it as very high.

Victimization experience
In the two communities, only 21 respondents had been victimized in the past year (5 in community A but 16 in community B). A chi-square test showed that the difference between the communities was highly significant. The crimes included theft of bicycles (four cases), theft of quilts (one case), theft of wallets (one case), theft without specifying the lost property (two cases), purse-snatching (one case), burglary (one case), robbery (three cases), assault (one case), one case in which the victim – a restaurant owner – reported that a customer did not pay the bill, and another six cases in which the victim did not specify the crime. When asked whether they reported it to the police, among the 21 victims 10 did not report, 10 reported, and 1 did not specify. Two of the victims who reported the case remarked that it was useless to report.

Security guards
Nearly all (96.7 per cent) respondents reported that there were security guards in their community. In community A, all of the respondents gave an affirmative answer, but in community B seven respondents (7.4 per cent) said there was no security guard. Among those who reported the existence of security guards, 87.3 per cent thought they were useful or somewhat useful. In community A, 96.5 per cent thought they were useful or somewhat useful, while in community B, the percentage was lower at 74.7 per cent. In community A, only 0.9 per cent of respondents regarded the security guards as not useful, while in community B, 21.7 per cent did so. This difference was also highly significant.

In the whole process, the interviewers were impressed that the differences observed in the analyses were reflected in the interviewees' verbal tones and facial expressions. In community A, when asked whether the security guards were useful, most respondents promptly gave an affirmative answer. For example, one female shopkeeper said, 'Of course they are important, very important; otherwise the situation would be in a mess.' An aged respondent was very satisfied with the military-style daily training programme for the security guards in community A. Another aged respondent even mentioned that more attention should be paid to the security guards' material and spiritual needs. But one respondent complained there were too many security guards in community A. On the contrary, the respondents in community B seemed to confuse the security guards with the local policemen. From their facial expression in responding to this question, it appeared they were not satisfied with the security guards, but, interestingly enough, they still thought they were useful to some degree. One respondent answered, 'They are useless! They always bullied the migrant workers.' The same respondent reported that he was once beaten by a security guard (but he did not regard it as a victimization experience). Another interviewee said, 'They are not useful. It is exactly those security guards who commit crime!' Another respondent remarked that security guards were useless because they would not intervene even in a fight.

Police presence in the community
In the two communities, similar percentages of respondents claimed that they saw the policemen 'very often'. But in community A, fewer people chose 'sometimes' (21.4 per cent versus 36.2 per cent), while more chose 'seldom' (38.5 per cent versus 25.5 per cent), a difference that was significant. Generally, the police presence in community B was greater. In the model community, that same female shopkeeper said, 'I seldom see policemen here. Otherwise it would be terrible.' So, for her, police presence in a community perhaps signified the presence of problem families or residents.

Satisfaction with the police
Over half (52.6 per cent) of respondents were satisfied with the police, more than one-quarter (28 per cent) were not satisfied, and one-tenth (10.9 per cent) chose 'don't know'. The difference between the communities was highly significant. In community A, 78.2 per cent were satisfied with the police, while in community B only 34.8 per cent were. Consequently, those who were dissatisfied in community B far outnumbered those in community A (52.2 per cent versus 10.9 per cent). It is interesting that in community A no one was 'very dissatisfied' while in community B only one (1.1 per cent) was very satisfied.

As mentioned above, the respondents in community B had difficulty in distinguishing the security guards from the local policemen. A large number of respondents from both communities did not know whether they were satisfied with the police because they seldom had contact with them. Some respondents from community A reported they were satisfied with the police because TV showed that police officers were very brave and important in fighting crime. As in their attitudes to security guards, respondents from community B were obviously less satisfied with the police. One respondent complained that policemen always treated the migrants roughly. Another said he was very dissatisfied with the police, because they always 'swaggered around and made a show of their strength' (*yao wu yang wei*). Still another respondent reported he was very dissatisfied with the police because they always arrested the 'good people' (law-abiding people). One respondent said he was not satisfied because some public security officers committed theft and even robbery. But one interviewee sympathized with the police because he thought the police force was limited and they had too many things to take care of at the same time.

The data in area two have shown that the two communities are very different from each other. In community B, the crime problem was more salient and prevalent, more respondents had previously been victimized, their feeling of safety was much lower, they perceived the chances of both personal and property victimization as much higher, and their attitudes were less positive about the local security force, including the security guards and policemen. Thus, the findings here were generally in accord with the qualitative data. Hence, the second hypothesis was supported: in community A, crime was perceived as less serious, there was less fear of crime, and the respondents' attitudes to the police and security guards were more positive.

Area three

Awareness of the programme

As reported in Table 8.6, 70.6 per cent of respondents claimed that they had heard something about the crime-prevention programme of BLSCC. In community A, 92.3 per cent had heard about it, while in the other community less than half (43.6 per cent) knew of such a programme. The difference was highly significant. Among those who had heard about the programme, 69.2 per cent thought it was useful to some degree. But, with respect to BLSCC usefulness, there was a significant difference between the communities. Among those who had heard about the programme from community A, 75.7 per cent thought it was useful and 21.4 per cent not useful, while in community B, the percentages were 52.5 per cent and 45.0 per cent, respectively.

Change of relationship between residents
In terms of relationship between residents, nearly half (43.6 per cent) thought there was no change at all, 37.4 per cent thought it was better, while 6.6 per cent of them thought it was worse. The perception of change was different at the community level. In communities A and B, 41.9 per cent and 31.9 per cent, respectively, thought it was better. More respondents in B than in A chose 'worse' and the gap was even larger: 12.8 per cent and 1.7 per cent, respectively. Given that the percentages for 'no change' were the same (43.6 per cent), the difference was significant.

Installation of anticrime measures
Approximately one-quarter (24.9 per cent) reported that in the last year they had installed some anticrime measures, mainly antiburglary doors, windows, safes, etc. Although more people from community B did so, the difference was not significant. This is largely because in community A the basic anticrime facilities were installed even before the residents moved in. So in community A, the new anticrime measures were extra security measures taken by the residents, while in community B it was to meet the basic requirements for crime prevention.

Change of community physical appearance
Over half (55.5 per cent) of the respondents thought it was better, followed by 23.7 per cent for 'no change' and 12.8 per cent for 'worse'. Comparing community B with community A, more people thought it was better (64.1 per cent versus 50.0 per cent) and worse (19.6 per cent versus 7.8 per cent) as well. On the contrary, a larger percentage in community A reported 'no change' (31.9 per cent versus 14.1 per cent). The difference was highly significant. In the process of the interview, many respondents from community B recognized the physical change in the community. However, they said the change mostly resulted from a citywide campaign to clean up the city before a national exhibition was due to be held in Shenzhen.

As noted previously, in community B, a large-scale clean-up campaign was initiated after the launch of BLSCC, and a large number of 'illegal structures' were demolished. The residents in community

Table 8.6 Cross-tablulation of area three by community

Variable	Responses				χ^2
BLSCC					
Awareness	Not heard of	Heard of		Total	59.55***
A	9/7.7	108/92.3		117	
B	53/56.4	41/43.6		94	
n/%	62/29.4	149/70.6		211	
Usefulness	Useful	Not useful	(No opinion)	Total	8.02*
A	78/75.7	22/21.4	(3/2.9)	103	
B	21/52.5	18/45.0	(1/2.5)	40	
n/%	99/69.2	40/28.0	(4/2.8)	143	
Change of relationship between residents	Better	No change	Worse	(No opinion)	Total	11.00**
A	49/41.9	51/43.6	2/1.7	(15/12.8)	117	
B	30/31.9	41/43.6	12/12.8	(11/11.7)	94	
n/%	79/37.4	92/43.6	14/6.6	(26/12.3)	211	
Installation of anticrime measures	No	Yes			Total	2.74
A	80/70.8	33/29.2			113	
B	65/81.3	15/18.8			80	
n/%	145/75.1	48/24.9			193	
Change of community's physical appearance	Better	No change	Worse	(No opinion)	Total	18.55***
A	58/50.0	37/31.9	9/7.8	(12/10.3)	116	
B	59/64.1	13/14.1	18/19.6	(2/2.2)	92	
n/%	117/56.3	50/24.0	27/13.0	(14/6.7)	208	

Table 8.6 continues overleaf

Table 8.6 continued

Variable	Responses				χ^2
Crime change	Better	No change	Worse	(No opinion)	Total	17.91***
A	54/46.2	46/39.3	4/3.4	(13/11.1)	117	
B	36/38.3	32/34.0	21/22.3	(5/5.3)	94	
n/%	90/42.7	78/37.	25/11.8	(18/8.5)	211	
Change of feeling of safety	Safer	No change	Less safe	(No opinion)	Total	12.64**
A	32/27.4	73/62.7	2/1.7	(10/8.5)	117	
B	15/16.0	63/67.0	12/12.8	(4/4.3)	94	
n/%	47/22.3	136/64.5	14/6.6	(14/6.6)	211	
Change of personal victimization	Increasing	No change	Decreasing	(No opinion)	Total	11.19**
A	4/3.4	68/58.1	29/24.8	(16/13.7)	117	
B	14/14.9	60/63.8	13/13.8	(7/7.4)	94	
n/%	18/8.5	128/60.7	42/19.9	(23/10.9)	211	
Change of property victimization	Increasing	No change	Decreasing	(No opinion)	Total	5.25
A	6/5.2	80/69.0	22/19.0	(8/6.9)	116	
B	12/12.9	62/66.7	11/15.8	(8/8.6)	93	
n/%	18/8.6	142/67.9	33/15.8	(16/7.7)	209	

*$P < 0.05$; **$P < 0.01$; ***$P < 0.001$.

B therefore did recognize the obvious change. But in community A, the physical environment was always pleasant so the residents there perceived less change.

Crime change
Over two-fifths (42.7 per cent) of respondents thought that the 'situation of public security' was better, 37 per cent did not perceive any change, and 11.8 per cent thought it was worse. At the community level, more from community A reported it was better (46.2 per cent versus 38.3 per cent) and no change (39.3 per cent versus 34.0 per cent), while fewer thought it was worse (3.4 per cent versus 22.3 per cent). The difference was highly significant. Again, the data should be understood by taking into account the original level of crime in the two communities.

Change of feeling of safety
Nearly two-thirds (64.5 per cent) of respondents reported no change of feelings of safety when walking alone at night in the community in the past year, over 22.3 per cent felt safer, and 6.6 per cent less safe. In terms of individual communities, more respondents from community A reported 'safer' (27.4 per cent versus 16.0 per cent) and fewer respondents 'no change' (62.4 per cent versus 67.0 per cent) and 'less safe' (1.7 per cent versus 12.8 per cent). The difference was again highly significant.

Change of personal victimization
In terms of the chances of being victimized in violent assaults or hooliganism in the past year, overall, 60.7 per cent reported 'no change', 19.9 per cent 'decreasing' and 8.5 per cent 'increasing'. In community A, more claimed that the likelihood of victimization was 'decreasing' (24.8 per cent versus 13.8 per cent) and fewer thought it was 'increasing' (3.4 per cent versus 14.9 per cent) or had not changed (58.1 per cent versus 63.8 per cent). This difference also was highly significant between the communities.

Change of property victimization
Concerning chances of theft or burglary in the community, two-thirds (67.9 per cent) reported no change, 15.6 per cent 'decreasing' and 8.5 per cent 'increasing'. At the community level, more from community A claimed that risks were 'decreasing' (19.0 per cent versus 11.8 per cent) or there was 'no change' (69.0 per cent versus 66.7 per cent),

and fewer thought that risks were 'increasing' (5.2 per cent versus 12.9 per cent). But this difference was not statistically significant.

As indicated above, BLSCC has gained considerable awareness among the residents and was perceived as 'useful' by a large proportion of them, although in community A more residents were aware of it and ranked it more positively. With regard to the evaluation measures, the respondents' perception was mixed. The most obvious perceived change was 'change of community physical appearance', especially in community B. 'Crime change' was also perceived as obvious in both communities. For the other items, nearly half chose 'no change'. Moreover, as shown in Table 8.6, a significant proportion of respondents from both communities could not come up with a definite answer to the questions. The high level of 'no opinion' made it more difficult to measure the different perception of programme effectiveness between communities. As stressed repeatedly, all the results should be interpreted by taking into account the original level of the individual measures in the communities.

In order to detect the differential effect of the programme in the two communities, a t-test was applied to test for difference between them. First, six items (change of residents' relationship, change of community physical appearance, crime change, change of feeling of safety, change of personal victimization, and change of property victimization) were taken to constitute a scale of programme effectiveness. Second, the response of 'no opinion' was incorporated with 'no change', and all three levels of responses (better, no change/ no opinion, and worse) were graded from 1 to 3. Lastly, a general score for every respondent was computed by the Statistical Package for the Social Sciences (SPSS). The reliability coefficient of the scale was 0.78. The t-test result indicated that the difference between the two communities was highly significant ($t = 10.5$, $P < 0.001$).

To sum up area three, a large proportion of the respondents had some awareness of BLSCC. They gave a positive evaluation to its general usefulness, and other individual measures of perceived change, including changes in relationship, physical appearance, crime, feelings of safety, risks of personal and property victimization. In terms of individual measures of perceived changes between communities, although results from the chi-square tests were mixed, the t-test showed a highly significant difference. This conforms to my observations, feedback from the interviewees and comments from the respondents.

Conclusion

This chapter presented the findings on BLSCC from two communities: a 'model' versus a 'non-model'. Two sources of data were employed: site visits, observations and interviews with the community residents and cadres (qualitatively), and the community survey (quantitatively). On the basis of the qualitative data source, the two communities stood in a stark contrast: 'order and peace' versus 'disorder and fear'. However, from the survey data, the two communities were less different in terms of three aspects of community life: (1) mutual help, social networks, and interaction; (2) crime and security inside communities; (3) perception of BLSCC effectiveness. Specifically, the results relating to the first and third aspects were mixed, while the results relating to the second aspect were very different between the two communities. Thus, concerning the three hypotheses corresponding to the three aspects of community life as introduced earlier in Chapter 2, only the second was fully supported by the survey data.

The chapter also investigated whether the amount of social capital underlay the success or achievement of BLSCC. By the conceptualizations of 'social capital', 'community' and 'community crime prevention' as discussed previously, social capital, or rather 'bonding social capital', was operationalized as mutual help between neighbours, *tongxiang* relationships, participation in community activities, perception of neighbours' intervention behaviour, and intervention in pickpocketing inside people's communities. In terms of bonding social capital, the two communities turned out not to be significantly different from each other on all the measures of social capital. But since social capital includes both bonding and bridging aspects, the comparison of the two communities should also examine the difference in the stock of bridging social capital.

In terms of bridging social capital, community A surpassed community B. First, as shown in the data concerning the second aspect of community life, respondents from community A held more positive attitudes to the security guards and the police, one element of bridging social capital. Second, because it was established as a model, the Shenzhen government and Wanxia, the SOE which managed community A, invested heavily in it (although the actual amount was not specified or available). For example, as noted, community A had very good exercise and sports amenities and other recreational facilities for residents. At the time of my fieldwork, I learned that a large-scale residents' amenity centre was being planned. No similar facility was available to residents of community B. Third, because community A was a model of citywide and even national fame, it attracted more and more resources, further increasing its bridging social capital. For example, companies that conduct promotional activities in the community are expected to pay a certain amount in fees, which could be used to fund further BLSCC activities. Thus, as discussed before, in community A, funding for BLSCC was not a problem. Also because of its fame, many agencies and companies chose to give community A free and voluntary services, such as film screenings, and doctors to diagnose and treat patients. Through these activities, residents in community A had more information and exposure to various sources of support as well as enjoying certain free services.

In a nutshell, community A had more stock of social capital, particularly bridging social capital, than community B, and thus it was more successful in implementing BLSCC. Without doubt, in this process, many factors played their parts, especially governmental support.

Notes

1 The information about its performance in the early period was from two other reports submitted to the city office of BLSCC.
2 The police officer was assigned to community A when it was first opened. During my fieldwork, when I asked whether I could meet him, I was told he had been promoted to chief of the local police station.
3 The source of the information is a journal article. In order to maintain the anonymity of the village, I chose not to mention the source of the article.
4 The exact number was not reported. The source referred to it as 'a double-digit figure'.
5 The report was from *Shenzhen SEZ Daily*, 28 September 1999. 'Three-company (*san pei*) girls' initially was used to refer to girls working in entertainment venues such as clubs or dancing parlours as company of their male customers in dancing, singing or drinking. '*San*' means three and '*pei*' means company (in dancing, singing and drinking). The term has evolved to denote prostitutes in China.
6 While I was waiting downstairs to meet the cadres of the neighbourhood committee, I met this woman. She was from an inland province. She and her husband managed a factory at home. The husband was responsible for marketing and selling the products in Shenzhen. But for over one year, he did not send any money and owed some of his friends money. She heard that her husband had a 'second wife' in that village. So she

came to find out whether it was true. In the process of telling her story, she kept crying. She later told me that they had two children, the elder of whom was 15 years old. By that time, she had found her husband, but he denied having a mistress. I noticed a wound on her hand and asked whether she had had a fight with her husband. She admitted it and told me that she would kill her husband and the 'second wife' and then commit suicide if the story turned out to be true. She looked very distressed and disoriented at that moment, and made other remarks a typical Chinese woman would make if she discovered an extramarital affair.

Chapter 9

Conclusion

This book has mainly explored three issues: community crime prevention, social capital, and the nexus between community crime prevention and social capital. The exploration has been pursued at two levels: theoretical and empirical. At the theoretical level, the literature in the West concerning community crime prevention and social capital was reviewed extensively, and the theoretical link between them was established. At the empirical level, the data from Shenzhen were employed to demonstrate to what extent the nexus could be maintained. In this chapter, first the theoretical and empirical explorations are summarized. Then, the issues pertinent to the nexus between social capital and community crime prevention are revisited, including formal/informal social control, public/private control, inclusion/exclusion, and the role of the state. Finally, the issues about the future direction of social control and its study in China are examined.

Theoretical exploration

Community crime prevention emerged in the 1970s in Western societies concomitant with three facilitating factors: (1) the theoretical reorientation that saw in criminology a revived interest in the community as opposed to the individual, attention to the offence as opposed to the offender, and focus on the status of the victim as opposed to that of the offender; (2) the changing nature of crime problems, in terms of their quality and quantity, according to various

Conclusion

sources such as official statistics and victim surveys, and in terms of their impact on public perception of crime and feeling of security; (3) the perceived inefficiency of the criminal justice system, which warranted a partnership between different governmental agencies and the public in crime prevention. The emergence of community crime prevention notwithstanding, it was pointed out that the current landscape of crime prevention is characterized by a coexistence of the community approach and the traditional 'get-tough' approach or, in Garland's (2000) words, a contradictory dualism of adaptive and non-adaptive responses. This point was further supported by a review of the location of the community approach to crime prevention in the general theoretical framework of crime prevention.

In the literature, social capital is basically represented by three perspectives: social capital as social networks, as civic engagement, and as trust (Lin 2000). In this research, Lin's conceptualization of social capital was adopted, defining it as 'the investment in embedded resources in social networks with expected returns' (Lin 2000, 2001a, 2001b). Being so defined, social capital embodies two aspects: the networks and the resources flowing between them. It is stressed that social capital can produce both positive and negative results, thus calling attention to negative social capital. When utilized to depict the characteristics of a collective, two aspects of social capital need to be distinguished: bonding and bridging social capital. According to Putnam (2000), bonding social capital accumulates in the course of informal social interactions that families and people from the same locality engage in through their daily lives, while bridging social capital connects communities and organizations to others. In this sense, Putnam (2000) stressed that bonding social capital is exclusive because it tends to be inward-looking and to reinforce exclusive identities and homogeneous groups, while bridging social capital is inclusive because it is outward-looking and encompasses people across diverse social cleavages. But, depending on the circumstances, both bridging and bonding social capital can produce positive social effects.

The distinction between bonding and bridging social capital, to a very large extent, is congruous with the differentiation between 'strong ties' and 'weak ties', or 'closure' and 'structural holes' in the literature of social networks. It is stressed that both 'closure' and 'structural holes' are important for a collective, such as a company, to achieve optimal performance. With the above conceptualization, Burt (2001) constructed a model to integrate the two dimensions of 'network closure within group' and 'non-redundant contacts beyond group' (Figure 3.1). According to this model, performance is highest when in-group closure is high and when there are many non-redundant contacts beyond the group. On the contrary, performance is lowest when in-group closure is low and when there are few non-redundant contacts beyond the group.

Thus, in order to optimize its performance, a social structure, such as a company or a community, should combine both bonding and bridging social capital (or utilize 'closure' and 'structural holes'); that is, be both inclusive (inward-looking) and exclusive (outward-looking). This is congruous with the conceptual framework on social capital advanced by Woolcock (1998). This comprehensive framework incorporates four dimensions of social capital: strong ties between family members and neighbours; weak ties with outside community and between communities; formal institutions (including laws and norms); and state–community interactions.

Apparently, the two dimensions of social capital are parallel to the two dimensions of community – 'horizontal' and 'vertical', as pointed out by Hope (1995). Further, by reviewing the theoretical models of community crime prevention: social disorganization, opportunity reduction and 'broken windows', the nexus between social capital and community crime prevention can be established. More specifically, in relation to social disorganization theory, the basic systemic model by Bursik and Grasmick (1993), and the non-recursive model by Rose and Clear (1998) implicitly or explicitly support the internal and external dimensions of social capital in community crime prevention. In relation to the opportunity-reduction model, more attention should be paid to the accumulation of social capital inside communities, such as informal social control exercised by community residents, instead of merely setting up physical barriers and target-hardening measures. Finally, as regards the 'broken windows' thesis, community policing should focus more on bottom-up, problem-solving policing and partnership building, so as to generate more social capital both inside and outside the community for the purpose of preventing crime.

Based on the above theoretical reasoning and drawing on the conceptualization of social capital by Burt (2001), a model was constructed to depict the dimensions of social capital and crime level inside a community (Figure 3.4). That is, when bonding and bridging social capital are both strong, the level of crime inside the community is low; while when bonding and bridging social capital are both weak, the level of crime inside the community is high.

While the above exploration stays at the theoretical level as based on the Western literature, the presentation of social control in China generally and the crime-prevention programme of BLSCC in Shenzhen particularly moved the focus to an evidence-based level in a non-Western context. This pursuit constituted the major contribution of this study.

Empirical testing

To put BLSCC into perspective, prior to the presentation of BLSCC in Shenzhen, I examined the embodiment of social capital and its Chinese version, *'guanxi'*, in Chinese society, and crime and social control in China. By examining Confucianism in contrast to legalism in China, the organization of Chinese society, and *guanxi*, I demonstrated that social capital is widely employed in Chinese society. I also pointed out that prior to the full-swing reform and opening up of social structures in more recent times, Chinese rural society was characterized by strong bonding social capital and weak bridging social capital. Yet *guanxi* continues to penetrate every aspect of social life even in the reform era. Given the stigma associated with *guanxi*, its negative effects have often been overemphasized (i.e. corruption and special favours) at the expense of its positive effects on social life in China.

More specifically, social capital is a characteristic of social control in China. This was corroborated by the examination of several prominent social institutions in China: the household registration system, neighbourhood committees, work units, and public security organs. At the community level, either a neighbourhood or a work unit, due to the high immobility of the population and high intervention by the state associated with the mode of a planned economy, bonding social capital was strong, while bridging social capital was weak, an observation somewhat incongruous with the conventional understanding of Chinese society. With the intense informal social control produced by strong social capital inside the community, the level of crime was low.

With the mode of economy transformed from the planned economy to the market economy in the reform era, the mobility of the population has increased rapidly, as evidenced by the emergence of the social group called 'the floating population', and the social ties at the community level have undergone great changes. Concomitant with this process, crime rates have escalated, feelings of insecurity have increased, and the discourse on crime has changed in parallel with the experience in Western countries in the process of industrialization and modernization.

Shenzhen, as a vanguard in reform and opening up, epitomizes the present and future of the whole country, as vividly articulated in the popular saying, 'Shenzhen today is the inland areas tomorrow'. Since its establishment as a SEZ in 1979, its rapid economic development has run parallel to a growing population and soaring crime rates. Shenzhen's economic success has made it a Mecca for the floating population. There is a distinction between the population with the Shenzhen *hukou* and the population without, and the latter population in Shenzhen now accounts for a very large proportion of its total population. Thus, the problems and issues allegedly associated with the floating population have become more acute in this economic 'vanguard'. According to the official crime reports, the floating population has become disproportionately over-represented among those convicted of crime in Shenzhen. Accordingly, crime-prevention measures, to a very large extent, have been geared toward this part of the population.

BLSCC developed in Shenzhen in the early 1990s, as well as in other parts of the country. It was intended as a forceful counter-measure to increasing crime rates when the old system of social/crime control was under challenge in the reform and opening-up era. It reflected the essence of the prevention side of the duality between prevention and punishment in the general crime policy of 'comprehensive management of social order', which was established in the early 1980s. The developmental process of BLSCC in Shenzhen can be summarized as following the steps of 'seed' (1992–3), 'bud' (1994), 'blossom' (the first three-year plan for 1995–7), and 'fruit' (the second three-year plan from 1998 onwards).

The measures adopted in BLSCC are partly politically driven and partly pragmatic, and thus a grasp of them by and large can be generalized to understanding other spheres of social life in China. The measures were grouped into four aspects: organizational features (ideological mooring, leadership responsibility system, and mass prevention and mass management), safety measures (police as the main force, private security services, situational measures, and management of the floating population), civilization measures (moral education, promoting harmonious relationship, building community culture, and improvement of the environment), and the BLSCC rating system. In the process of delineating the measures, a large number of official documents were quoted in order to keep the original flavour of the official treatment of BLSCC, which has shown a preference for slogans and numbers in the official language, a proneness to moor local activities against the large national political

Conclusion

climate, and a tendency towards issuing official directives in crime prevention.

The presentation of the development and measures of BLSCC has demonstrated that, compared with the various initiatives of community crime prevention in the West, BLSCC includes certain common measures and techniques that are widely adopted in the West, but at the same time reflects certain Chinese characteristics. The BLSCC initiative has demonstrated that social capital can be employed to underlie the rationale of this community crime-prevention programme, a further testimony to the usefulness of social capital in examining Chinese society generally and Chinese social crime control in particular.

The above macrolevel study of BLSCC in Shenzhen was supplemented and corroborated by a microlevel study of BLSCC in two local contrasting communities: a 'model' and a 'non-model' community with a 'pass' based on the rating system. The data were gathered through site visits, participant observation, in-depth interviewing, and a community survey. This process demonstrated the value and significance of this study: the unequal social and political resources in individual communities were demonstrated, social networks inside local communities were measured, public perception of crime and security issues and their different distribution in individual communities were examined, and measures pertinent to the effectiveness of crime-prevention programmes were employed, and hence the actual and differential implementation of BLSCC at the community level was presented.

Most importantly, the usefulness of social capital in community crime prevention was further tested at the community level. Social capital was conceptualized as comprising the following measures at the community level: mutual help between neighbours, *tongxiang* ties, community activities, neighbours' reaction when respondents were robbed or attacked, and respondents' own reaction to an imagined pickpocketing scenario. Chi-square analyses showed that the difference between the two communities was not as substantial on some key factors as predicted from the qualitative data gathered from the communities. While this conceptualization mainly covered bonding social capital, supplementation of the available qualitative data showed that, in the model community, bridging social capital, in the form of a more positive attitudes to the police and security guards, more direct government investment and more social investment from the local level as a result of the community's designation as a model even at the national level, was stronger, and this to a very large extent accounted for its success in implementing BLSCC, not to mention the actual difference from the non-model community in social-economic status.

The nexus revisited

As the literature review has shown, the nexus between community crime prevention and social capital in the West warrants attention to the following problems and issues: formal versus informal social control, public versus private control, exclusion versus inclusion, and the fundamental role of the state. In the following discussion, I examine the salience, manifestation and significance of these problems and issues based on the Chinese experience as presented in this study.

Formal/informal

The social control system in China features a unique combination of formal and informal methods, with a strong emphasis on the latter. As Troyer *et al.* (1989: 6) observed, 'In order to understand the dynamics of social control in China, one must begin by examining its informal control network. This is where the pressure to conform is pervasive and intense.' However, they stressed that, in China, 'An informal social control system is actually controlled by Chinese officials' (1989: 6). As Turk (1989: 273) observed:

> It is not that Chinese control is informal where ours is formal; rather it is that social control is formally invested in less formal structures – in human groups more than in social institutions. For instance, mediation committees – that ubiquitous presence in Chinese social control – are local groups that are legitimized and often trained by the Ministry of Justice. Formal agencies make informal groups the locus of social control.

This interlinking of the formal with the informal is corroborated by the examination of the social institutions of *hukou, danwei*, neighbourhood committees and the police prior to the full development of the market economy. Thus, it is hard to distinguish formal from informal social control in the Chinese context. Because of the blurring between the two, to a certain extent it is more accurate to address the informal control mechanisms in the Chinese context as equivalent to grass-roots involvement. Moreover, as noted earlier, while in the West the new initiatives in crime prevention aim to increase informal control at the community level, in China the heavy involvement of the masses and informal agencies always constitutes one of the important characteristics of the Chinese approach to crime prevention.

With the reform and opening-up deepening and broadening, the landscape of social control in China has been transformed to feature a combination of Westernization, socialism and Chinese characteristics, as argued by Xu (1995). Previously low in population mobility, the Chinese – for example, in their neighbourhoods and their work units – were always under an all-encompassing surveillance by people within that very social environment, a 'formalization' of natural surveillance. This pervasive surveillance, as imposed by the *hukou, danwei,* and neighbourhood committees, constituted a powerful informal control network (via social pressure, gossip and 'neighbour' intervention) under which people were obliged to conform. However, the reform era necessitated the establishment of a formal legal system complying with international standards and conducive to economic activities, on the one hand, and the transformation of the informal control system on the other hand. This is demonstrated by the changing role assumed by the four prominent social institutions of the PSB, *hukou, danwei,* and neighbourhood committees.

In Shenzhen, the PSB was actively engaged in professionalization and formalization, as, for example, through the adoption of the patrolling system and the crime-reporting hotline 110. Understandably, all the other agencies joined in the professionalization movement, in order to adapt to the new social and economic environment. However, the PSB still upholds the mass line, and still puts great emphasis on establishing a good relationship with the masses. This is manifested in the 'four-ones', 'four-haves' and similar slogans. *Hukou*, together with its registration and all its associated social welfare support, has been impinged upon under the economic reform. However, *hukou*, even the compromised 'blue-card' *hukou*, still functions to identify migrants as 'outside workers', and by that very identification it still functions to exercise control over the migrants.

Neighbourhood committees, albeit often with acute budget difficulties, still function as one of the important parts of the grass-roots control system. Meanwhile, corresponding to the different demands of the new era, the staff, structure, and accountability of neighbourhood committees are in the process of adaptation. Specifically, they are under challenge from other newly emerging organizations, which are perceived to be more efficient by local residents, such as the office of housing management. Thus, their role has often been downgraded and discounted. The *danwei* system has undergone the most marked change in terms of its function in social control. With the marketization of the most necessary products and the abolition of rationing, SOEs have unloaded many of their traditional welfare functions. Thus, due to the collapse of the interdependence between social welfare and social control within the *danwei* system, the *danwei*'s role in social control has also substantially diminished. In the foreign-owned, private, and joint enterprises, this role has been greatly undermined and is even disappearing. With the work unit form of control undermined and new forms of control emerging slowly, Lau (2001) argues that a socio-political control crisis has arisen.

According to the inverse relationship between formal and informal control in mobilizing law and order agencies suggested by Black (1980), the growth of formal control in China should lead to the decline in informal control. Xu even envisaged that due to the influence of the Western model, the existing 'extensive, intrusive community surveillance would be *replaced* by a professional police force and individuals would regain freedom in a wide range of spheres' (1995: 84; emphasis added). She regarded such a development as 'a progressive change'. But as illustrated above, although the formal control mechanisms, such as the police are undergoing professionalization, the informal control mechanisms (or the grass-roots involvement) still play an important role and are far from being replaced. For instance, in BLSCC the 'mass prevention and mass management' is particularly emphasized. Thus, under the current scenario, informal control mechanisms coexist with the formal control mechanisms, with both contributing to the maintenance of a social order pertinent for the sustainable development of the socialist market economy in China. The balancing of the informal with the formal mode has been observed in the West – for example, by Horwitz (1990). He argued that, despite the expanded symbolic and actual presence of law and other formal control in everyday life (as reflected by the 'litigation crisis'), 'the dominant focus on law and governmental social control systems and the peripheral place allocated to the extralegal handling of disputes in the study of social control is unjustified' (1990: 7). However, as noted in Shenzhen, the partnership approach between the formal and the informal modes of social control has encountered difficulties, a situation similar to that in the West.

Public/private control

Based on the Western experience, a mixture of private and public control is supposed to facilitate the prevention of crime. Compared with the West, the distinction between the private and public spheres in China is less obvious, or, more accurately, the private sphere was underdeveloped or suppressed due to the dominant role of public ownership (including state ownership and collective ownership) associated with the planned economy. Hence, the social space in a particular entity such as a neighbourhood is open to all residents, a fact that is conducive to the accumulation of bonding social capital. Social/crime control becomes everyone's business, and the masses are extensively mobilized in this pursuit, as evidenced by the continuation of the mass-line approach. But as Shearing suggests, the principle that 'the private becomes the public, and the public becomes the private' (1992: 419) results in the loss of the individual's protection from unfettered state intrusion.

The reform era has seen the growth of private ownership and the rapid expansion of the private sphere. A particularly significant initial step in this process was the 'household responsibility system' in the countryside, which was characterized by the assignment of land to individual households, division of village collective properties, and lease of village enterprises by individual peasants. The rationale underlying this new system was that individuals or households should take responsibility for farming the land or managing the village enterprises. This saw a substantial improvement of agricultural output throughout the country, and a boom in 'village and township enterprises', especially along the eastern coastline. This has brought about one of the most significant consequences: the accelerated stratification of Chinese society (see e.g. Bian 2002). While, in the past, the dominant ideology was equalitarianism, as expressed in the popular saying of 'eating from the same big pot', in the reform era it has changed to 'getting rich is glorious'.

In the spirit of the responsibility system, the private sector has taken more responsibility for preventing crime, and private investment has grown in the form of target-hardening measures or the development of defensible space as a response to increasing crime. Since what individuals and households can invest depends on their economic status, their risk of being victimized by crime has changed. Further, as a result of the 'hardening' and 'defending' of individual properties and households, the social space between neighbours has shrunk substantially, and hence the social ties have attenuated, as illustrated by some of the older residents who complained about this in the model community. This development has caused adverse effects on the stock of social capital inside the community, and subsequently on the objective of social control and crime prevention.

One of the most overt steps in the privatization of security is the emergence of the private security industry. In Shenzhen, the security guards at the community level play an important role in preventing crime and maintaining public feeings of safety, whatever positive or negative economic or social changes individual communities undergo. But privatization has contributed to the unequal chances of victimization at both the individual and the community level, as evidenced in communities A and B. The development of private security makes possible the sharing of the crime prevention role previously played solely by the public police. Although it has expanded rapidly to overtake the public police in terms of personnel and investment in the West, the private security industry is under the direct guidance of the PSB in China. Given rapid developments in the whole society, the status of private security industry as 'junior partners' (Shearing 1992) is predicted to change in the foreseeable future. For example, by December 2005, the number of security guards had reached four million nationwide, and in Beijing, security guards outnumbered the police (*China News Net* 2005). Without doubt, the further growth of the private security industry will widen the gap between the rich and the poor in terms of victimization and feelings of security.

Thus, while the expansion of the private sphere is associated with a vibrant economy and more individual freedom, it simultaneously leads to a more stratified society. This is expected to have adverse effects on the integration of different elements in individual communities and subsequently on the accumulation of bonding social capital. As Wang (2002: 8) observed, tensions arise in community development and community integration in the new era of China for the following two reasons: (1) community members vary in their expectations and interests, which may conflict; (2) the modernization has destructive effects on community awareness. He proceeded to argue that since community development resources are increasingly compartmentalized or privatized, it has become a real problem to make the owners of these resources release them for community development. He particularly called attention to 'the social strata that own more social resources and need not ask the help of others'. This observation applied to community A in Shenzhen, where the residents were more wealthy and thus tended to be more successful in implementing BLSCC. Further, with the gap of social-economic status widening, it is envisaged that cooperation and collaboration between communities will become more difficult, jeopardizing the building of bridging social capital. The new changes in the internal and external dynamics of the community will hinder the building of partnership between the private and public for the control and prevention of crime.

Inclusion/exclusion

As the analysis of social capital in China has shown, social structures such as a neighbourhood or work unit, were characterized by a high level of inclusion (strong bonding social capital) and a high level of exclusion (low bridging social capital), a scenario associated with and reinforced by the lack of state-approved population mobility in the pre-reform era. The most dramatic example was the separation of the urban residents from the rural residents. In the reform era, that situation has been difficult to maintain. Of particular importance have been the rural migrants 'floating' to the urban areas. Inside a community where migrants and non-migrants reside together, migrants are excluded or at least seen as a special group, as in community B. There are also special communities where migrants are concentrated, such as the Zhejiang Village and Xinjiang Village in Beijing. Sufficient evidence shows that the floating population may now constitute the excluded 'underclass' or de facto lumpenproletariat in Chinese cities.

According to Crowther (2000), the 'underclass' in the West refers to a variety of underlying factors or groups: educational failure; underemployment or unemployment and job insecurity; social and spatial isolation; dependency on state-provided welfare; teenage mothers; racial discrimination; participation in the informal economy; and a propensity to engage in criminal and disorderly behaviour. While, for example, in the United States, in relation to the underclass thesis, race is of particular significance, in the Chinese context, the migrants' treatment as an 'underclass' is mainly based on their rural *hukou* status assigned on the basis of their rural origin. Contingent on that *hukou* status, they are associated with a variety of factors, corresponding to the factors listed above for their Western counterparts: educational deprivation for themselves and their children in the cities; underemployment or unemployment and job insecurity, social and spatial isolation, lack of state-provided welfare, *hukou*-driven discrimination, *alleged* participation in the informal economy, and *alleged* propensity to engage in criminal and disorderly behaviour.

There are essentially two perspectives on the 'underclass': the structural and the behavioral (see reviews by Crowther 2000: 151). The structural perspective concentrates on the processes that produce socio-economic inequality, poverty, social exclusion and social polarization. The behavioural perspective holds individuals to be culpable for their own and their family's poverty. In the Chinese context, while the formation of an underclass based on the floating population status can be attributed to the structural perspective, the popular wisdom holds to the behavioural perspective. This further increased their exclusion in the cities and reduced the underclass's opportunities for full civic engagement.

As Crowther pointed out, in the UK, 'on the basis of the still politically influential behavioral perspective any failures of government policy may be ascribed to the characterological deficiencies of the "underclass"' rather than structural factors' (2000: 154). Accordingly, he argued, despite changes in the political economy and the reforms of the police, the policing of the underclass remains the basic mandate of the police in all industrial societies. In China, as shown in the measures for managing the floating population, migrants actually become the convenient target of aggressive policing and any government-initiated crime-prevention activity.

In current Chinese society, the migrants are not the only excluded group. To follow the previous argument about the increasing stratification of Chinese society, there has increasingly emerged a class of urban poor. For example, there is the large number of laid-off workers from the SOEs (their former *danwei*) as a result of economic restructuring, regardless of their urban *hukou*. This section of the new urban poor will join the migrants to become the 'underclass'. The underclass tend to be the target of three levels of exclusion provided by Young (1999): economic exclusion from the labour market, social exclusion between people in civil society, and the ever-expanding exclusionary activities of the criminal justice system and private security. Thus, substantial efforts should be made to integrate them for the sake of the stability of the whole society.

The role of the state

In the above discussions on formal/informal social control, public/private control, and inclusion and exclusion, there is an underlying theme: the role of the state. As reviewed earlier, according to the

Conclusion

Weberian perspective, the state is more than the government. But in the Chinese context, the state is associated with both the government and the Party. At this juncture, it is necessary to point out that several scholars in China studies (e.g. Sue 1988; Dutton 1992; Dutton and Lee 1993) have rejected the conceptualization of the Chinese state as 'totalitarian' or 'despotic'. In examining Chinese policing strategies in the period of economic reform, Dutton and Lee (1993) challenged the 'cold war approach' of treating the Chinese state as 'the omnipotent despotic state', although they did not deny the arbitrary and extralegal nature of many forms of detention and control in China. They suggested that the arbitrary policing methods, rather than being merely the inevitable consequence of an authoritarian regime, were the inevitable consequence of economic reform and had considerable popular support.

If the Western literature shows more of a 'state–society' dichotomy, in Chinese society the state and the society can actually coexist, as cogently argued by Sigley when examining family-planning policies in China.

> Granted that Chinese governmental discourse is devoid of certain liberal forms of reasoning as they are understood in the work of governmentality, and it is hence misleading to pose the question of individual and market autonomy in terms of a *'distance'* between state and society, it is possible then to perceive a form of governmental reasoning in which the market and highly specific forms of technical intervention in daily life can *coexist*. (1996: 477; emphasis added)

Yang (1994) admitted that to apply the modern Western social dynamic of state and civil society to an understanding of China ran the risk of imposing one interpretive framework on a different social and historical context. So in her discussion on *guanxi*, instead of civil society, she used a native Chinese term in common use, *minjian*, which refers to 'a realm of people-to-people relationship which is non-governmental or separate from formal bureaucratic channels' (1994: 288). However, in spite of *minjian*'s different contours from its equivalent in the West, she still regarded discussions of civil society and the state as relevant to what is happening in China today.

In comparing the Chinese *'minjian'* with the emergence of civil society in Western Europe, where stress is put on individual rights, and in Eastern Europe, where stress is put on independent associations and institutions, Yang (1994: 294) argued,

> Given the difficulties of independent group formation in the present Chinese political context, the inability of the legal system to protect individuals and associations and the relative weakness of a discourse of 'rights' and of 'individualism' in the culture, the prognosis of civil society according to the European model does not look good in China. Perhaps we must focus on informal group and individual units for the seeds of an autonomous realm in China.

Thus, she conceptualized the Chinese *minjian* as 'in-between the individual and society' and 'in-between the individual and groups or associations'.

Although Yang confined her discussion to the conventional understanding of 'civil society' as opposed to the state, her depiction of *minjian* did suggest a non-conventional framework for civil society in China. In fact, Solinger's (1993) review of the bond between the state and civil society showed a basic ambiguity: civil society may either be distinguished from the state or inextricably ensnared within the state. If the latter perspective of ambiguity is taken, it is consistent with Woolcock's comprehensive observation about social capital wherein the state itself constitutes one part of social capital. In this regard, the Chinese context offers an example for reconsidering how to involve the state in the production of social capital and subsequently in preventing crime.

In the examination of community development in China, Wang observed, 'Advancing the idea of community development and promoting the community development movement are associated with politics' (2002: 5). As he pointed out, although since the initiation of reforms the growth of extra-governmental political forces has given rise to a scenario of complex interactions between governmental and extra-governmental politics, the extra-governmental politics is still underdeveloped. He argued that, 'the previous "community-based" activities were part of organized and planned governmental work, while the goal sought by the current community development is to realize the relatively independent and stable operation of community affairs' (Wang 2002: 6). In other words, they are essentially self-regulating and self-investing community help.

But Wang (2002) conceded that community residents in China lack experience of self-governance and the ability to realize community self-government, and this he attributed to the rather slow maturation of civil society in Chinese cities. Wang also used the native term *minjian* to denote non-governmental organizations. When listing the entities or actors taking part in community development, he included *minjian zuzhi* (which he rendered as 'civilian organizations'), together with governmental bodies, the subdistrict offices as agencies of the government, neighbourhood committees, subdistrict-based enterprises and institutions and community residents.[1] Clearly included in the list are both state and non-state entities. But he cogently pointed out the problems related to the non-state involvement in China:

> For a long time, a tradition of mass participation has developed in China, but it is mostly limited to the sphere of implementation, that is, the masses are mobilized to implement decisions made by the leadership of the Party and the government, evolving thereby into a power-elite dominated pattern of participation. (Wang 2002: 7)

In the spirit of the literature in the West, this is an approach of 'top-down' rather than 'bottom-up' in community development. However, as shown above, community crime prevention in the West should be from a 'bottom-up' approach based on identifying community problems and their solutions.

Wang (2002) observed that the Chinese government no longer automatically resorts to political mobilization and direct intervention in community affairs, yet its desire for the maintenance of social stability has not weakened. However, my fieldwork in Shenzhen showed that, in implementing BLSCC, political mobilization and direct intervention were still widely used regardless of market forces. But as Wang (2002) suggested, even in the era of the widespread penetration of market forces, the government should play a more active role in promoting community development in view of the following factors: (1) enterprises and institutions lack the zeal to participate in community development; (2) civilian organizations committed to the cause of community development are underdeveloped; (3) for a long time, community residents have been accustomed to relying on the government. Despite the necessity of government involvement, he stressed that 'while the government should shoulder responsibility for community development, it should not overstep its authority' (Wang 2002: 7).

The active involvement of the state in community affairs is further evidenced in the establishment of trade unions in the various new and emerging enterprises. Unlike its Western counterpart, the trade union in Chinese work units mainly performs social welfare functions (Lau 2001). With the marketization of the welfare benefits previously provided by the work units, the trade union in the new era is granted the role of protecting stability in the enterprises, the main responsibility being 'preventing and defusing labor unrest' (Lau 2001). Above all, trade unions have been controlled by the Chinese government, both before and after the economic reform. But they are not established in many private or foreign-owned enterprises. The official union statistics indicated that trade unions had been set up in about 40 per cent of newly founded overseas companies, and only 54.7 per cent of employees at those firms had become union members, and in the private sector and in township enterprises, only one-sixth and one-seventh of workers were union members, respectively (*South China Morning Post* 2002d). In many foreign-owned enterprises where the trade unions are absent, fraternities of migrant workers from the same native place are established, whose de facto role alarmed the government (Lau 2001). Further, disputes between workers and employers have become commonplace,[2] and these are seen as potential threats to social stability. Thus, the government initiated a campaign in 2001 to 'set up unions where there are workers' (*South China Morning Post* 2002d). As Lau (2001) observed, although the state's economic reform programme had undermined the social control function of the former work units and prohibited the trade union from assuming the assigned duties of social control in the new enterprises, the government initiatives in increasing the presence of the trade union demonstrates the active involvement of the state in the maintenance of social stability, albeit in a different manner from that in the West.

Concerning the nexus of social capital and crime prevention, the role of the state is further shown in mediating the social and political effects on crime and crime prevention in the local communities. In his critique of the broken widows theory, Matthews (1992) argued that the relationship between incivility, crime and community decline is far more complicated than a causal sequence from incivility to crime to community decline. In particular, he stressed the effects of economic and political development, rather than incivility alone, on the level of crime in communities. For example, in terms of the relation between incivility, neighbourhood decline and fear of crime, he cited Lewis and Salem's (1986) argument that the community's political and social resources appeared to constitute a major mediating force between the perception of crime and other neighbourhood problems and the subsequent expression of fear. But he observed that such resources played little role in the broken windows thesis; for example, political organizations through which policies would have to be channelled and the prime movers in the process of urban decline such as corporations, industrial and finance capital, and political groupings.

In the conceptualization of community crime prevention in this study, the broken windows thesis becomes the rationale for a partnership for crime prevention, whereby different government agencies, community organizations and the public collaborate and cooperate in the pursuit of crime prevention. But in the framework of social capital underpinning community crime prevention, the aspect of bridging social capital takes into account the effect of political and social factors on crime and crime prevention in communities. Above all, mediating the differential effects of any political and social factors impinging on particular communities becomes an important role of the state.

Looking forward into the future

In this study, I delineated the problems and promises in the areas of crime and crime prevention in the Chinese context. Here I particularly stress certain prospective aspects and new challenges in future China studies.

Concerning the methodological endeavours I made in the process of conducting this study, I encountered certain obstacles in the field. I believe those obstacles apply to China studies in general. But things seem to be changing rather rapidly. In several annual meetings on crime and its control in greater China convened by the Center for Criminology of the University of Hong Kong, officials from the Peoples' Public Security University, the Ministry of Public Security, the Ministry of Justice and other provincial departments were invited to attend. The attendees were extraordinarily cautious in presenting crime and the countermeasures against crime in the mainland, which were and are surrounded by secrecy, but they gave the impression that they were far more open-minded than before. It might not be over-optimistic to foresee that they will go even farther in this direction. This open-mindedness bodes well for the undertaking of more rigorous evidence-based criminological research in the mainland, and ultimately for the healthy development of the discipline of criminology. Although the development of criminology has undergone a detour in the mainland (see Kang and Zhao 1998; Pearson 2002), we may hope that the new tendencies will bring it more in line with an international perspective.

As observed by Garland and Sparks (2000: 6), criminology has developed in three major social settings or matrices: (1) the world of the academy – of social science and scholarly discourse; (2) the world of government – of crime control and criminal justice; (3) the world of culture – including mass-mediated popular culture and political discourse. However, they noted a striking divergence between national penal policy and criminological research, a gap which has been growing over the last decade. According to them, this divergence was earlier pointed out by Radzinowicz (1999: 469, quoted in Garland and Sparks 2000: 5): 'What I find profoundly disturbing is the gap between "criminology" and "criminal policy", between the study of crime and punishment and the actual mode of controlling crime.... The stark fact stands out that, in the field of criminal justice, in spite of the output of criminological knowledge, a populist political approach holds sway.'

The current situation is similar in both China and the West: a 'populist political approach' predominates. But, according to the above observations, in the West it is because well-developed criminological knowledge is not employed by governments to direct criminal policies and crime control. In China, it can be said that it is because criminology is underdeveloped, partly due to excessive governmental intervention and outdated disciplinary set-up in tertiary educational institutions. In terms of the latter, criminology is affiliated to the law departments in universities and is always undertaken by scholars with a speciality in criminal law, a fact that, to a certain extent, hinders the diversity of perspectives in criminology. This calls for more government support for the healthy and dependent growth of the discipline of criminology, on the one hand, and, on the other hand, more active deployment of criminological output in guiding governmental decision-making in crime and crime control.

Concerning the third perspective of criminology by Garland and Sparks (2000), the mass media and the publication industry in China are subject to more governmental control. But, as Kinkley (2000) demonstrated in his book *Chinese Justice, the Fiction: Law and Literature in Modern China*, the law on publication and literary production is undergoing rapid development in the reform era of China regardless of political influences. With the Chinese society becoming more open, criminology and its related literature will reach the popular culture in a more profound way, and thus it should lead to more public understanding of the discipline.

Notwithstanding the optimism expressed above, crime and criminal policy are still subject to the prevailing political climate, and certain political techniques still play their role in the field of crime control. To take 'learning from models' as an example, Shenzhen became a model for economic reform and opening up in the whole country, and community A was elevated to a citywide model in implementing BLSCC and even became 'the first civilized village' of the nation. With the initiation of the 'go west' movement to pursue a balanced economic development around the country and entry to the World Trade Organization, Shenzhen's prestigious status has increasingly lost its significance. This led to the loss of a wide range of policy-induced privileges, and ultimately may have an adverse impact on future economic and civic development. The case of Shenzhen shows the impact of national policies on local development. In fact, community A is also subject to political influences. As noted above, community A is managed by Wanxia, a state-owned property company. The emergence of community A to a large extent illustrates the role of political manoeuvre. For example, in the field, I was informed by one of the employees in the management office of community A that Wanxia and the government were directing attention away from community A to another newly emerging community in its vicinity. Thus, in community A, there was a sense of an imminent loss of favour at the political level. I paid close attention to any further development of this issue; and during my subsequent return trips to Shenzhen, I was frequently reminded by my informants that that newly emerging community was much more under the spotlight. From the relevant agencies and departments, I was able to find reports submitted by the new community on their achievement, in the same manner as community A did in its prime time as a model LSCC. My informants even kindly advised me to shift focus to the new community because of their understanding that the old one had lost its research value. This illustrates their perception of political value, the impact of politics on research, and the deep penetration of 'learning from models' in the Chinese psyche. Thus, it can be envisaged that it takes time for more fundamental changes to take place.

    China studies tend to focus more on the urban areas and the coastal regions of China. In regard to the vast areas of the countryside and the inland regions, less is known. With the implementation of the 'go west' movement, it is expected that cross-cultural researchers with an interest in China will direct their attention to the western regions to gain a fuller understanding of the mysterious 'Middle Kingdom'. Growing up in the countryside of central China, I personally experienced the huge gap between urban and rural areas in China.

Certainly, with the reforms slowly at first and now rapidly spreading, the countryside is also undergoing a tremendous transformation, which will have a profound impact on the national development, considering the large rural land and population. This further calls for a diversion of more academic attention to the countryside. For example, as I have observed on my visits to the countryside during recent years, the grass-roots organizations are increasingly losing relevance to the rural villagers, and the local clans organized around the same family name are gaining more and more influence in local affairs. A deeper understanding of the clan and the role it plays in local social control will enrich our perspectives on local social relationships, social capital and local social control in the new era of China.

Notes

1 Here 'subdistrict' is equivalent to 'street office' (*jiedao ban*), as shown in Figure 5.1 on the hierarchy of administrative structure in China.
2 For example, in 2001, there were 12,580 disputes between workers and employers in Shenzhen, and more than half occurred in the private sector (*South China Morning Post* 2002d).

Appendix

Survey questions

Area one: Social networks, cohesion and mutual help within the community

1. In the past year, did your neighbours ask you to watch their home or look after their children while they were away?
   a. Yes.
   b. No.
2. In the past year, did you ask your neighbours to watch your home or look after your children while you were away?
   a. Yes.
   b. No.
3. Do you know any *tongxiang* (fellow villagers, townsmen or provincials) living in the same community? If you got into trouble, would you ask them for help?
   a. Don't know any.
   b. Know some but would not ask them for help.
   c. Know some and would ask them for help.
4. Were there any cultural activities or other recreational activities in your community in the past year, and did you take part in any of them?
   a. There are no such activities at all.
   b. There were some activities, and I took part in them.
   c. There were some activities, but I did not take part in them.
5. If you were being attacked or robbed, how do you think your neighbours would react?
   a. Come to my assistance.

b. Call the police.
   c. Avoid getting involved.
   d. Show their sympathy and support after the event.
   e. Other.
6. If you were in the following situation, what would you do?
   (1) You are walking in your community in the afternoon. In front of you, a man is walking slowly. He is in his twenties, of slight build, and dressed like a construction worker. Just in front of him, there is an old lady. Suddenly, you see the man stealing a purse from her. What would you do?
   a. Stop the man on the scene.
   b. Seek help from others to stop the man.
   c. Report it to the security guards or the police.
   d. Shout, 'Stop thief.'
   e. Shout, 'Watch out, someone is stealing a purse.'
   f. Would be so scared that I would avoid getting involved and keep walking.
   g. None of my business; I would avoid getting involved and keep walking.
   h. Inform the old lady after the event.
   i. Other.
   (2) If that situation happened at the same time but outside your own community, what would you do?
   a. Stop the man at the scene.
   b. Seek help from others to stop the man.
   c. Report it to the security guards or the police.
   d. Shout, 'Stop thief.'
   e. Shout, 'Watch out, someone is stealing a purse.'
   f. Would be so scared that I would avoid getting involved and keep walking.
   g. None of my business; I would avoid getting involved and keep walking.
   h. Inform the old lady after the event.
   i. Other.

Area two: Crime, fear of crime and the attitudes towards the security guards and police

7. What are the major problems in your community?
   a. hygiene and sanitation.
   b. Health service.

c. Problems with floating population and house renting.
   d. Laid-off (*xia gang*) workers.
   e. Car parking.
   f. The problem of *zhi'an* ('public security').
   g. Public transport.
   h. Children's school education.
   i. Illegal buildings (*wei zhang jian zhu*).
   j. Family planning.
   k. Fire.
   l. Other.
8. The following is a list of certain types of crime that can be problems in some communities. Please choose those that you think are the real problems in your own community.
   a. Breaking into houses.
   b. Bicycle theft.
   c. Auto theft.
   d. Violence and fighting.
   e. Gambling.
   f. Drunkenness.
   g. Robbery.
   h. Sale or use of drugs.
   i. Prostitution.
   j. Sexual assault (hooliganism against women).
   k. Swindling.
   l. Gang activity.
   m. Triads.
   n. Others.
9. Do you think migrants are more likely to commit crime or other illegal activities?
   a. Yes.
   b. No.
   c. No opinion.

Questions 11, 13, and 15 are for area three (they are put here for the continuity of the interview)

10. Do you feel that it is safe to walk alone at night in your community?
    a. Very safe.
    b. Somewhat safe.
    c. Unsafe.
    d. Very unsafe.
    e. No opinion.

11. Has there been any change in the aforementioned feeling of safety in the past year?
    a. Better.
    b. Worse.
    c. No change.
    d. No opinion.
12. What do you think are your chances of being the victim of violence or other assault in this community?
    a. Very high.
    b. High.
    c. Low.
    d. Very low.
    e. No opinion.
13. In the past year, do you think the chances aforementioned have changed?
    a. Increasing.
    b. Decreasing.
    c. No change.
    d. No opinion.
14. What do you think about your chances of being the victim of robbery, theft or burglary in this community?
    a. Very high.
    b. High.
    c. Low.
    d. Very low.
    e. No opinion.
15. In the past year, do you think the chances aforementioned have changed?
    a. Increasing.
    b. Decreasing.
    c. No change.
    d. No opinion.
16. In the past year, have you been the victim of any crime?
    a. Yes (go to Q17).
    b. No (go to Q19).
17. If 'Yes', what was it?
18. If 'Yes', did you report it?
    a. Yes.
    b. No.
19. Are there any security guards in your community?
    a. Yes (go to Q20).
    b. No (go to Q21).

20. If 'Yes', do you think they help maintain security in this community?
    a. Very helpful.
    b. Somewhat helpful.
    c. Not helpful.
    d. No opinion.
21. Do you often see the policemen from the local police station (*pai chu shuo*) in this community?
    a. Very often.
    b. Often.
    c. Sometimes.
    d. Never.
22. Are you satisfied with the police's work?
    a. Very satisfied.
    b. Satisfied.
    c. Dissatisfied.
    d. Very dissatisfied.

Area three: General knowledge and overall impression of BLSCC

23. Have you heard anything about BLSCC?
    a. Yes (go to Q24).
    b. No (go to Q25).
24. If 'Yes', what do you think about BLSCC?
    a. Very useful.
    b. Somewhat useful.
    c. Not useful.
    d. No opinion.
25. How do you think the relationship between the residents in the community has changed recently?
    a. Better.
    b. Worse.
    c. No change.
    d. No opinion.
26. Have you taken any new anticrime measures in your home in the past year?
    a. Yes (go to Q27).
    b. No (go to Q28).
27 If 'Yes', what was it?

28. Is there any change of the physical appearance of your community recently?
    a. Better.
    b. Worse.
    c. No change.
    d. No opinion.
29. In the past year, do you feel that the *zhi'an zhuang kuang* ('the situation of public security') in this community is worse, is better or has not changed?
    a. Better.
    b. Worse.
    c. No change.
    d. No opinion.

Questions 11, 13, and 15 from area two

11. Has there been any change in the aforementioned feeling of safety in the past year?
    a. Better.
    b. Worse.
    c. No change.
    d. No opinion.
13. In the past year, do you think the chances aforementioned have changed?
    a. Increasing.
    b. Decreasing.
    c. No change.
    d. No opinion.
15. In the past year, do you think the chances aforementioned have changed?
    a. Increasing.
    b. Decreasing.
    c. No change.
    d. No opinion.

Demographic questions

D1. Community:
    a. Community A.
    b. Community B.

D2. Gender:
- a. Male.
- b. Female.

D3. Age:
- a. Under 25.
- b. 26–35.
- c. 36–45.
- d. 46–55.
- e. 56–65.
- f. 66 and over.

D4. Time lived in the community:
- a. Under 1 year.
- b. 1–2 years.
- c. 2–10 years.
- d. Over 10 years.

D5. Status of residence:
- a. Permanent.
- b. Temporary.

D6. Education:
- a. Less than junior high school.
- b. Junior high school.
- c. Senior high school.
- d. College.
- e. Postgraduate.

D7. Occupation:
- a. Civil servants.
- b. Employee in state-owned enterprises.
- c. Employee in private sector.
- d. Employee in foreign company.
- e. Teacher.
- f. Student.
- g. Unemployed.
- h. Retired.

D8. Type of residence:
- a. Own.
- b. Rent.
- c. Live with relatives or friends.
- d. Other.

References

Ayres, I. and Braithwaite, J. (1992) *Responsive Regulation: Transcending the Deregulation Debate*. Oxford: Oxford University Press.

Baker, M.H., Nienstedt, B.C., Everett, R.S. and McCleary, R. (1983) 'The Impact of a Crime Wave: Perceptions, Fear, and Confidence in the Police', *Law and Society Review*, 17 (2): 319–36.

Bakken, B. (2000) *The Exemplary Society: Human Improvement, Social Control, and the Dangers of Modernity in China*. Oxford: Oxford University Press.

Bakken, B. (2004) 'Moral Panics, Crime Rates and Harsh Punishment in China', *Australian and New Zealand Journal of Criminology*, 37 (Supple): 67–89.

Bakken, B. (2005) 'Comparative Perspectives on Crime in China', in B. Bakken (ed.), *Crime, Punishment, and Policing in China*. New York: Rowman and Littlefield.

Banton, M. (1980) 'Foreword', in J.M. Hough and R.V. Clarke (eds), *The Effectiveness of Policing*. Aldershot: Gower, pp. vii–xii.

Bellair, P.E. (1997) 'Social Interaction and Community Crime: Examining the Importance of Neighbor Networks', *Criminology*, 35 (4): 677–704.

Bennett, R.B. (1991) 'Development and Crime: A Cross-National, Time-series Analysis of Competing Models', *Sociological Quarterly*, 32 (3): 343–63.

Bennett, T. (1996) 'Introduction', in T Bennett (ed.), *Preventing Crime and Disorder: Targeting Strategies and Responsibilities*. Cambridge: Cambridge University Press.

Bian, D. (1997) 'Investigation of University Graduates in the Shenzhen Police Force'. *Public Security Research*, 51 (1): 43–6.

Bian, Y. (1994) 'Guanxi and the Allocation of Urban Jobs in China', *China Quarterly*, 140, 971–99.

Bian, Y. (1997) 'Bringing Strong Ties Back In: Indirect Ties, Network Bridges, and Job Searches in China', *American Sociological Review*, 62: 366–85.

Bian, Y. (2001) 'Guanxi Capital and Social Eating in Chinese Cities: Theoretical Models and Empirical Analyses', in N. Lin, K. Cook and R.S. Burt (eds), *Social Capital: Theory and Research*. New York: Aldine De Gruyter.

Bian, Y. (2002) 'Chinese Social Stratification and Social Mobility', *Annual Review of Sociology*, 29: 91–116.

Bian, Y. and Ang, S. (1997) 'Guanxi Networks and Job Mobility in China and Singapore', *Social Forces*, 75 (3): 981–1005.

Black, D. (1980) *The Manners and Customs of the Police*. New York: Academic Press.

Blakely, E.J. and Snyder, M.G. (1997) *Fortress America: Gated Communities in the United States*. Washington, DC and Cambridge, MA: Brookings Institution and Lincoln Institute of Land Policy.

Blanchard, A. and Horan, T. 2000. 'Virtual Communities and Social Capital', in G.D. Garson (ed.), *Social Dimensions of Information Technology: Issues for the New Millennium*. Hershey, PA: Idea Group Publishing.

Bottoms, A.E. and Wiles, P. (1996) 'Understanding Crime Prevention in Late Modern Societies', in T. Bennett (ed.) *Preventing Crime and Disorder: Targeting Strategies and Responsibilities*. Cambridge: Cambridge University Press.

Bourdieu, P. (1985) 'The Forms of Social Capital', in J.G. Richardson (ed.), *Handbook of Theory and Research for the Sociology of Education*. New York: Greenwood, pp. 24–158.

Bracey, D.H. (1989) 'Policing the People's Republic', in R.J. Troyer, J.P. Clark and D.G. Rojek (eds), *Social Control in the People's Republic of China*. New York: Praeger, pp. 130–40.

Braithwaite, J. (1989) *Crime, Shame and Reintegration*. Cambridge: Cambridge University Press.

Braithwaite, J. (1999) 'Restorative Justice: Assessing Optimistic and Pessimistic Accounts', in M. Tonry (ed.), *Criminal Justice: A Review of Research*. Chicago: University of Chicago Press, pp. 1–127.

Braithwaite, J. (2000) 'The New Regulatory State and the Transformation of Criminology', in D. Garland and R. Sparks (eds), *Criminology and Social Theory*, Oxford: Oxford University Press, pp. 47–70.

Brantingham, P.L. and Faust, F.L. (1976) 'A Conceptual Model of Crime Prevention', *Crime and Delinquency*, 22 (3): 284–96.

Brewer, J.D., Guelke, A., Hume, I., Moxon-Browne, E. and Wilford, R. (eds) (1996) *The Police, Public Order and the State* (2nd edn). London: Macmillan.

Broadhurst, R.B. (2002) 'Bridging the Gap – Transnational Organized Crime: Introduction', *Proceedings of the Transnational Organized Crime Conference*. Centre for Criminology: University of Hong Kong.

Brogden, M. (1999) 'Community Policing as Cherry Pie', in R.I. Mawby (ed.), *Policing Across the World: Issues for the Twenty-First Century*. London: UCL Press.

Brown, M. and Polk, K. (1996) 'Taking Fear of Crime Seriously: The Tasmanian Approach to Community Crime Prevention', *Crime and Delinquency*, 42 (3): 398–420.
Bursik, R.J. (1988) 'Social Disorganization and Theories of Crime and Delinquency: Problems and Prospects', *Criminology*, 26: 519–51.
Bursik, R.J. and Grasmick, H.G. (1993) *Neighborhood and Crime*. New York: Lexington Books.
Burt, R.S. (1992) *Structural Holes*. Cambridge, MA: Harvard University Press.
Burt, R.S. (2001) 'Structural Holes versus Network Closure as Social Capital', in N. Lin, K. Cook, and R.S. Burt (eds), *Social Capital: Theory and Research*. New York: Aldine De Gruyter.

Cain, M. (2000) 'Orientalism, Occidentalism and the Sociology of Crime', in D. Garland and R. Sparks (eds), *Criminology and Social Theory*. Oxford: Oxford University Press.
Cao, F. (1997) *The Fifth Peak: Crime in Contemporary China*. Beijing: China Today Press.
Carr, P. (2003) 'The New Parochialism: The Implications of the Beltway Case for Arguments Concerning Informal Social Control', *American Journal of Sociology*, 108: 1249–91.
Carson, W.G. (2004a) 'Is Communalism Dead? Reflections on the Present and Future Practices of Crime Prevention: Part One', *Australian and New Zealand Journal of Criminology*, 37: 1–21.
Carson, W.G. (2004b) 'Is Communalism Dead? Reflections on the Present and Future Practices of Crime Prevention: Part Two', *Australian and New Zealand Journal of Criminology*, 37: 192–210.
Carson, W.G. (2007) 'Calamity or Catalyst: Futures for Community in Twenty-First-Century Crime Prevention', *British Journal of Criminology*, 47: 711–27.
Chan, A. and Cheung, T.S. (1998) 'Confucianism, Particularism, and the Asian Financial Crisis', Unpublished Manuscript.
Chan, L.W. (1993) *The Myth of Neighborhood Mutual Help*. Hong Kong: Hong Kong University Press.
Chang, J. (1998) 'The Guanxi Factor: Accounting Ethics in China', *Australian CPA*, 68 (8): 44–6.
Chen, W. (1998) 'Economic Reform and Social Instability in Rural China', in J. Zhang and X. Li (eds), *Social Transition in China*. Lanham, MA: University Press of America.
Chen, Z. (1989) 'The Theoretical Analysis and Practical Study of the Psychology of Face', in G. Yang (ed.), *The Psychology of the Chinese*. Taipei: Guiguan Publishing House.
Cheung, Y.W. and Cheung, W.T. (2000) 'Social Capital and Recovery from Drug Addiction: Findings of a Study of Treated Drug Addicts in Hong Kong', *Hong Kong Journal of Sociology*, 1: 29–51.

China Law Yearbook (1987–2007) Beijing: China Law Yearbook Press.

China News Net (2005) (6 December) 'The Number of Security Guards Reached Four Million and in Beijing the Police Was Outnumbered by Security Guards' [Accessed 2 November 2007]. Available from: http://news.sina.com.cn/c/2005-12-06/10577635232s.shtml.

Clark, J.P. (1989) 'Conflict Management Outside the Courtroom of China', in R.J. Troyer, J.P. Clark and D.G. Rojek (eds), *Social Control in the People's Republic of China*. New York: Praeger, pp. 57–69.

Clarke, R. and Weisburd, D. (1994) 'Diffusion of Crime Control Benefits: Observations of the Reverse of Displacement', in R. Clarke (ed.), *Crime Prevention Studies*, 2. New York: Criminal Justice Press.

Clarke, R.V. (1995) 'Situational Crime Prevention', in M. Tonry and D.P. Farrington (eds), *Building a Safer Society: Strategic Approaches to Crime Prevention*. Chicago and London: University of Chicago Press.

Clarke, R.V. (ed.) (1997) *Situational Crime Prevention: Successful Case Studies* (2nd edn). Guilderland, NY: Harrow and Heston.

Cohen, L.E. and Felson, M. (1979) 'Social Change and Crime Rate Trends: A Routine Activity Approach', *American Sociological Review*, 44 (4): 588–608.

Cohen, S. (1985) *Visions of Social Control*. Oxford: Polity Press.

Cohen. S. (1989) 'The Critical Discourse on "Social Control": Note on the Concepts as a Hammer', *International Journal of the Sociology of Law*, 17 (3): 347–57.

Coleman, J.S. (1990) *Foundations of Social Theory*. Cambridge, MA: Belknap Press of Harvard University Press.

Colletta, N.J. and Cullen, M.L. (2000) *Violent Conflict and the Transformation of Social Capital: Lessons from Cambodia, Rwanda, Guatemala, and Somalia*. Washington, DC: World Bank.

Cornish, D.B. and Clarke, R.V. (eds) (1986) *The Reasoning Criminal: Rational Choice Perspectives on Offending*. New York: Springer-Verlag.

Crawford, A. (1997) *The Local Governance of Crime: Appeals to Community and Partnerships*. Oxford: Clarendon Press.

Crawford, A. (1998) *Crime Prevention and Community Safety: Politics, Policies and Practices*. London and New York: Longman.

Crawford, A. and Jones, M. (1996) 'Kirkholt Revisited: Some Reflections on the Transferability of Crime Prevention Initiatives', *Howard Journal of Criminal Justice*, 35 (1): 21–39.

Crowther, C. (2000) 'Thinking About the "Underclass": Towards a Political Economy of Policing', *Theoretical Criminology*, 4 (2): 149–67.

Cullen, F.T. (1994) 'Social Support as An Organizing Concept for Criminology: Presidential Address to the Academy of Criminal Justice Sciences', *Justice Quarterly*, 11 (4): 527–59.

Curran, D.J. and Cook, S. (1993) 'Growing Fears, Rising Crime: Juveniles and China's Justice System', *Crime and Delinquency*, 39 (3): 296–315.

Currie, E. (1988) 'Two Visions of Community Crime Prevention', in T. Hope and M. Shaw (eds), *Communities and Crime Reduction*. London: HMSO.

Currie, E. (1996) 'Social Crime Prevention Strategies in a Market Society', in J. Muncie, E. McLaughlin and M. Langan (eds), *Criminological Perspectives: A Reader*. London: Sage.

Curtis, L.A. (1988) 'The March of Folly – Crime and the Underclass', in T. Hope and M. Shaw (eds), *Communities and Crime Reduction*. London: Home Office Research and Planning Unit, pp. 180–203.

Dahrendorf, R. (1985) *Law and Order*. London: Stevens.

Dasgupta, P. and Serageldin, I. (2000) 'Preface', in P. Dasgupta and I. Serageldin (eds), *Social Capital: A Multifaceted Perspective*. Washington, DC: World Bank.

Davis, M. (1990) *City of Quartz: Excavating the Future in Los Angeles*. London: Verso.

Deng, X. and Cordilia, A. (1999) 'To Get Rich Is Glorious: Rising Expectations, Declining Control, and Escalating Crime in Contemporary China', *International Journal of Offender Therapy and Comparative Criminology*, 43 (2): 211–29.

Dikotter, F. (2002) *Crime, Punishment and the Prison in Modern China*. Hong Kong: Hong Kong University Press.

Du, J. (1997) 'Police – Public Relations: A Chinese View', *Australian and New Zealand Journal of Criminology*, 30: 87–94.

Dubo, F. and Emmons, D. (1981) 'The Community Hypothesis', in D.A. Lewis (ed.), *Reactions to Crime*. Beverly Hills, CA: Sage.

Dutton, M. (1992) *Policing and Punishment in China: From Patriarchy to 'the People'*. Cambridge: Cambridge University Press.

Dutton, M. and Lee, T.F. (1993) 'Missing the Target? Police Strategies in the Period of Economic Reform', *Crime and Delinquency*, 39 (3): 316–36.

Eisner, M. (2001) 'Modernization, Self-control and Lethal Violence', *British Journal of Criminology*, 41: 618–38.

Ekblom, P. (1996) 'Towards a Discipline of Crime Prevention', in T. Bennett (ed.), *Preventing Crime and Disorder: Targeting Strategies and Responsibilities*. Cambridge: University of Cambridge Press.

Ekblom, P. and Pease, K. (1995) 'Evaluating Crime Prevention', in M. Tonry and D.P. Farrington (eds), *Building a Safer Society: Strategic Approaches to Crime Prevention*. Chicago: University of Chicago Press, pp. 585–662.

Ekblom, P. and Tilley, N. (2000) 'Going Equipped: Criminology, Situational Crime Prevention and the Resourceful Offender', *British Journal of Criminology*, 40: 376–98.

Emerson, R.M., Fretz, R.I. and Shaw, L.L. (1996) *Writing Ethnographic Fieldnotes*. Chicago: University of Chicago Press.

Engstad, P. and Evans, J.L. (1980) 'Responsibility, Competence and Police Effectiveness in Crime Control', in R.V.G. Clarke and J.M. Hough (eds), *The Effectiveness of Policing*. Aldershot: Gower.

Epstein, E.J. and Wong, S.H.Y. (1996) 'The Concept of "Dangerousness", in the People's Republic of China and Its Impact on the Treatment of Prisoners', *British Journal of Criminology*, 36 (4): 472–500.

Fang, Y. 1988. 'Public Security Organization', in M. Findlay, and U. Zvekic (eds), *Analysing (in)formal Mechanisms of Crime Control: A Cross-cultural Perspective*. Rome: United Nations Social Defence Research Institute.

Farrall, S., Bannister, J., Ditton, J. and Gilchrist, E. 2000. 'Social Psychology and the Fear of Crime: Re-Examining a Speculative Model', *British Journal of Criminology*, 40: 399–413.

Fei, X. (1948/1992) *From the Soil: The Foundations of Chinese Society* (transl. G.G. Hamilton and W. Zheng). Berkeley, CA: University of California Press.

Felson, M. (1986) 'Linking Criminal Choices, Routine Activities, Informal Control and Criminal Outcomes', in D.B. Cornish and R.V. Clarke (eds), *The Reasoning Criminal: Rational Choice Perspective on Offending*. New York: Springer-Verlag, pp. 119–28.

Feng, Z. (1995) 'Police/public Relation and Community Policing in the New Era', *Public Security Research*, 40 (2): 22–5.

Findlay, M. and Zvekic, U. (1988) *Analysing (in)formal Mechanisms of Crime Control: A Cross-Cultural Perspective*. Rome: United Nations Social Defence Research Institute.

Formby, W.A. and Smykla, J.O. (1981) 'Citizens Awareness in Crime Prevention: Do they really Get Involved?', *Journal of Police Science and Administration*, 9 (4): 398–403.

Forrest, R. and Kearns, A. (2000) 'Social Cohesion, Social Capital and the Neighborhood'. Paper Presented to ESRC Cities Programme Neighbourhoods Colloquium, Liverpool.

Foster, J. and Hope, T. (1993) *Housing, Community and Crime: The Impact of the Priority Estates Project*. Home Office Research Study No. 131. London: HMSO.

Fu, H. (1990) Police Reform and Its Implication for Chinese Social Control', *International Journal of Comparative and Applied Criminal Justice*, 14 (1/2): 41–8.

Fu, H. (1993) 'The Security Service Company in China', *Journal of Security Administration*, 16 (2): 35–44.

Fu, H. (1994) 'A Bird in the Cage: Police and Political Leadership in Post-Mao China', *Policing and Society*, 4: 277–91.

Fu, H. (2005a) 'Re-education Through Labour in Historical Perspective', *China Quarterly*, 184: 811–30.

Fu, H. (2005b) 'Zhou Yongkang and the Recent Police Reform in China', *Australian and New Zealand Journal of Criminology*, 38 (2): 241–53.

Fukuyama, F. (1999) *The Great Disruption: Human Nature and the Reconstitution of Social Order*. London: Profile Books.

Garland, D. (1985) *Punishment and Welfare: A History of Penal Strategies*. Aldershot: Gower.
Garland, D. (1996) 'The Limits of the Sovereign State: Strategies of Crime Control in Contemporary Society', *British Journal of Criminology*, 36 (4): 445–71.
Garland, D. (1997) '"Governmentality" and the Problem of Crime', *Theoretical Criminology*, 1 (2): 173–214.
Garland, D. (1999) 'The Commonplace and the Catastrophic: Interpretations of Crime in Late Modernity', *Theoretical Criminology*, 3 (3): 353–64.
Garland, D. (2000) 'The Culture of High Crime Societies', *British Journal of Criminology*, 40 (3): 347–75.
Garland, D. (2001) *The Culture of Control: Crime and Social Order in Contemporary Society*. Oxford: Oxford University Press.
Garland, D. and Sparks, R. (2000) 'Criminology, Social Theory, and the Challenge of Our Times', in D. Garland and R. Sparks (eds), *Criminology and Social Theory*. Oxford: Oxford University Press, pp. 1–22.
Geertz, C. (1990) 'History and Anthropology', *New Literary History*, 21 (2): 321–35.
Giddens, A. (1990) *The Consequences of Modernity*. Cambridge: Polity Press.
Gilling, D. (1994) 'Multi-agency Crime Prevention in Britain: the Problem of Combining Situational and Social Strategies', in R.V. Clarke (ed.), *Crime Prevention Studies*, vol. 3. Monsey, NY: Criminal Justice Press.
Gong, Z. (1998) 'Research on Deng Xiaoping's Yanda Theory', *Journal of Chinese People's Public Security University*, 75 (5): 49–53.
Graham, J. and Bennett, T. (1995) *Crime Prevention Strategies in Europe and North America*. Helsinki, Finland: European Institute for Crime Prevention and Control Affiliated with the United Nations.
Granovetter, M.S. (1974) *Getting a Job: A Study of Contacts and Careers*. Cambridge, MA: Harvard University Press.
Grant, G. (1989) 'The Family and Social Control: Traditional and Modern', in R.J. Troyer, J.P. Clark and D.G. Rojek (eds), *Social Control in the People's Republic of China*. New York: Praeger, pp. 17–25.
Gui, W. (1998) 'Reflection on the Construction of Spiritual Civilization and Crime Prevention', *Juvenile Prevention Research*, 1: 35–40.
Guo, X. (1998) 'Research on Modern Chinese Crime and Its Control Strategy', *Journal of Central Management Cadre Institute on Politics and Law*, 8 (4): 1–10.
Guyot, D. (1991) *Policing As Though People Matter*. Philadelphia: Temple University Press.

Hagan, F. (1997) *Research Methods in Criminal Justice and Criminology* (4th edn). Boston: Allyn and Bacon.
Hamilton, G.G. and Zheng, W. (1992) 'Introduction' and 'Epilogue', in X. Fei (ed.), *From the Soil: The Foundations of Chinese Society*. Berkeley, CA: University of California Press.

He, C. (2006) (February 8). 'The Police Sent 85% of Officers to the Local Level', *China Youth Daily* [Accessed 18 February 2008]. Available from http://news.xinhuanet.com/politics/2006-02/08/content_4149311.htm.

He, N. and Marshall, I.H. (1997) 'Social Production of Crime Data: A Critical Examination of Chinese Crime Statistics', *International Criminal Justice Review*, 7 (1): 46–64.

Heath, L. (1984) 'Impact of Newspaper Crime Reports on Fear of Crime: Multimethodological Investigation', *Journal of Personality and Social Psychology*, 47 (22): 263–76.

Heiland, H., Shelley, L.I. and Katoh, H. (eds) (1991) *Crime and Control in Comparative Perspective*. Berlin: Walter de Gruyter.

Heimer, M. and Thogersen, S. (eds) (2006) *Doing Field Work in China*. Copenhagen: NIAS Press.

Hindelang, M.J., Gottfredson, M.R. and Garofalo, J. (1978) *Victims of Personal Crime: An Empirical Foundation for a Theory of Personal Victimization*. Cambridge, MA: Ballinger.

Hood, R. and Hoyle, C. (2008) *The Death Penalty: A Worldwide Perspective* (4th edn). New York: Oxford University Press.

Hope, T. (1995) 'Community Crime Prevention', in M. Tonry and D.P. Farrington (eds), *Building a Safer Society: Strategic Approaches to Crime Prevention*. Chicago: University of Chicago Press, pp. 21–90.

Hope, T. and Hough, M. (1988) 'Area, Crime and Incivility: A Profile from the British Crime Survey', in T. Hope and M. Shaw (eds), *Communities and Crime Reduction*. London: Home Office Research and Planning Unit.

Hope, T. and Murphy, J.I. (1983) 'Problems of Implementing Crime Prevention: The Experience of a Demonstration Project', *Howard Journal*, 22: 38–50.

Hope, T. and Shaw, M. (eds) (1988) *Communities and Crime Reduction*. London: Home Office Research and Planning Unit.

Horwitz, A.V. (1990) *The Logic of Social Control*. New York and London: Plenum Press.

Hough, J.M. and Clarke, R.V.G. (eds) (1980) *The Effectiveness of Policing*. Aldershot: Gower.

Huang, J. (1996) 'The Change and Trend of Criminal Cases in Shenzhen', *Research on Juvenile Delinquency*, 13 (10–11). 24–27.

Huang, Z. and Luo, J. (1997) 'Preliminary Exploration of the New Characteristics of the Management of Public Security Work in Shenzhen: Reflection on the Experience of Shezhen BLSCC', in *Shenzhen Political and Legal Yearbook*. Shenzhen: Haitian Press, pp. 2–10.

Hunter, A.J. (1985) 'Private, Parochial and Public Social Orders: The Problems of Crime and Incivility in Urban Communities', in G.D. Suttles and M.N. Zald (eds), *The Challenge of Social Control: Citizenship and Institution Building in Modern Society*. Norwood, NJ: Ablex, pp. 230–42.

Huphes, G. (2007) *The Politics of Crime and Community.* New York: Palgrave Macmillan.

Jacobs, J. (1961) *The Death and Life of Great American Cities.* New York: Random House.

Jiang, B. and Dai, Y.S. (1990) 'Mobilize All Possible Social Forces to Strengthen Public Security – A Must for Crime Prevention', *Police Studies,* 13 (1): 1–9.

Jiang, X. and Luo, F. (eds) (1996) *Handbook of Policing: Public Security Management.* Beijing: Qunzhong Press.

Jiao, A.Y. (1997) 'Crime Control Through Saturated Community Policing: A Corporate Policing Model', *International Journal of Comparative and Applied Criminal Justice,* 21 (1): 79–89.

Johnson, E.A. and Monkkonen, E.H. (1996) *The Civilization of Crime: Violence in Town and Country Since the Middle Ages.* Urbana and Chicago: University of Illinois Press.

Johnston, L. (1992) *The Rebirth of Private Policing.* London and New York: Routledge.

Johnston, L. (1996) 'What Is Vigilantism?', *British Journal of Criminology,* 36 (2): 220–36.

Johnston, L. (1999) 'Private Policing: Uniformity and Diversity', in R.I. Mawby (ed.), *Policing Across the World: Issues for the Twenty-First Century.* London: UCL Press.

Johnston, P., Rhodes, W. and Carrigan, K. (2000) *Estimation of Heroin Availability 1995–1998,* NCJ 187082. Available at: http://www.whitehousedrugpolicy.gov/gov/pdf/heroin_1995_1998.pdf.

Kang, S. and Zhao, G. (1998) 'The Establishment and Development of Criminology in New China', *China Legal Studies,* 4: 23–6.

Kang, S., Feng, S. and Hao, H. (eds) (1998) *Crime Prevention and Control in the 21st Century.* Beijing: Police Officers Education Press.

Kelling, G.L. and Coles, C.M. (1996) *Fixing Broken Windows: Restoring Order and Reducing Crime in Our Communities.* New York: Touchstone.

Kennedy, B.P., Kawachi, I., Prothrow-Stith, D., Lochner, K. and Gupta, V. (1998) 'Social Capital, Income Inequality, and Firearm Violent Crime', *Social Science and Medicine,* 47 (1): 7–17.

Killias, M. and Clerici, C. (2000) 'Different Measures of Vulnerability in Their Relation to Different Dimensions of Fear of Crime', *British Journal of Criminology,* 40 (3): 437–50.

Kinkley, J.C. (2000) *Chinese Justice, the Fiction: Law and Literature in Modern China.* Stanford, CA: Stanford University Press.

Klein, M.W. and Gatz, M. (1989) 'Professing the Uncertain: Problems of Lecturing on Chinese Social Control', in R.J. Troyer, J.P. Clark, and D.G. Rojek (eds), *Social Control in the People's Republic of China.* New York: Praeger.

Lab, S.P. (1988) *Crime Prevention: Approaches, Practices and Evaluations*. Cincinnati, Ohio: Anderson.
LaFree, G.D. and Kick, E.L. (1986) 'Cross-National Effects of Development, Distributional and Demographic Variables on Crime: A Review and Analysis', *International Annals of Criminology*, 24: 213–36.
Lanier, M., and Henry, S. (1998) *Essential Criminology*. Boulder, CO: Westview Press.
Lash, S. and Urry, J. (1994) *Economies of Signs and Space*. London: Sage.
Lau, R.W.K. (2001) 'Socio-political Control in Urban China: Changes and Crisis', *British Journal of Sociology*, 52 (4): 605–20.
Laub, J.H., Nagin, D.S. and Sampson, R.J. (1998) 'Good Marriages and Trajectories of Change in Criminal Offending', *American Sociological Review*, 63 (2): 225–38.
Lavrakas, P.J. (1995) 'Community-based Crime Prevention: Citizens, Community Organizations, and the Police', in L.B. Joseph (ed.), *Crime, Communities, and Public Policy*. Chicago: University of Chicago Press.
Lederman, D., Loayza, N. and Mendendez, A.M. (2002) 'Violent crime: Does Scial Capital Matter?', *Economic Development and Cultural Change*, 50: 509–39.
Lee, B.A., Oropesa, R.S., Metch, B.J. and Guest, A.M. (1984) 'Testing the Decline-of-Community Thesis: Neighborhood Organizations in Seattle, 1929 and 1979', *American Journal of Sociology*, 89 (5): 1161–88.
Leighton, B. (1988) 'The Community Concept in Criminology: Toward a Social Network Approach', *Journal of Research in Crime and Delinquency*, 25 (4): 351–74.
Levrant, S. Cullen, F.T., Fulton, B. and Wozniak, J.F. (1999) 'Reconsidering Restorative Justice: The Corruption of Benevolence Revisited?' *Crime and Delinquency*, 45 (1): 3–27.
Lewis, D.A. and Salem, G. (1986) *Fear of Crime: Incivility and the Production of a Social Problem*. New Brunswick, NJ: Transaction.
Li, X. (1998) 'Crime and Policing in China', Occasional Seminars, Australian Institute of Criminology. Available online at: www.aic.gov.au/conferences/occasional/xiancui.html.
Liang, D. and Yang, H. (eds) (1994) *Public Security Strategies in the Shenzhen SEZ*. Shenzhen: Haitian Press.
Lin, N. (1986) 'Conceptualizing Social Support', in N. Lin, A. Dean and W. Edsel (eds), *Social Support, Life Events, and Depression*. Orlando, FL: Academic.
Lin, N. (1989) 'Chinese Family Structure and Chinese Society', *Bulletin of the Institute of Ethnology*, 65: 382–99.
Lin, N. (1998) 'Guanxi: A Conceptual Analysis', in A. So, N. Lin and D. Poston (eds), *The Chinese Triangle of Mainland, Taiwan, and Hong Kong: Comparative Institutional Analysis*. Westport, CT: Greenwood.

Lin, N. (2000) 'Social Capital: Social Networks, Civic Engagement, or Trust?', Keynote Speech at the Annual Meeting of the Hong Kong Sociological Association, Hong Kong University of Science and Technology.

Lin, N. (2001a) 'Building a Network Theory of Social Capital', in N. Lin, K. Cook, and R.S. Burt (eds), *Social Capital: Theory and Research*. New York: Aldine De Gruyter.

Lin, N. (2001b) *Social Capital: A Theory of Social Structure and Action*. Port Chester, NY: Cambridge University Press.

Lin, N., Cook, K. and Burt, R.S. (eds) (2001) *Social Capital: Theory and Research*. New York: Aldine De Gruyter.

Liu, J. (1999) 'Social Capital and Covariates of Reoffending Risk in the Chinese Context', *International Criminal Justice Review*, 9: 39–55.

Liu, J. (2005) 'Crime Patterns During the Market Transition in China', *British Journal of Criminology*, 45: 613–33.

Liu, J. (2006) 'Modernization Theory and Crime Patterns in China', *Journal of Criminal Justice*, 34: 119–30.

Liu, J., Zhang, L. and Messner, S.F. (2001) 'Introduction: Impact of Market Transition – Changing Crime and Social Control in China', in J. Liu, L. Zhang and S.F. Messner (eds), *Crime, Justice, and Social Control in the Changing Chinese Society*. West Port, CT: Greenwood Publishing, pp. xi–xvi.

Liu, R. and Tang, J. (1997) 'Public Security Situation 1996–1997', in L. Jiang and X. Lu (eds), *Social Blue Book: Analysis and Prediction of Social Situation in China 1996–1997*. Beijing: China Social Sciences Press.

Liu, J., Zhou, D., Liska, A., Messner, S., Krohen, M., Zhang, L. and Zhou, L. (1998) 'Status, Power, and Sentencing in China', *Justice Quarterly*, 15 (2): 289–300.

Loader, I. and Walker, N. (2001) 'Policing as a Public Good: Reconstituting the Connections between Policing and the State', *Theoretical Criminology*, 5 (1) 9–35.

Lu, C. and Zhao, H. (1999) 'Reflection on the Legislation of Comprehensive Prevention of Crime', *Juvenile Delinquency Research*, 200–201 (2–3): 50–4, 27.

Lu, H. (1998) *Community Policing – Rhetoric or Reality? The Contemporary Chinese Community-Based Policing System in Shanghai*. PhD Thesis. Arizona State University.

Lupton, D. (1999) 'Dangerous Places and the Unpredictable Stranger: Constructions of Fear of Crime', *The Australia and New Zealand Journal of Criminology*, 32 (1): 1–15.

Lurigio, A.J. and Rosebaum, D.P. (1986) 'Evaluation Research in Community Crime Prevention: A Critical Look at the Field', in D.P. Rosenbaum (ed.), *Community Crime Prevention: Does it Work?* Beverly Hlls, CA: Sage, pp. 19–45.

Ma, J. (1998) 'Reflection on Public Security Mass Work in the New Era', *Journal of Beijing People's Police Officers Institute*, 3: 10–15.

Ma, L.J.C. and Xiang, B. (1998) 'Native Place, Migration and the Emergence of Peasant Enclaves in Beijing', *The China Quarterly*, 155: 546–81.
Mandel, M.J., Magnusson, P., Ellis, J.E., DeGeorge, G. and Alexander, K.L. (1993) 'The Economics of Crime', *Business Week* (13 December): 72–75, 78–81.
Markowitz, F., Bellair, P.E., Liska, A.E. and Liu. J. (2001) 'Extending Social Disorganization Theory: Modeling the Relationship Between Cohesion, Disorder, and Fear', *Criminology*, 39: 293–320.
Matthews, R. (1992) 'Replacing "Broken Windows": Crime, Incivilities and Urban Change', in R. Matthews and J. Young (eds), *Issues in Realist Criminology*. London: Sage.
Mauer, M. (1997) 'Racial Disparities in Prison Getting Worse in the 1990s', *Overcrowded Times*, 8 (1): 8–13.
Maxfield, M. and Babbie, E. (2005) *Research Methods for Criminal Justice and Criminology*. Belmont: Wadsworth.
Melossi, D. (2000) 'Changing Representation of the Criminal', in D. Garland and R. Sparks (eds), *Criminology and Social Theory*. Oxford: Oxford University Press, pp. 149–82.
Meng, X. (1994) 'Chinese Rural Men in the Transfer of the Rural Labor Force', *Social Sciences in China*, 15 (1): 109–118, 224.
Messner, S.F., Baumer, E.P. and Rosenfeld, R. (2004) 'Demensions of Social Capital and Rates of Criminal Homicide', *American Sociological Review*, 69 (6): 882–903.
Miethe, T. and Meier, R. (1994) *Crime and Its Social Context: Toward an Integrated Theory of Offenders, Victims, and Situations*. Albany, NY: State University of New York Press.
Miller, L.S. and Hess, K.M. (1998) *The Police in the Community: Strategies for the 21st Century*. Belmont, CA: West/Wadsworth.
Mingpao Daily (2002) 'Mistress Village Left in Despair', 6 August, p. D07.
Murphy, C. (1988) 'Community Problems, Problems Communities, and Community Policing in Toronto', *Journal of Research in Crime and Delinquency*, 25 (4): 392–410.

National Statistical Bureau (2006) (16 March) 'Press Release of the Main Statistics from the 1% Census'. Retrieved 1 September 2007 from http://www.stats.gov.cn/tjgb/rkpcgb/qgrkpcgb/t20060316_402310923.htm.
Nelken, D. (1985) 'Community Involvement in Crime Control', *Current Legal Problems*, 38: 259–67.
Newman, G., Clarke, R.V. and Shoham, S.G. (eds) (1997) *Rational Choice and Situational Crime Prevention: Theoretical Foundations*. Dartmouth: Ashgate.

O'Leary, V. (1988) 'Editor's Comments', *Journal of Research in Crime and Delinquency*, 5 (4): 1–3.
Onyx, J. and Bullen, P. (2000) 'Measuring Social Capital in Five Communities', *Journal of Applied Behavioral Science*, 36 (1): 23–42.

Pantazis, C. (2000) '"Fear of Crime", Vulnerability and Poverty: Evidence from the British Crime Survey', *British Journal of Criminology*, 40: 414–36.

Pawson, R. and Tilley, N. (1994) 'What Works in Evaluation Research?', *British Journal of Criminology*, 34 (3): 291–306.

Pearson, G. (2002) 'Introduction: Crime and Criminology in China', *British Journal of Criminology*, 42: 235–9.

Pease, K. (1994) 'Crime Prevention', in M. Magure, R. Morgan and R. Reiner (eds), *The Oxford Handbook of Criminology*. Oxford: Clearendon Press, pp. 659–704.

Peterson, R.D., Krivo, L.J. and Harris, M.A. (2000) 'Disadvantage and Neighborhood Violent Crime: Do Local Institutions Matter?', *Journal of Research in Crime and Delinquency*, 37 (1): 31–63.

Podolefsky, A.M. (1985) 'Rejecting Crime Prevention Programs: The Dynamics of Program Implementation in High Need Communities', *Human Organizations*, 44 (1): 33–40.

Portes, A. (1998) 'Social Capital: Its Origins and Applications in Modern Sociology', *Annual Review of Sociology*, 24: 1–24.

Potapchuk, W.R., Crocker, J.P. and Schechter, W.H. Jr. (1997) 'Building Community with Social Capital: Chits and Chums or Chats with Change', *National Civic Review*, 86 (2): 129–39.

Putnam, R.D. (1993a) 'The Prosperous Community: Social Capital and Public Life', *American Prospect*, 13: 35–42.

Putnam, R.D. (1993b) *Making Democracy Work: Civic Traditions in Modern Italy*. Princeton, NJ: Princeton University Press.

Putnam, R.D. (1995) 'Bowling Alone: America's Declining Social Capital', *Journal of Democracy*, 6 (1): 65–78.

Putnam, R.D. (2000) *Bowling Alone: The Collapse and Revival of American Community*. New York: Simon and Schuster.

Radzinowicz, L. (1999) *Adventures in Criminology*. New York: Routledge.

Radzinowicz, L. and Hood, R. (1990) *The Emergence of Penal Policy in Victorian and Edwardian England*. Oxford: Clarendon Press, pp. 91–112.

Reiss, A.J. (1986) 'Why Are Communities Important in Understanding Crime?', in A.J. Reiss and M. Tonry (eds), *Communities and Crime*. Chicago: University of Chicago Press, pp. 1–34.

Research Team of the Ministry of Public Security Project on 'Research and Evaluation on Public Feelings of Safety' (1991) 'Public Feeling of Security in Our Country has improved', *Public Security Research*, 20 (6): 53–7.

Rose, D.R. and Clear T.R. (1998) 'Incarceration, Social Capital, and Crime: Implications for Social Disorganization Theory', *Criminology*, 36 (3): 441–80.

Rose, D. and Clear, T. (2002) 'Incarceration, Reentry and Social Capital: Social Networks in the Balance'. Paper prepared for the 'From Prison to Home' conference, Washington, DC (30–31 January 2002). Available from: http://aspe.hhs.gov/hsp/prison2home02/rose.pdf.

References

Rose, N. (1996) 'The Death of the Social? Re-figuring the Territory of Government', *Economy and Society*, 25 (3): 327–56.

Rose, N. (2000) 'Government and Control', in D. Garland and R. Sparks (eds), *Criminology and Social Theory*. Oxford: Oxford University Press, pp. 183–208.

Rosenbaum, D. (1988) 'Community Crime Prevention: A Review and Synthesis of the Literature', *Justice Quarterly*, 5 (3): 323–95.

Rosenbaum, D.P. (ed.) (1986) *Community Crime Prevention: Does it Work?* London: Sage.

Rosenbaum, D.P. and Lavrakas, P.J. (1995) 'Self-Reports About Place: The Application of Survey and Interview Methods to the Study of Small Areas', in J.E. Eck and D. Weisburd (eds), *Crime and Place: Crime Prevention Studies*, Vol. 4. Monsey, NY: Criminal Justice Press and Washington, DC: Police Executive Research Forum.

Rosenbaum, D.P., Lurigio, A.J. and Davis, R.C. (1998) *The Prevention of Crime: Social and Situational Strategies*. Belmont, CA: West/Wadsworth.

Rosenfeld, R., Messner, S.F. and Baumer, E.P. (2001) 'Social Capital and Homicide', *Social Forces*, 80: 283–309.

Saegert, S., Winkel, G. and Swartz, C. (2002) 'Social Capital and Crime in a New York City's Low-Income Housing', *Housing Policy Debate*, 13 (1): 189–226.

Sampson, A., Stubbs, P. and Smith, D. (1988) 'Crime, Localities and the Multi-agency Approach', *British Journal of Criminology*, 28 (4): 478–93.

Sampson, R.J. (2002) 'Transcending Tradition: New Directions in Community Research, Chicago Style', *Criminology*, 40 (2): 213–30.

Sampson, R.J. and Laub, J.H. (1992) 'Crime and Deviance in the Life Course', *Annual Review of Sociology*, 18: 609–27.

Sampson, R.J. and Laub, J.H. (1993) *Crime in the Making: Pathways and Turning Points Throughout Life*. Cambridge, MA: Harvard University Press.

Sampson, R.J. and Raudenbush, S.W. (2004) 'Seeing Disorder: Neighborhood Stigma and the Social Construction of 'Broken Windows', *Social Psychology Quarterly*, 67 (4): 319–42.

Sampson, R.J., Morenoff, J.D. and Gannon-Rowley, T. (2002) 'Assessing "neighborhood effects": Social processes and New Directions in Research', *Annual Review of Sociology*, 28: 443–78.

Sampson, R.J., Raudenbush, S.W. and Earls, F. (1997) 'Neighborhoods and Violent Crime: A Multilevel Study of Collective Efficacy', *Science*, 277: 918–24.

Sampson, R.J. and Raudenbush, S.W. (2001) 'Disorder in Urban Neighborhoods – does It Lead to Crime?', National Institute of Justice, NCJ 186049. Available at: http://www.wjh.harvard.edu/soc/faculty/sampson/articles/2001_NIJ_Raudenbush.pdf.

San, G. (1995) *Prostitution in China: Past and Present*. Beijing: Law Press.

Schneider, A.L. (1987) 'Coproduction of Public and Private Safety: An Analysis of Bystander intervention, "Protective Neighborhood", and Personal Protection', *Political Research Quarterly*, 40: 611–30.
Shaw, C.R. and McKay, H.D. (1969) *Juvenile Delinquency and Urban Areas* (2nd edn). Chicago: University of Chicago Press.
Shaw, V.N. (1996) *Social Control in China: A study of Chinese Work Units*. London: Praeger.
Shearing, C.D. and Stenning, P.C. (eds) (1987) *Private Policing*. Newbury Park, CA: Sage.
Shearing, C.D. (1992) 'The Relation Between Public and Private Policing', in M. Tonry and N. Morris (eds), *Modern Policing*. Chicago: University of Chicago Press.
Shelley, L.I. (1981) *Crime and Modernization: The Impact of Industrialization and Urbanization on Crime*. Carbondale and Edwardsville, IL: Southern Illinois University Press.
Shenzhen Legal Daily (1999) 'Sending Rice, Sending Gas and "Sending Warm" To the Masses Was Only a Drama' (25 September).
Shenzhen Political and Legal Yearbook (SZPLY) (1996–2008) Shenzhen: Haitian Press.
Shenzhen Special Economic Zone Yearbook (1985–1996) Shenzhen: Shenzhen SEZ Yearbook Press.
Shenzhen Statistical Bureau (2007) Shenzhen Population and Economy in 2006. Retrieved 1 September 2007 from http://www.sztj.com/pub/sztjpublic.
Shenzhen Yearbook (1997–2006) Shenzhen: Shenzhen Yearbook Press.
Sherman, L. (1990) 'Police Crackdowns: Initial and Residual Deterrence', in M. Tonry and N. Morris (eds), *Crime and Justice: A Review of Research*, 12. Chicago: University of Chicago Press, pp. 1–48.
Sherman, L.W. (1992) 'Attacking Crime: Police and Crime Control', in M. Tonry and N. Morris (eds), *Modern Policing*. London: University of Chicago Press, pp. 159–230.
Sherman, L.W., Gottfredson, D.C. and MacKenzie, D.L. (1997) *Preventing Crime: What Works, What Doesn't, What's Promising*. Washington, DC: National Institute of Justice. Available at: http://www.ncjrs.org/works/index.htm.
Shi, Q. and Meng, Z. (eds) (1996) *The Explanation and Application of the Newly Revised 'Regulation on the Punishment of Public Security Offenders'*. Beijing: Chinese People's Public Security University Press.
Shichor, D. (1985) 'Effects of Development on Official Crime Rates 1967–1978: Homicide Rates and Larceny Patterns Differ Greatly', *Sociology and Social Research*, 70: 96–110.
Shue, V. (1988) *The Reach of the State: Sketches of the Chinese Body Politic*. Stanford, CA: Stanford University Press.
Siegel, L.J. (1998) *Criminology: Theories, Patterns, and Typologies* (6th edn). Belmont, CA: West/Wadsworth.

Sigley, G. (1996) 'Governing Chinese Bodies: the Significance of Studies in the Concept of Governmentality for the Analysis of Government in China', *Economy and Society*, 25 (4): 457–82.
Situ, Y. and Liu, W. (1996a) 'Restoring the Neighborhood, Fighting Against Crime: A Case Study in Guangzhou City, People's Republic of China', *International Criminal Justice Review*, 6: 89–102.
Situ, Y. and Liu, W. (1996b) 'Transient Population, Crime, and Solution: The Chinese Experience', *International Journal of Offender Therapy and Comparative Criminology*, 40 (4): 293–99.
Skinner, G.W. (1964) 'Marketing and Social Structure in Rural China, Part I', *Journal of Asian Studies*, 24 (1): 3–43.
Skinner, G.W. (1965a) 'Marketing ad Social Structure in Rural China, Part II', *Journal of Asian Studies*, 24 (2): 195–228.
Skinner, G.W. (1965b) 'Marketing and Social Structure in Rural China, Part III', *Journal of Asian Studies*, 24 (3): 363–99.
Skinner, G.W. (1971) 'Chinese Peasants and the Closed Community: An Open and Shut Case', *Comparative Studies in Society and History*, 13 (3): 270–81.
Skocpol, T. (1985) 'Bringing the State Back In: Strategies of Analysis in Current Research', in P.B. Evans, D. Rueschemeyer and T. Skocpol (eds), *Bringing the State Back In*. Cambridge: Cambridge University Press.
Skogan, W.G. (1990) *Disorder and Decline: Crime and the Spiral of Decay in American Neighborhoods*. New York: Free Press.
Skogan, W.G. (1994) *Contacts Between Police and Public: Findings from the 1992 British Crime Survey*. Home Office Research Study No. 134. London: HMSO.
Skogan, W.G. and Wycoff, M.A. (1986) 'Storefront Police Offices: The Houston Field Test', in D.P. Rosenbaum, *Community Policing: Does It Work?* Beverly Hills, CA: Sage.
Skogan, W.G., Hartnett, S.M., DuBois, J., Comey, J.T., Kaiser, M. and Lovig, J.H. (2000) 'Problem Solving in Practice: Implementing Community Policing in Chicago', NCJ 179556. NIJ Research Report.
Solinger, D.J. (1993) 'China's Transients and the State: A Form of Civil Society', *Politics and Society*, 21 (1): 91–122.
Solinger, D.J. (1999) *Contesting Citizenship in Urban China: Peasant Migrants, the State, and the Logic of the Market*. Berkeley, CA: University of California Press.
South China Morning Post (1999) 'Security Guards in Guangzhou "Poorly Trained"', 31 March (Internet Edition).
South China Morning Post (2001) 'China's "Apartheid"', 3 July, Focus (Internet Edition).
South China Morning Post (2002a) 'Hong Kong Men Farewell their Concubines', 25 July, p. EDT3 (Internet Edition).
South China Morning Post (2002b) 'It Is a Dirty Job But Everyone Wants to Do It', 21 July (Internet Edition).

South China Morning Post (2002c) 'Second to None', 25 July (Internet Edition).
South China Morning Post (2002d) 'Union Drive Targets New Firms', 13 August, p. FRN7 (Internet Edition).
Stepan, A. (1978) *The State and Society: Peru in Comparative Perspective*. Princeton, NJ: Princeton University Press.
Stern, R.H. (1997) 'China: A most Favored Nation or a Most Feared Nation – the PRC's Latest Anti-crime Campaign and a Possible U.S. Response', *George Washington Journal of International Law and Economics*, 31 (1) 119–40.
Stewart, J.E. and Cannon, D.A. (1977) 'Effects of Perpetrator Status and Bystander Commitment on Responses to a Simulated Crime', *Journal of Police Science and Administration*, 5 (3): 318–23.

Tan, X. and Xue, K. (1997) 'The Thinking Concerning the Strengthening of Police Force Under the New Situation', in *Shenzhen Political and Legal Yearbook*. Shenzhen: Haitian Press.
Tanner, H.M. (1999) *Strike Hard! Anti-Crime Campaigns and Chinese Criminal Justice 1979–1985*. Ithaca, NY: East Asia Program, Cornell University.
Tanner, M.S. (2000) 'State Coercion and the Balance of Awe: The 1983–1986 "Stern Blows" Anti-crime Campaign', *China Journal*, 44: 93–125.
Taylor, I. (1999) *Crime in Context: A Critical Criminology of Market Societies*. Oxford: Polity Press.
Thurston, A.F. and Pasternak, B. (eds) (1983) *The Social Sciences and Fieldwork in China: Views from the Field*. Boulder, CO: Westview Press.
Tian, J. (1998) 'The Analysis of the Social Background of *Yanda*', *Journal of Chinese People's Public Security University*, 72 (2): 12–16.
Tonry, M. (1995) *Malign Neglect: Race, Crime, and Punishment in America*. New York: Oxford University Press.
Tonry, M. and Farrington, D.P. (eds) (1995) *Building a Safer Society: Strategic Approaches to Crime Prevention*, in M. Tonry (ed.), *Crime and Justice: A Review of Research*, vol. 19. Chicago: University of Chicago Press.
Trevaskes, S. (2003) 'Yanda 2001: Form and Strategy in a Chinese Anti-crime Campaign', *Australian and New Zealand Journal of Criminology*, 36 (3): 272–92.
Trevaskes, S. (2007) 'Severe and Swift Justice in China', *British Journal of Criminology*, 47: 23–41.
Trojanowicz, R.C. (1986) 'Evaluating a Neighborhood Foot Patrol Program: The Flint, Michigan, Project', in D.P. Rosenbaum (ed.), *Community Policing: Does it Work?* Beverly Hills, CA: Sage.
Troyer, R.J. and Rojek, D.G. (1989) 'Introduction', in R.J. Troyer, J.P. Clark and D.G. Rojek (eds), *Social Control in the People's Republic of China*. New York: Praeger, pp. 3–10.
Troyer, R.J., Clark, J.P. and Rojek, D.G. (eds) (1989) *Social Control in the People's Republic of China*. New York: Praeger.

Tulloch, M. (2000) 'The Meaning of Age Differences in the Fear of Crime: Combining Quantitative and Qualitative Approaches', *British Journal of Criminology*, 40: 451–7.

van Dijk, J. (1990) 'Crime prevention Policy: Current state and Prospects', in G. Daiser and H-J. Albrecht (eds), *Crime and Criminal Policy in Europe, Criminological Research Report*, vol. 43. Freiburg: Max Planck Institute, pp. 205–20.

van Dijk, J. and de Waard, J. (1991) 'A Two Dimensional Typology of Crime Prevention Projects', *Criminal Justice Abstracts*, 23: 483–503.

van Dijk, J.J.M. (1994) 'Understanding Crime Rates: on the Interaction between the Rational Choices of Victims and Offenders', *British Journal of Criminology*, 34 (2): 105–21.

Vold, G.B. and Bernard, T.J. (1986) *Theoretical Criminology*. New York: Oxford University Press.

Wacquant, L. (2001) 'Deadly Symbiosis: When Ghetto and Prison Meet and Mesh', *Punishment and Society*, 3 (1): 95–133.

Walder, A.G. (1986) *Communist Neo-Traditionalism: Work and Authority in Chinese Industry*. Berkeley, CA: University of California Press.

Walklate, S. (1996) 'Community and Crime Prevention', in E. McLaughlin and J. Muncie (eds), *Controlling Crime*. London: Sage, pp. 293–332.

Waller, I. and Welsh, B. (1999) 'International Trends in Crime Prevention: Cost-Effective Ways to Reduce Victimization', in *Global Report on Crime and Justice*, United Nations, Office for Drug Control and Crime Prevention, Center for International Crime Prevention. New York and Oxford: Oxford University Press.

Wang, C. (1999) 'Ten Urgent Problems Facing the Public Security Organs', *Public Security Research*, 63 (1): 55–8.

Wang, F. (2004) 'Reformed Migration Control and New Targeted People: China's Hukou System in the 2000s', *China Quarterly*, 177: 115–32.

Wang, G., Qin, L. and Nie, G. (1998) 'Reflection on Scientific Yanda Strategy', *Journal of Chinese People's Public Security University*, 74 (4): 94–8.

Wang, L., Wang, X., Luo, X. and Jiao, J. (1998) 'Comprehensive Management of Public Security', in Y. Xiao, J. Liu and P. Wei (eds), *The Encyclopedia of Crime Prevention in China*. Beijing: People's Court Press, pp. 315–67.

Wang, P. and Chen, M. (1998) 'Community Prevention', in Y. Xiao, J. Liu and P. Wei (eds), *The Encyclopedia of Crime Prevention in China*. Beijing: People's Court Press, pp. 476–523.

Wang, S. (2002) 'On the Politics and Participation in the Development of Urban Communities in China', *Social Sciences in China*, 23 (2): 3–13.

Wang, W., Wang, L. and Sun, M. (1999) *An Overview of the Practice of Ban'an Industry in China*. Beijing: Police Officers' Educational Press.

Wellman, B. (1979) 'The Community Question: The Intimate Networks of East Yorkers', *American Journal of Sociology*, 84 (5): 1201–31.

Wiener, M.J. (1990) *Reconstructing the Criminal: Culture, Law and Policy in England 1830–1914*. Cambridge: Cambridge University Press.

Williams, P. and Dickson, J. (1993) 'Fear of Crime: Read All About It? The Relationship between Newspaper Crime Reporting and Fear of Crime', *British Journal of Criminology*, 33 (1): 33–56.

Wilson, J.Q. (1996) 'Foreword', in G.L. Kelling and C. Coles (eds), *Fixing Broken Windows: Restoring Order and Reducing Crime in Our Communities*. New York: Simon and Schuster, pp. 1–10.

Wilson, J.Q. and Kelling, G.L. (1982) 'The Police and Neighborhood Safety: Broken Windows', *Atlantic Monthly*, 127: 29–38.

Wilson, J.Q. and Kelling, G.L. (1989) 'Making Neighbourhoods Safe', *Atlantic Monthly*, 263: 46–52.

Wong, K.C. (2000) 'Community Policing in Comparative Context: P.R.C. vs. U.S.A.' Available at: http://www.polizei-newsletter.de/documents/Community_PolicinginChWong.pdf.

Wong, K.C. (2002) 'Police Reform in China in the 1990s', *British Journal of Criminology*, 42 (2): 281–316.

Wong, S.W. (1999) 'Delinquency Control and Juvenile Justice in China', *Australia and New Zealand Journal of Criminology*, 32 (1): 27–41.

Woolcock, M. (1998) 'Social Capital and Economic Development: Towards a Theoretical Synthesis and Policy Framework', *Theory ad Society*, 27 (2): 151–208.

Woon, Y. (1999) 'Labor Migration in the 1990s: Homeward Orientation of Migrants in the Pearl River Delta Region and Its Implications for Interior China', *Modern China*, 25 (4) 475–512.

Wright, A.F. (1977) 'The Cosmology of the Chinese City', in G.W. Skinner (ed.), *The City in Late Imperial China*. Stanford, CA: Stanford University Press.

Xin, K.R. and Pearce, J.L. (1996) 'Guanxi: Connections as Substitutes for Formal Institutional Support', *Academy of Management Journal*, 39 (6): 1641–58.

Xu, X. (1995) 'The Impact of Western Forms of Social Control on China: A Preliminary Evaluation', *Crime, Law and Social Change*, 23 (1): 67–87.

Yang, C. (1994) 'Public Security Offences and Their Impact on Crime Rates in China', *British Journal of Criminology*, 34 (1): 54–68.

Yang, J. (1998) 'The Situation and Developmental Paradigm of the Mass Prevention and Mass Management Team in Shanghai', *Juvenile Delinquency Research*, 2: 16–25.

Yang, M.M.H. (1994) *Gifts, Favors, and Banquets: The Art of Social Relationships in China*. London: Cornell University Press.

Yang, S. (1996) 'Research on Crime Problem and its Control Pattern in the Transitional Period', *Modern Law*, 4: 57–60, 106.

Yao, Y. (2001) 'Social Exclusion and Economic Discrimination: Current Conditions of Peasant Immigrants in East China', *Strategy and Management*, No. 3. *Selected Abstracts in Social Sciences in China* (transl. by S. Chen), Summer 2002.

Young, J. (1988) 'Risk of Crime and Fear of Crime: A Realist Critique of Survey-based Assumptions', in M. Maguire and J. Pointing (eds), *Victims of Crime: A New Deal*. Milton Keynes: Open University Press.

Young, J. (1992) 'Ten Points of Realism', in J. Young and R. Mathews (eds), *Rethinking Criminology: The Realist Debate*. London: Sage, pp. 24–68.

Young, J. (1999) *The Exclusive Society: Social Exclusion, Crime and Difference in Late Modernity*. London: Sage.

Yu, D., Zheng, X. and Su, T. (eds) (1997) *The Encyclopaedia for Chiefs of Local Police Station*. Beijing: Red Flag Press.

Zhang, L. Messner, S.F. and Liu, J. (2007) 'Criminological Research in Contemporary China: Challenges and Lessons learned from a Large-Scale Criminal Victimization Survey', *International Journal of Offender Therapy and Comparative Criminology*, 51: 110–21.

Zhang, Q. (ed.) (2002) *The Theory and Practice of Yanda Policy*. Beijing: China Prosecution Press.

Zhong, L.Y. and Broadhurst, R.G. (2007) 'Building Little Safe and Civilized Communities: Community Crime Prevention with Chinese Characteristics?', *International Journal of Offender Therapy and Comparative Criminology*, 51 (1): 52–67.

Zhong, Z. (1999) (2 March) 'The Route to Long-Term Public Security: Reflection of the Eight-year work on Comprehensive Management of Public Security', *Legal Daily*, pp. 1–2.

Glossary

an'quan wenming xiaoqu jianshe	安全文明小区建设	Building Little, Safe and Civilized Communities
baijia zhengming	百家争鸣	a hundred schools contending with each other
bangjiao	帮教	help and education
bao wei ke	保卫科	a public security department
ben	本	symptoms
biao	标	cause
cha yu ge ju	差序格局	the differential model of association
chi fa guo fan	吃大锅饭	eat from the same big pot
chuangshou	创收	income creating
chunqiu	春秋	the period of Spring and Autumn
da	打	punishment
da fang bingju, yi fang wei zhu	打防并举, 以防为主	combine both punishment and prevention with the focus placed on prevention

da sao chu	大扫除	to do thorough cleaning
dai lao	大佬	big brother
daijia lun	代价论	cost theory
dan wei	单位	work unit
dang'an	档案	dossier keeping
daxue	大学	Great Learning
daode lunsang	道德沦丧	corrupted morality
diyuan	地缘	geographic ties
du	毒	drugs
du	赌	gambling
fajia	法家	legalism
fang	防	prevention
fen fang	分房	housing assignment
fengbi guanli	封闭管理	closed system of management
fengjian canyu	封建残余	feudal remnants
fenshu kenru	焚书坑儒	burning the books and burying the Confucianists
gaigekaifang	改革开放	economic reform and opening up
gang	纲	dyadic social ties
gong'an	公安	Public Security Bureau
gongshi	攻势	offensives
gu	古	the past

guan qi men lai gao jianshe	关起门来搞建设	closing the door to construct a socialist state
guanxi xue	关系学	the art of knowledge of *guanxi*
guoqing	国情	national status quo
houjin bogu	厚今薄古	emphasizing the present and denigrating the past
hu kou	户口	household registration
huang	黄	pornography
huji minjing	户籍民警	registration policeman
Jiating zeren zhi	家庭责任制	household responsibility system
jiazhong chufa	加重处罚	increased punishment
jilu chufa	纪律处罚	administrative discipline
jin	今	the present
jingshen huapo	精神滑坡	spiritual slide
juweihui	居委会	neighbourhood committee
kui zeng jia pin	馈赠佳品	a product which is the best choice for gift-giving
laojiao	劳教	re-education through labour
li	礼	manners, ritual, etiquette, propriety or rites
lianfang dui	联防队	social order joint protection team
lianhe ban'an	联合办案	jointly handle cases
liudong renkou	流动人口	floating population (migrants)

liumang tuanhuo fenzi	流氓团伙份子	hooligan gang elements
min-fen	民愤	public outrage
minjian	民间	in-between the individual and society; in-between the individual and groups or associations
minjian zuzhi	民间组织	civilian organizations
pai chu suo	派出所	a local police station
pilin pikong	批林批孔	criticizing Lin Biao and criticizing Confucius' campaign
pingtianxia	平天下	make the land under heaven peaceful
qijia	齐家	attain a harmonious family relationship
qin shao nian	青少年	the youth
qunfang qunzhi	群防群治	mass prevention and mass management
qunzhong luxian	群众路线	mass line
rujia	儒家	Confucianism
sai lao	细佬	followers
shehui zhi'an zonghe zhili	社会治安综合治理	comprehensive management of social order
siheyuan	四合院	the traditional Chinese compounds house
tequan	特权	special privilege
tiaojie	调解	mediation

tie fan wan	铁饭碗	an iron rice bowl
tong bu lun	同步论	synchronism theory
tongxiang	同乡	people from the same village or province
tuan ti ge ju	团体格局	the organizational model of association
weizhang jianzhu	违章建筑	illegal buildings
xiagang	下岗	laid off
xiao	孝	filial piety
xiaomie fanzui	消灭犯罪	to eliminate crime
xinyang weiji	信仰危机	faith crisis
xiushen	修身	cultivate one's moral character
xue lei feng	学雷锋	learn from Leifeng
xue yuan	血缘	blood ties
yanda	严打	strike hard
yangwu yundong	洋务运动	the Westernization Movement
yao wu yang wei	耀武扬威	swaggered around and made a show of strength
yigu feijin	以古非今	to employ the past to negate the present
you zhongguo tese shehui zhiyi	有中国特色社会主义	Socialism with Chinese characteristics
zan zhu zheng	暂住证	temporary residence permit
zhanguo	战国	the period of Warring States
zhi'an	治安	public security

Glossary

zhi'an zhuangkuang	治安状况	the situation of public security
zhiguo	治国	run a country
zhiwu fanzui	职务犯罪	crime of misconduct in office
zhiwu jingji fanzui	职务经济犯罪	economic crime of misconduct in office
zhongdian renkou	重点人口	the targeted population
zhongguo tese	中国特色	the Chinese characteristics
zhongxue weiti, xixue weiyong	中学为体, 西学为用	Chinese learning should be for its essence, and Western learning for practical use
zi bei	自卑	inferiority complex
zi da	自大	superiority complex
zichan jieji geren zhuyi	资产阶级个人主义	bourgeois individualism
zili kouliang chenzhen hukou	自理口粮城镇户口	urban *hukou* for those with self-supplied grain
zou hou men	走后门	go through the back door
zuo hao shi	做好事	do good deeds

Index

Added to the page number, 'f' denotes a figure and 't' denotes a table.

administrative hierarchy 115
administrative offences *see* public security offences
'anticorruption' campaign 134
'arms race' effect 66
association, models of 80–1

BLSCC in Shenzhen 7, 142–5, 177–80, 216–18
  civilization measures *see* spiritual civilization, measures
  Community A *see* Community A
  Community B *see* Community B
  Community C *see* Community C
  Community D 21, 173, 174
  Community E 21–2, 168–9
  comparisons between Communities A and B 189–210, 217–18
    awareness of the programme 203–4, 205t, 208
    change of community physical appearance 204, 206t, 207
    change of relationships between residents 204, 205t
    community activities 190, 191t, 192, 195
    crime prevalence inside communities 195–6, 199t, 206t, 207
    feeling of safety 197t, 200, 206t, 207
    installation of anticrime measures 204, 205t
    intervention rates 191t, 192–4, 195
    major community problems 195, 197t
    migrants' criminality 196, 197t, 200
    mutual help between neighbours 190, 191t, 195
    personal victimization 197t, 200, 206t, 207
    police presence 198t, 202
    property victimization 198t, 200–1, 206t, 207–8
    satisfaction with the police 198t, 202–3
    security guards 198t, 201–2
    tonxiang relationship 190, 191t, 195

victimization experience 198t, 201
developmental process 143, 216
effect of social capital 209–10, 217
funding 154–6
officially claimed outcome 144–5
organizational features 147–57, 216
  ideological mooring 147–8
  leadership responsibility system 148–52
  mass prevention and mass management *see* mass prevention and mass management, in Shenzhen
rating system 158–9, 167, 176–7
safety measures 157–71, 216
  management of floating population *see* floating population, in Shenzhen
  police *see* Shenzhen PSB
  situational measures 162–3
  SSC *see* SSCs
blue card *hukou* 15, 219
bonding social capital 55–6, 70, 75, 213, 214
  in the Chinese context 85, 127, 179, 215
  and the success or achievement of BLSCC 209
  see also localized social capital
'bridging relational networks' 61
bridging social capital 55–6, 68, 69, 70, 71, 72, 75, 213, 214
  in the Chinese context 10, 85, 127, 179, 215, 229
  and the success or achievement of BLSCC 209–10, 217–18
broken windows theory 49, 51, 194
  and the nexus between community crime prevention and social capital 67, 214, 228–9
Building Little, Safe and Civilised Communities *see* BLSCC

capitalist societies, crime patterns 97
'cellularity' model, Skinner's 82, 84
cha-xu-ge-ju (differential model of association) 80–1
Chicago Area Project 62
China Law Yearbook 99
'Chinese characteristics' (*zhongguo tese*) approach to modernization 23, 26
Chinese Justice, the Fiction: Law and Literature in Modern China 230
Chinese society 80–5
  Fei's 'ripple' model 80–2, 84
  networks 81
  rural nature 82
  Shue's 'honeycomb' model 82–5
  Skinner's 'cellularity' model 82, 84
civic engagement, social capital as 55, 213
civil society, and the state 225–6
civilization
  and criminological development 99
  see also Elias's civilization theory; 'material civilization'; spiritual civilization
closure of social networks 56–8, 213–14
CMSO 10, 131–41, 177, 216
  balancing aspects 141
  guiding principle 134
  problems in implementation 134
  promulgation 131–2
    problems 132–3
  as a 'social systematic project' 133
  and spiritual civilisation 133
  theorization and conceptualization 133
Cohen's model of social control 1, 43–4
'collective efficacy' 61
collectivist ethos x, 142
community

definition 4
dimensions 41–2, 214
see also individual/community dyad; virtual communities
Community A 19–21, 163, 174, 178
  building community culture 175
  community survey see community survey
  comparisons between Community B and see BLSCC in Shenzhen, comparisons between Communities A and B
  investment 154–5
  order and peace 182–6
  participant observation 31–2
  political influences 231
  security guards 160, 183
Community B 21, 174, 175, 186–9
  cleaning up the environment 188–9
  community survey see community survey
  comparisons between Community A and see BLSCC in Shenzhen, comparisons between Communities A and B
  crime problems 186–8
  funding 155
  in-depth interviews 32–3
  security guards 160
Community C x, 21, 173, 174, 175
  funding 155
  in-depth interviews 32–3
  security guards 160
community crime prevention 2–5, 53–4
  and BLSCC 177
  context for emergence 45–51
    nature of crime problems 48–50
    perceived inefficiency of the criminal justice system 3, 50–1, 213
    theoretical reorientation see theoretical reorientation
  and community crime prevention
  and the criminal justice system 4–5
  effectiveness 4
  evaluation 4
  facilitating factors 212–13
  phases of development 54
  strategies 3–4
  and the strike-hard campaign 141
community crime prevention and social capital 6, 9, 41–74, 179, 217–18
  nexus between 58–68, 214
    and broken windows theory 67, 214, 228–9
    and opportunity reduction 54, 64–7, 214
    role of the state 228
    and social disorganization theory 59–64, 67, 194, 214
  problems and issues 68–73
community culture, building 175
Community D 21, 173, 174
community development in China 226–7
Community E 21–2, 168–9
community policing 67, 214
  in China 122
community survey 34–9
  hypotheses 38–9
  measurement of variables 34–8, 233–9
    awareness, and perceived effectiveness of BLSCC 38, 237–8
    crime, fear of crime and attitudes to the security guards and police 37, 234–7
    mutual help, social networks and interaction 34, 233–4
  sample 34, 35–6t
    demographic questions 238–9

community-based control mechanisms 125–6
community/individuals dyad 46–7
Comprehensive Management of Social Order *see* CMSO
computer-mediated communication 41
Confucianism 22
  and criminals 110
  tenets on social control 78
  versus legalism 76–80
contradictory dualism 2, 45, 72, 213
corporate security management 124
corruption, and the strike-hard campaign 140
'cost theory' (*daijia lun*), and development and crime 110–11
CPTED ('crime prevention through environmental design') 59, 162
Crawford's model of social control 44
crime
  changes in problems 48–50
  development and ix–x, 1, 96–9, 110–11
  fear of 1, 49, 66
  media portrayals 49
  nature 48
  non-recursive model 62–4
  perceptions 49, 108–9
  relationship with spiritual civilization 148
  social capital and 58, 64, 68
  systemic model 59–62, 214
  welfare approach 2, 3
  see also economic crime; gang crime; 'street crime'; youth crime
crime in China 95–111, 125, 215
  by migrants 15–16, 163–4
  as a morally charged problem 172–4
  perceptions 108–11
  in Shenzhen 18, 19t, 20t
crime displacement 53, 66

'crime as normal in mechanical societies' 108–9
crime prevention
  conceptualization 51–4
    public health model 52
    social/situational approach 53
    Tonry and Farrington's four-level model 53–4
  multiagency approach 3, 69
  objectives 51–2
  see also community crime prevention
'crime prevention through environmental design' (CPTED) 59, 162
crime rates
  growth 1, 48
  in China ix–x, 7, 99, 100–1t, 110
  tensions between communitarianism and xii
  in Shenzhen 18, 19t, 20t
crime and social control in China 8–9, 94–129
crime statistics 8, 16, 28, 99–108
  categories 102–3, 104–6t
  clearance rates 99–100, 100–1t
  quality and accuracy 98, 99
criminal justice system
  and community crime prevention 4–5
  exclusionary activities 71
  perceived inefficiency 3, 50–1, 213
criminal offences 108t
  distinction between public security offences and 102–3
criminals
  representation 109–10
  see also offenders
criminological studies 22–6, 229
  dilemmas within 22–3
  dilemmas without 23–6
  see also Shenzhen criminological study
'criminologies of everyday life' 47–8
criminology

development 229
gap between criminal policy and 230
perspectives 212, 230
and regulation and control 2
'criminology of the self',
'criminology of the Other' and 2, 47
critical ecology 59
cultural adaptation, theory 44, 46–7

daijia lun ('cost theory'), and crime and development 110–11
'dangerousness', concept 109–10
danwei
changes 166, 178
cooperation with other control mechanisms 124
and *guanxi* 89
and housing 119
and social capital 126–7
and social control 6, 118–20, 220
data
availability and collecting 28
see also crime statistics; secondary data analysis
The Death and Life of Great American Cities 5
defensible space 5, 54, 59, 66, 162, 221–2
Deng Xiaoping, and the strike-hard campaign 137
deportation 169–70
design ecology 59
development *see* economic development
developmental crime prevention 54
deviant place hypothesis 64
differential model of association (*cha-xu-ge-ju*) 80–1
'diffusion of benefits' 53
displacement 53, 66
Durkheim, Emile 96, 108–9

East versus the West 23, 25–6

economic crime 102, 134
economic development ix–x, 6–7
crime and ix–x, 1, 96–9, 110–11
in Shenzhen 17–18
economic discrimination, and migrants 15
economic exclusion 71
economic reform and open-door policy xi, 3, 6, 13, 23, 73, 95, 219
economic stratification x, 221, 222–3, 224
effectiveness, definition 4
egocentrism 81
Elias's civilization theory 97
methodological difficulties and limitations 98
environment, purification 176
'environments of trust' 41
evaluation
of community crime prevention 4
of the strike-hard campaign 140
exclusion
dyad between inclusion and 70–1, 223–4
levels 71
of migrants 15, 178
'exemplary society', China as 80
external resources, solicitation 61, 63

Farrington and Tonry's four-level model of crime prevention 53–4
fear of crime 1, 49, 66
Fei's 'ripple' model of Chinese society 80–2, 84
'filial piety' (*xiao*) 77
'Five Standards for Shenzhen BLSCC' 158–9, 167, 176–7
floating population x, 7, 14, 215, 223
in Shenzhen 163–71, 216
management of the 'three-no population' 167–70
management via the rented housing units 167

management via temporary *hukou* and temporary residence permits 14–15, 165–7, 169
and public legal education 170
and second-border management 165
seeking cooperation from the origin provinces 170–1
see also migrants
fortress society 53, 66
'four a's' activity 158
'four ones', principle 154, 174
'four-haves' activity 158, 174

gaige kaifang 6, 13, 23, 73, 95, 219
gang crime, and the strike-hard campaign 140
Garland's analysis of social control 1–2, 44–5, 49, 72, 94, 109, 213
'generalized social capital' *see* bridging social capital
globalization 41, 42
'go west' movement 231
gongshi ('seasonal offensives') 136–7
gu (past) versus *jin* (present) 22–3, 24–5
guanxi 6, 10, 75, 81, 85–91, 94, 215
conceptualizations 86–7
convergence between social capital and 90, 91
layers of meaning 85
negative effects 90–1
sources 89–90
use contexts 89–91
guanxi-xue 87–8, 90
popular and official discourses 88
'guardianship' 65

Han dynasty 76, 79
hardened targets *see* target-hardening measures
harmonious relationships, promoting 174

'history of the present' framework 94
'honeycomb' model, Shue's 82–5
Hong Kong triads 187
'horizontal' capital *see* localized social capital
household registration system *see hukou*
household responsibility system 6–7, 14, 83, 142, 221
huang, du and *du* (pornography, gambling and drugs), phenomena 172–4
hukou
cooperation with other control mechanisms 124–5
influence on intervention 194
migration and 7, 14–16, 164
registration 113
and social control 6, 112–14, 178, 219
urban and rural registration status 113–14
see also temporary *hukou*

illegal structures 167–8
in-depth interviews 32–3
inclusion, dyad between exclusion and 70–1, 223–4
individualism x, 81
individuals/community dyad 46–7
industrialization, effect on criminality 96–7
informal social control 58, 66–7, 214
in China 6, 126
programmes 54
relationship between formal and 69
in China 218–20
integrative ecology 59
intimate handlers 65

jin (present) versus *gu* (past) 22–3, 24–5

271

juweihui see neighbourhood committees

law, power of 77–8
law enforcement
    crime prevention by 53
    see also policing
leadership responsibility system, BLSCC 148–52
'learning from models' 148, 231
    in Community A 184–5
legalism, Confucianism versus 76–80
li 77, 79
    power of law versus the power of 77–8
lifestyle theory 64–5
liudong renkou see floating population
localization 41–2
localized social capital 55–6, 67–8
    see also bonding social capital
LSCCs (Little, Safe and Civilised Communities) 142
    eligibility for 143

Mao 82–3, 84
    'collective' approach 142
mass line 10, 95, 111, 117, 221
    and policing 121–2, 123, 178–9, 219
mass prevention and mass management 152–7
    and multiagency cooperation 156
    problems 156
    in Shenzhen 153–7, 220
        in Community A 183
        and the SSC and security guards 160
'material civilization' 131
media
    portrayal of crime 49
    role in BLSCC activities 153
Mediation Committee 116, 124
migrants 224
    in Community B 187–8
    crime by 15–16, 163–4
        comparisons in Communities A and B 196, 197t, 200
    exclusion and economic discrimination 15, 178
    in Shenzhen xi
    see also floating population
migration and the *hukou* system 7, 14–16, 164
minjian 225–6
minjian zuzhi 227
misconduct by Party and state officials, and the strike-hard campaign 140
models/heroes, learning from *see* 'learning from models'
modernity, re-embedding effects 25
modernization 24–5, 222
    'Chinese characteristics' (*zhongguo tese*) approach 23, 26
    effect on criminality 96–7, 99
        methodological difficulties and limitations for measurement 98
moral education 171–4
moral outrage, as a reaction to crime 109
multiagency approach
    and mass prevention and mass management 156
    to crime prevention 3, 69

negative social capital 213
neighbourhood committees
    cooperation with other control mechanisms 124–5
    and economic reform 117–18
    functions 115–16
    judicial organs and 116
    personnel 116–17
    and social capital 126–7
    and social control 6, 115–18, 178, 219–20
    sub-committees 115f, 116
networks *see* social networks

non-recursive model of crime 62–4, 67, 69, 214
'nothing works' 2

offence-focused theoretical traditions 47
offenders
  motivation 47
  representation 46
  see also criminals
one-child policy x
openness and economic reform xi, 3, 6, 13, 23, 73, 95, 219
Opium War 23
opportunity reduction 54, 64–7, 214
'opportunity thesis' of the relationship between development and crime 98
organizational model of association (*tuan-ti-ge-ju*) 80–1
'overnight city', Shenzhen as xi, 12

parochial social control 60–1
participant observation, site visits and 30–2
partnership approach to crime prevention 54, 67, 69
  see also 'preventative partnership'
past(*gu*) versus the present (*jin*) 22–3, 24–5
penal population 49–50
People's Republic of China *see* PRC
physical environment, purification 176
police-public relationship 3, 50–1, 67, 70, 123
  improving 158
policing 3, 50–1, 70
  in China 120–3
    in Community A 184
    comparisons between Communities A and B 198t, 202–3
    components 120

cooperation with other control mechanisms 124–5
leadership 121
levels 120–1
mass line and 121–2, 123, 178–9, 219
numbers 121
police powers 122–3
reform 123
responsibilities 122
see also community policing; private policing; problem-based policing; Shenzhen PSB; social policing
'political economy of community' 61
political influences on criminal policy 230–1
The Politics of Crime and Community 2–3
population in Shenzhen 16–17
pornography, gambling and drugs (*huang, du* and *du*), phenomena 172–4
PRC 6, 23, 26, 82
  and the *hukou* system 112–13
present (*jin*) versus the past (*gu*) 22–3, 24–5
'preventative partnership' 1, 45, 72
prevention of crime *see* crime prevention
primary crime prevention 52
Priority Estates Project 49
prison population 49–50
private policing 70
  exclusionary activities 71
  see also security guards
private security service *see* SSCs
private social control 60
  relationship between public and 69–70
  in China 221–3
problem-based policing 67
property crime 96–7, 98
proximity hypothesis 64
public, perceptions of crime 49

273

public health model of crime prevention 52
public legal education 170
Public Security Bureau in Shenzhen see Shenzhen PSB
public security offences 108t
　distinction between criminal offences and 102–3
public security organs see policing, in China
public social control 60, 61, 69
　relationship between private and 69–70
　in China 221–3
public-police relationship see police-public relationship
punishment, and the strike-hard campaign 141
'punitive segregation' 1
purification of the environment 176
'pyramid of morality' 78

Qin dynasty 76, 79, 112
qunzhong luxian see mass line

rational choice theory 65–6
reform and open-door policy xi, 3, 6, 13, 23, 73, 95, 219
rented housing units, managing the temporary population via 167
residents' committees see neighbourhood committees
'resourceful offender', concept 47
responsibilization strategy 70
restorative justice 126
'ripple' model, Fei's 80–2, 84
routine activities theory 47–8, 65, 66
rujia see Confucianism
rural China
　diversion of academic attention to 231–2
　and the hukou system 113–14
　nature of society 10, 82
　and social capital 85, 215
　waves of development 82–4

work units 118
rural nature of Chinese society 82

seasonal 'offensives' (gongshi) 136–7
'second revolution' 95
second-border management 165
secondary crime prevention 52
secondary data analysis 29–30
Security and Defence Committee 116, 124
security guards 159–61, 222
　in Community A 183
　comparisons between Community A and Community B 198t, 201–2
security service companies see SSCs
'severe and rapid punishment' campaign 135
Shenzhen xi, 12, 13–18, 216
　BLSCC in see BLSCC in Shenzen
　crime rates 18, 19t, 20t
　hukou and migration 14–16
　population and economic growth 16–18
　'special battles' (gongshi) 136–7
'Shenzhen City Assessment Measures on Leadership Responsibility System for CMSO' 150
Shenzhen criminological study 12–40
　five communities 18–22
　methodological challenges and research methods 27–39, 229
　community survey see community survey
　in-depth interviews 32–3
　secondary data analysis 29–30
　site visits and participant observation 30–2
　research questions and significance 7–9
Shenzhen PSB 157–9, 178–9, 219
　comparisons between

Communities A and B 198t, 202–3
and security guards 161
Shue's 'honeycomb' model of Chinese society 82–5
site visits and participant observation 30–2
situational crime prevention 53
  overlaps between community crime prevention and 54
  in Shenzhen 162–3
  see also defensible spaces; target-hardening measures
'six evils' campaign 103
Skinner's 'cellularity' model of Chinese society 82, 84
social capital
  community crime prevention and *see* community crime prevention and social capital
  concept 5–6, 54–8, 213
  convergence between *guanxi* and 90, 91
  crime and 58, 64, 68
  dimensions 214
  effect on success or achievement of BLSCC 209–10, 217
  see also bonding social capital; bridging social capital
social capital in China 6, 75–93, 215
  and social control 126–7, 215
social control
  in modern Western societies 43–5
  relationship between formal and informal 69
  in China 218–20
  theories 1–2
    Cohen's 1, 43–4
    Crawford's 44
    Garland's 1–2, 44–5, 49, 72, 94, 109, 213
  see also informal social control; parochial social control; private social control; public social control

social control in China 24, 26, 110, 111–27, 179
  community-based 125–6
  Confucian tenets 78
  crime and 8–9, 94–129
  danwei see danwei
  household registration *see hukou*
  neighbourhood committees *see* neighbourhood committees
  network of control mechanisms 124–5
  public security organs (the police) *see* policing, in China
  relationship between formal and informal 218–20
  social capital and 126–7, 215
social crime prevention 53
social disorganization theory 59–64, 67, 194, 214
social ecology theory 59
social exclusion 71
  of migrants 15, 178
social intertexture, study of 130
social networks
  in Chinese society 81
  closure 56–8, 213–14
  density 56
  social capital as 55, 213
social policing 24, 25
social sciences research 27–8
social stability 24–5
'socialism with Chinese characteristics' 6, 23, 137
socialist societies, crime in 97, 110
society, Chinese *see* Chinese society
solicitation of external resources 61, 63
'special battles' (*zhuanxiang douzheng*) 136–7
spiritual civilization 131
  in Community A 185
  connection with CMSO 133
  measures 171–6, 216
    building community culture 175

moral education 171–4
promoting harmonious relationships 174
purification of the environment 176
relationship between levels of crime and 148
'spiritual pollution' 131
SSCs 159–61, 222
regulation 160–1
state
and Confucianism 76–7
and legalism 76–7
relationship between segmentary and bureaucratic 78–9
role 5, 70, 71–3, 179, 224–9
theorizations regarding 2
stratification x, 221, 222–3, 224
'street crime', and the strike-hard campaign 134
street offices 115
'strike severe blows against economic crime' campaign 135
strike-hard campaign 110, 131, 135–41
backgrounds for 137–8
criticisms 138–40
evaluation 140
formula for 138
critique 139
main targets 135–6
and miscarriage of justice 141
overemphasis on punishment 141
singularity of goals 139
and 'street crime' 134
three forms 136–7
'strong ties' versus 'weak ties' 56, 213
structural holes 214
versus network closure 56–8, 213–14
sweeps 169–70
'synchronism theory' (*tongbu lun*), and crime and development 110–11

systemic model of crime 59–62, 214

target-hardening measures 5, 48, 53, 54, 64–5, 66, 221–2
in Shenzhen 157, 162–3
in Community A 182–3
comparisons between Communities A and B 204, 205t
temporary *hukou* 165–6
temporary residence permits (*zan zhu zheng*) 14–15, 166–7, 169
temporary settlement areas, establishment 167–9
'Ten Service Promises of the Shenzhen PSB' 158
tertiary crime prevention 52
theoretical reorientation and community crime prevention 45–8
individuals/community dyad 46–7
offender/offence dyad 47
offender/victim dyad 47–8
'three irons' 157, 162
'three preventions' 157, 162
'three-no population' 164
management 167–70
tongbu lun ('synchronism theory'), and crime and development 110–11
Tonry and Farrington's four-level model of crime prevention 53–4
tonxiang 34
trade unions 227–8
triads in Hong Kong 187
trust
social capital as 55, 213
see also 'environments of trust'
tuan-ti-ge-ju (organizational model of association) 80–1
'two civilisations', theory 131

'underclass' 71, 223–4
behavioural perspective 224

levels of exclusion 224
structural perspective 224
urban *hukou* (*zili kouliang chenzhen hukou*) 14
urban poor 224
urbanization, effect on criminality 96–7

'vertical' capital *see* bridging social capital
victims
and lifestyle theory 64–5
status 47–8
violent crime 96–7, 98
virtual communities 41, 42

'ways of lying', thesis 172
'weak ties' versus 'strong ties' 56, 213
'the web of informal crime control' 65
welfare approach to crime 2, 3

West versus the East 23, 25–6
Western societies, social control in modern 43–5
Westernization Movement (*yangwu yundong*) 23
work unit *see danwei*

xiao ('filial piety') 77

yanda see strike-hard campaign
youth crime 102, 107t, 140

zan zhu zheng (temporary residence permits) 14–15, 166–7, 169
Zhang Zhidong 23
zhongguo tese ('Chinese characteristics') approach to modernization 23, 26
zhuanxiang douzheng ('special battles') 136–7
zili kouliang chenzhen hukou (urban *hukou*) 14